GENDER AND IMMIGRATION

Gender and Immigration

Edited by

Gregory A. Kelson

and

Debra L. DeLaet

First published 1999 by
MACMILLAN PRESS LTD
Houndmills, Basingstoke, Hampshire RG21 6XS
and London
Companies and representatives
throughout the world

ISBN 0–333–74177–3 hardcover
ISBN 0–333–74178–1 paperback

A catalogue record for this book is available
from the British Library.

This book is printed on paper suitable for recycling and
made from fully managed and sustained forest sources.

10   9   8   7   6   5   4   3   2   1
08   07   06   05   04   03   02   01   00   99

Printed and bound in Great Britain by
Antony Rowe Ltd, Chippenham, Wiltshire

To Lori Andrews, J.D. and Nanette Elster, J.D.,
M.P.H. for the support and encouragement they
have given to me as a policymaker
Gregory A. Kelson

To my parents, Jack and Sandy DeLaet, for their
constant support and encouragement
Debra L. DeLaet

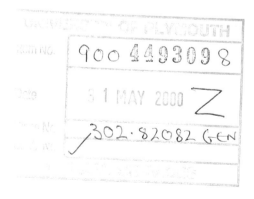

Contents

List of Tables

List of Contributors

Nandini Narain Assar is a Ph.D. candidate in sociology at the Virginia Polytechnic Institute and State University. She holds a BA with honors in Sociology from Miranda House College of Delhi University (India) and an MA in Sociology from the State University of New York, Binghamton. Her research interests include race and gender, immigration, political economy and women in development. She has also taught courses on gender relations and third world women and development.

Brigitte H. Bechtold is Professor of Sociology and Director of the Women Studies Program at Central Michigan University. She holds an MA in Economics from Michigan State University and a Ph.D. from the University of Pennsylvania. Her dissertation was entitled *French Macroeconomic Policies in the 1960s: An Econometric Evaluation*. She is the author of seven books and numerous articles dealing with economics.

Shu-Ju Ada Cheng is a Ph.D. student in sociology at the University of Texas at Austin. She holds a BA in Spanish from Fu-jen University (Taiwan), and an MA in International Studies and a graduate certificate in Women's Studies from the University of Oregon. Her research interests includes women's movements around the world, western and third world feminism, development theory, gender and development, and human rights.

Debra L. DeLaet is an Assistant Professor of Political Science at Drake University. She received her Ph.D. in Government and International Studies from the University of Notre Dame. Her research interests are in the areas of international migration, human rights, and international law and organizations. She is currently revising her manuscript, *U.S. Immigration Policy in an Age of Rights*, and is completing research on the most recent amendments to US immigration policy.

Ludmila Dziewięcka-Bokun is Associate Professor in Politics of the Faculty of Social Sciences at the University of Wrocław (Poland). She holds an MA with special Honours in Law and a Ph.D. in Political Science from the University of Wrocław. Her research is on modern social conflicts and on rebuilding the state–society relationship in post-communist European countries.

Sepali Guruge is an M.Sc. candidate in Nursing at the University of Toronto. Born in Sri Lanka, she was first educated there, and later in the

Soviet Union, and in Canada. Her research interests include immigrants and refugees' health issues and their access to health services. She currently works as a registered nurse at the Clarke Institute of Psychiatry in Toronto.

David Ip is Senior Lecturer in the Department of Anthropology and Sociology at the University of Queensland (Australia), and a Director of the Master's programme in Social Planning and Development. He was born in Hong Kong and educated there and in the United States. His main research areas are in the sociology of development, social planning, and social impact assessment. In recent years his research has concentrated on Australia's ethnic entrepreneurship and Asian immigrant communities as well as on the socio-economic development of China. He is co-author of *Asian Impressions of Multicultural Australia* and is also actively involved in consultancy work for the Australian International Development Assistance Bureau, now renamed AusAid.

Gregory A. Kelson is the founder and Executive Director of the Institute for Women and Children's Policy, an international policymaking think-tank. He is the author of three law review articles and has lectured extensively on international women and children's human rights. His current work involves monitoring government compliance to the Beijing Platform for Action, the rights of children in adoption cases, reparations for Asian comfort women, and gender-based persecution and political asylum.

Constance Lever-Tracy is Senior Lecturer in Sociology at the Flinders University of South Australia, Adelaide. She has lived, studied and worked in England, Israel, France, Africa and Australia, and has always been interested in the transnational networks that migrating people weave. Her initial work focused on the transnational culture created by militant industrial workers from around the world in Australia's factories. She has also studied the impact of returning immigrants in Malta. She is the coauthor (with Michael Quinlan) of *A Divided Working Class: Ethnic Segmentation and Industrial Conflict in Australia*.

Cecilia G. Manrique is Professor of Political Science/Public Administration at the University of Wisconsin-La Crosse, where she also serves on the faculty of the Women's Studies Department. She received her Ph.D. from the University of Notre Dame with areas of specialization in comparative politics and international relations. She has done extensive work in integrating computer applications including the Internet in a variety of courses. She has published widely in this field and has published the second edition of *The Houghton Mifflin Guide to the Internet for Political*

Science. She and her husband, Gabriel, have undertaken research together on the subject of immigration and immigrant faculty in the US.

Gabriel G. Manrique is Professor of Economics and chair of the Department of Economics and Finance at Winona State University, where he also serves on the faculty of interdisciplinary programs including the women's studies, international studies, and honors programs. He received his Ph.D. in Economics with a specialization in third world economic development and international economics from the University of Notre Dame. He has also served as a fellow at the Overseas Development Council and in the US Congress where he worked with the House Select Committee on Hunger. He is a native of the Philippines and his current research is on immigration and immigrant faculty in the US.

Lynn Morrison is a Ph.D. candidate in the Department of Anthropology at the University of Toronto. The focus of her dissertation is on sexual networking and the impact of HIV/AIDS in northern Thailand. Research on pediatric AIDS was also undertaken in Romania in 1991. Lynn has developed and implemented a peer education programme at Ryerson Polytechnic University, and also served as a committee member for "From All Walks of Life," Toronto's walk for AIDS.

Larissa I. Remennick is Assistant Professor in the Graduate Program in Medical Sociology, Department of Sociology and Anthropology at Bar-Ilan University, Israel. Born in Russia, she holds a Ph.D. in Sociology and Demography of Health from the Institute of Sociology, USSR Academy of Sciences, Moscow. Her research interests include women's health, social demography of fertility and birth control, and the sociology of health, illness and health care. Larissa has conducted a number of studies on acculturation, gender and health issues among Russian immigrants in Israel.

Lisa Simons is a Ph.D. student in international politics at the Graduate School of International Studies at Denver University. She holds a BA in political philosophy from Syracuse University and an M.Sc. in International Relations from the London School of Economics. She has taught classes in international relations, gender studies, political science, film studies, English composition and literature.

Kymberly Anne Snarr is currently pursuing her Masters of Science at the University of Toronto in the Department of Anthropology. Her current areas of interest include: multiculturalism, empowerment, and women's issues and HIV/AIDS in immigrant populations and the Caribbean.

Kathleen Staudt is Professor of Political Science at the University of Texas at El Paso. She holds an MA and Ph.D. in Political Science from the University of Wisconsin at Madison. She wrote *Free Trade? Informal Economies at the United States–Mexico Border*, has done consultation work for Partners for the Americas on Mexican family planners' training at the US–Mexico Border, and provided years of service for the Mexican Federation of Private Associations (FEMAP).

Preface

This volume is an outgrowth of a panel on gender and international migration on which both of the editors participated during the 1996 Annual Meeting of the International Studies Association in San Diego, California and a similar panel organized and chaired by Mr Kelson, with Dr DeLaet as the discussant. The primary objective of this edited volume is to apply a "gender-sensitive lens" to the study of international migration. In particular, the chapters in this volume explore the varied and complex ways in which women experience international migration. While the volume includes chapters on diverse groups of migrant women, several general questions frame this work. Does international migration provide women with an opportunity for liberating themselves from subordinate gender roles in their countries of origin, or are traditional gender roles perpetuated in the host societies? Do migrant women face new forms of subordination and discrimination in their host societies? To what extent is international migration driven by actors and institutions which exploit the social, economic, and political vulnerability of women across the globe?

One of the unique contributions of this work is that it includes chapters on women in a variety of occupational categories. Previous studies of migrant women have focused almost exclusively on migrant women working in the "unskilled" sector of the global economy. To be sure, the volume includes several chapters which focus on the economic vulnerability of migrant women in low-wage occupations, including Kathleen Staudt's chapter on women who work in the "informal economy" along the US–Mexico border and Shu-Ju Ada Cheng's chapter on domestic workers in East Asia. However, this volume complicates the ideological assumptions and theoretical implications of migration scholarship which *only* looks at these women. In an effort to provide a comprehensive overview of international female migration, this volume includes chapters on women in a variety of occupational categories. The chapter by Ip and Lever-Tracy looks at migrant women from Asia who work in business in Australia, and Nandini Assar's chapter explores the role of Indian women in family-owned hotel businesses in the US. Cecilia G. Manrique and Gabriel G. Manrique look at the case of "Third World" migrant women in higher education in the US. Moreover, this volume challenges the economically reductive approaches of earlier works by examining groups of migrant women who cannot rigidly be grouped into economic categories. Lisa Simons' chapter on mail order brides and Larissa Remennick's chapter on the experience of Jewish women from the former Soviet Union who have settled in Israel are illustrative of the social and political dimensions of female migration that are highlighted in this volume.

Although women migrate across international boundaries at roughly the same rate as men, most international migration scholarship assumes that international migration results primarily from the labor migration of male workers. Thus, while mainstream perspectives acknowledge that women migrate, they tend to assume that women do not migrate autonomously but, rather, that they merely follow men as their dependents. As a result, scholars feel that in order to understand the underlying forces which drive international migration, it is most important to understand male migration. The few studies which have explored international female migration have focused almost exclusively on the migration of women to work in the low-wage labor sector of the global economy. This volume challenges the simplicity of both of these analyses. By exploring the status of migrant women in a variety of categories, several of the chapters in this volume address the question of the motivations which lead women to migrate and, in this way, highlight the reality that female migration is neither driven by exactly the same determinants as male migration nor merely an economic phenomenon. In this way, the chapters in this volume will provide a more thorough understanding of both the process of international migration and how it is experienced by women, and hopefully will enrich the work of migration scholars and policymakers alike.

1 Introduction: The Invisibility of Women in Scholarship on International Migration

Debra L. DeLaet

I. INTRODUCTION

Although women migrate across international boundaries at roughly the same rate as men, a great deal of international migration scholarship has been based on the assumption that international migrants largely consist of male workers. According to this traditional assumption, women migrate only to join their husbands abroad, and economic factors are the underlying impetus for most migration flows. While few in number, existing studies of women and international migration challenge this simple view. These studies suggest that women migrate for a variety of complex reasons and that, in terms of migrants' adaptions to host societies, women experience migration in unique ways (Simon and Brettell, 1986; Phizacklea, 1983).

The lack of attention to women in studies of international migration is by no means unique to this issue. In general, the field of international relations has treated women as if they were insignificant actors. While different international relations perspectives focus on a variety of actors and issues, in every case, women remain 'hidden from international relations' (Halliday, 1994, p. 147). A growing body of feminist scholarship within internationals relations has challenged the notion that women are unimportant actors in global politics.[1] This feminist literature argues that fundamental assumptions in the mainstream perspectives on international relations are 'gender-biased'. According to Tickner, most scholarship in international relations has neglected the lived experiences and the viewpoints of women and, as a result, reflects a masculine bias which provides an incomplete and inaccurate portrayal of global politics. Similarly, Peterson and Runyan argue that a 'gender-sensitive lens' is necessary to provide a more complete and accurate view of world politics.

This volume represents an effort to apply a 'gender-sensitive lens' to the study of international migration. In particular, the chapters in this volume focus on the status of international female migrants in their host societies. Specifically, the chapters address one or more of the following questions. Does international migration provide women with an opportunity for liberating themselves from subordinate gender roles in their countries of origin, or are traditional gender roles perpetuated in the host societies? Do migrant women face new forms of subordination and discrimination in their host societies? To what extent is international migration driven by actors and institutions which exploit the social, economic, and political vulnerability of women across the globe? The authors answer these questions in various ways, and no consensus viewpoint emerges in this volume. The absence of consensus illustrates that the experience of women migrants is shaped not only by gender but also by such variables as class and culture. Although no consensus emerges, the common theme that runs through these chapters is that female migration is neither driven by exactly the same determinants as male migration nor do women experience migration in precisely the same way as men. Thus, these chapters illustrate that scholars can obtain a more complete understanding of the phenomenon of international migration by examining the unique elements of international female migration.

II. WOMEN AND INTERNATIONAL MIGRATION

In order to evaluate the status of international female migrants in their host societies, it is important to take into consideration the factors that drive women to leave their countries of origin. To this end, this section will provide an overview of the existing, though scant, research on the causes of international female migration. Women migrate internationally at nearly the same rate as men. Currently, women constitute just under 50 percent of international migration flows in most countries which receive international migrants as well as almost half of the stock of international migrants.[2] While men typically comprise the majority of migrants to developing countries, a majority of migrants to many developed countries in recent decades have been women (United Nations, 1994). In the case of the United States, which still receives the largest overall numbers of legal immigrants, women have constituted a majority of migration flows since the 1930s (Houstoun, Kramer, and Barrett, 1984). In general, women have predominated in migration flows to countries which favor migration for permanent resettlement whereas men have predominated in migration flows to countries which emphasize migrant labor (Zlotnik, 1995, p. 231).

In spite of the fact that women today migrate internationally in roughly the same numbers as men and evidence that the direction of female migration flows differs somewhat from male migration flows, the pervasive image of the international migrant as a male worker still persists in much of the scholarship on international migration. Scholars of international migration commonly assume that when women migrate, they do so as family 'dependents'. In this way, women are not seen as having a major influence over the choice to migrate and, hence, are seen as irrelevant to understanding why migration occurs (Brettell and Simon, 1986). Interestingly, one of the earliest theorists of international migration, E.G. Ravenstein, addressed female migration in his examination of migration within the United Kingdom in the late 1800s. Ravenstein, whose work is based on an application of classical economic liberalism to the analysis of migration, notes:

> Woman is a greater migrant than man. This may surprise those who associate women with domestic life, but the figures of the census clearly prove it. Nor do women migrate merely from the rural districts into the towns in search of domestic service, for they migrate quite as frequently into certain manufacturing districts, and the workshop is a formidable rival of the kitchen and scullery (p. 196).

Ravenstein's analysis suggests not only that women migrate autonomously but also that they do so for a variety of reasons. Unfortunately, most migration scholars have treated women as dependants rather than autonomous actors, and, as a result, women have been largely invisible in studies of international migration.

In order to highlight the visibility of women in actual migration flows and to examine the extent to which they are autonomous actors in these flows, it is necessary to consider the reasons women migrate. The few existing studies on this subject suggest that women migrate for a variety of reasons. These reasons include economic incentives, family unity, the desire to escape marital problems, and opportunities for more social independence (Morokvasic, 1984, pp. 896–9). Women also have fled their countries of origin to escape political violence and war. An exploration of four basic migration categories illustrates the multifaceted nature of international female migration.

A. Legal Migration for Family Reunification

Most women migrating for legal permanent resettlement have done so under policies designed to facilitate family reunification. An emphasis on family reunification in US immigration policy is one of the reasons that women have predominated in migration flows to this country (Zlotnik, 1995, p. 239). In fact, almost two-thirds of all legal immigrants to the United States have been women and children (Houstoun, Kramer, and Barrett, 1984, p. 913). The predominance of women in migration flows to the US also has been reinforced by the greater propensity of American males to marry foreigners, which likely results from the thriving mail-order bride industry in this country (Simons, this volume) as well as the fact that more men participate in the military and have been overseas in this capacity where they have had a greater opportunity to meet foreign women (Houstoun, Kramer, and Barrett, 1984, pp. 919–20; Tyree and Donato, 1986, pp. 32–3). Many European countries also made allowances for family reunification after halting labor migration in the early to mid-1970s. As a result, while overall immigration to Europe declined and return migration to the countries of origin increased, women often have comprised a high proportion of net migration in these cases since the 1970s (De Wenden and DeLey, 1986).

The case of family reunification demonstrates the way in which immi-gration policy can influence the composition of migration flows. In this case, policies emphasizing family reunification have made it more likely that women will migrate. On the surface, it might appear that the fact that most women migrate under family reunification provisions substantiates the notion that women migrate only as dependants and, hence, do not require serious scholarly attention. However, as will be shown below, women migrate, though at lower numbers, in other categories as well. Thus, while women comprise large numbers of family immigrants, it is a mistake to assume that women migrate solely for purposes of family unity.

Furthermore, family migration flows and women within these flows deserve serious scholarly attention for two basic reasons. First, family reunification policies reflect assumptions about women and gender roles and commonly are a result of the assumption that women are dependents (Lim, 1995, pp. 34–6; Boyd, 1995, pp. 84–6; Brettell and Simon, 1986, p. 6). A recent UN report on the international migration of women clearly summarizes how gender conceptions can play an important role in shaping international migration flows:

> throughout the world, the formulation of migration laws and regulations is influenced by prevailing conceptions of the family and of the roles that different family members ought to play. Women, as spouses or daughters, are traditionally assumed to have primarily non-economic roles under the assumption that their husbands or fathers are responsible

for satisfying the family's economic needs. These perceptions are translated into immigration regulations that, in some circumstances, can actually favour female migration by facilitating the admission of dependents. On the other hand, in countries that either restrict or discourage family reunification, or which admit mainly migrant workers, the migration of women will tend to be smaller than that of men. (United Nations, 1994, p. 69)

Prescribed gender roles not only shape policies in receiving countries, but they also will affect migration choices in countries of origin. Further attention to women and gender roles will be crucial in order to contribute to a complete and accurate understanding of the nature of family migration flows and the importance that family reunification plays in the immigration policies of many states.

Second, while family migration typically has been precipitated by labor migration to industrialized countries, family migration to advanced industrialized countries in recent decades has become an autonomous force and must be studied in its own right. Contrary to widespread opinion, governments have been able to reduce labor migration when restriction is desired, as demonstrated in the cases of the national origins quotas in the US in the 1920s and the European halt to guestworker migration in the 1970s. However, once family migration flows have been precipitated, they are more difficult to restrict, at least in liberal democracies because of support for civil rights and a belief in the importance of the family as a social unit (Houstoun, 1984, p. 918; Hollifield, 1992; DeLaet, 1995). Thus, family reunification remains one of the major avenues for female migration. While family migration initially may have been precipitated by labor migration, today family migration has a dynamic of its own. In order to completely understand international migration in general, then, the causes of family migration must be given greater attention. Because women predominate in these flows, it will be necessary for scholars to study female migrants.

B. Legal Employment-Based Immigration

While women have predominated in family migration flows to most advanced industrialized countries, women have comprised a much smaller proportion of employment-based permanent immigration. Nonetheless, women still have migrated for employment purposes in significant numbers. Over one-fourth of the labor migrants to Germany in 1907 were women. Similar proportions of immigrant workers to France in recent decades have been women (United Nations, 1994, p. 75). One-third of the skilled and unskilled workers admitted to the US in the 1970s were women, and a significant proportion of women also were admitted under the preference category for professionals of exceptional ability (Houstoun, Kramer, and Barrett, 1984, p. 926).[3] It is also important to note that even women who are not explicitly admitted as labor migrants often enter the labor market.

Much of the existing scholarship on women as migrants focuses on the migration of women from developing to developed countries to fulfill jobs in low-wage sectors or as private domestic workers. In this way, this research typically incorporates Marxist assumptions into a feminist analysis of unskilled female workers in the global economy. Clearly, many women who have migrated internationally have done so to take low-wage jobs in the garment industry, textiles, footwear, and electronics. Many women also migrate internationally to work as domestic help in private homes (Saskia Sassen-Koob, 1984; Morokvasic, 1983, 1984; Phizacklea, 1983).

Although low-wage labor migration has been an important part of the international migration flows of women, Marxist-feminist analyses do not provide a comprehensive overview of female labor migration. Female migration for employment purposes is a complex phenomenon involving women who cite a variety of reasons for migrating and who migrate under a wide range of occupational categories (United Nations, 1995, pp. 4–8). Evidence of women participating in low-wage sectors may be accurate, but it is incomplete. For example, in the US case, over 28 percent of the women who migrated under occupational preference categories in the 1970s entered under high-skilled occupations, including nurses, management, teachers, and administrators. Eighteen percent of women who migrated under the occupational categories were admitted to work in blue-collar jobs, and an additional 18 percent were admitted as clerical workers. Only 14 percent of these women were admitted as domestic workers (Houstoun, Kramer, and Barrett, 1984, p. 944). Clearly, many women migrated to fulfill labor needs in low-wage job sectors. Nevertheless, these figures also indicate that a significant number of women migrated to perform skilled jobs with higher wages. As a result, these figures challenge the strict Marxist focus on structural inequality as the primary determinant of employment-based migration.

The above discussion of female labor migration necessarily reflects only limited data. The few studies cited cannot provide the foundation for broad generalizations about female migration for employment-purposes. Far more research has been conducted on women who have migrated to work in low-wage sectors than on professional women who have migrated internationally or on the migration of skilled female workers. However, the relative lack of attention to these types of migration does not mean that these types of female labor migration are irrelevant. In fact, the focus on female labor migrants in low-wage sectors and the lack of attention to the migration of professional women and skilled female workers partly reflects limited data on female migrants resulting from biased assumptions about who migrates. This methodological dilemma was described in a recent UN report on the status of female migrants:

> because the evidence available tends to be partial, incomplete, or down-right biased, it suggests that women who participate in labour migration tend to be selected from the lower rungs of the socio-economic scale, that they usually undertake the most menial or otherwise unappealing jobs, and that, if they migrate at all, it is because of the dire needs of their families. In reality, a more comprehensive assessment of female labour migration would likely show that women from all types of back-grounds and a variety of occupations are involved. (United Nations, 1995, p. 3)

In order to address this methodological dilemma, an important area for future research will be to explore the range of economic activities in which female migrants participate (United Nations, 1995, pp. 2–3).

C. Illegal or Undocumented Migration

Women also have comprised a significant proportion of undocumented immigrants in a variety of countries.[4] Indeed, while many scholars have viewed illegal immigration as a flow dominated by single male workers, illegal immigration often entails the movement of whole families (Boyd, 1989, p. 649). Additionally, single women also migrate illegally in signifi-cant numbers. For example, survey research suggests that between 35 and 50 percent of the undocumented migrants from Mexico to Los Angeles in the 1970s were women. Importantly, only approximately 30 percent of the undocumented female migrants in these surveys were married, with just over an additional 25 percent living with a partner. The data does not indi-cate whether or not the women in these cases migrated specifically to join their spouses or partners. Regardless, at least 45 percent of the female respondents migrated independently.[5] Legalization programs in various countries also provide evidence that women migrate illegally in significant numbers. In the US, women accounted for roughly 45 percent of the 1.5 million individuals who participated in the legalization program created under the Immigration Reform and Control Act of 1986[6] (Zlotnik, 1995, 237; United Nations, 1994, pp. 77–8). Women accounted for 47 percent of those immigrants legalized under a 1974 program in Argentina, and 47 percent of immigrants legalized in Venezuela in 1980 were women. The numbers were smaller in some recent legalizations in European countries, though they are still significant. Seventeen percent of the migrants legalized in France in 1981–2 were women, and women comprised 28 percent of migrants legalized in Italy in 1987 and 1988 (United Nations, 1994, 78). In West Germany, family members of guestworkers who did not meet requirements for legal family reunification migrated illegally in significant numbers (Goodman, 1987, 236). The evidence that large numbers of women have migrated illegally to a variety of countries poses serious challenges to the pervasive image of the undocumented migrant as a male worker.

The limited data on undocumented female migrants also suggest that these women migrate illegally for a variety of reasons, though economic incentives commonly are the most prevalent motivation. For example, in the survey research on undocumented female migrants from Mexico to Los Angeles in the 1970s cited above, the researchers also gathered data on the women's reasons for migrating. Roughly 50 percent of these undocumented migrants came to the US with the intention of working, and about 70 percent cited economic incentives as a very important reasons for migrating. In spite of the fact that economic incentives were a primary motivation for migration among the majority of these women, the undocumented female immigrants cited a number of important reasons for migrating. Almost 46 percent said family unity was a very important reason for migrating; 64 percent stated that personal benefits ('to see and do things and have a better life') were a very important consideration; and, almost 40 percent of the women stated that the ability to offer their children more opportunities was a very important reason that they had migrated illegally.[7] Clearly, economic incentives were a key consideration for most of these illegal female migrants, the majority of whom worked in factories, restaurants, retail, or in domestic service. Nonetheless, their decision to migrate was shaped by a variety of additional factors. Moreover, at least 30 percent of these women did not cite economic considerations as a very important motivation (Simon and DeLey, 1984, p. 1214). Broad generalizations cannot be drawn about the motivations of undocumented female migrants from this one study of illegal migrants to Mexico to Los Angeles. However, the study does suggest that it will be important for migration scholars to investigate women who migrate illegally and their motivations rather than just to assume that illegal migrants tend to be single men who migrate solely for economic reasons.

D. Refugee Migration

A common perception exists that women are disproportionately represented in refugee flows. According to figures released by the UN High Commissioner for Refugees in 1993, 80 percent of the 19 million refugees in the world were women and children. However, a recent study by the United Nations suggests that this figure should be regarded with some reservations. As with all migrants, statistics on refugees are incomplete, and typically data on sex is not collected. The perception that women and children are disproportionately represented in refugee flows, especially in developing countries, 'is simply a recognition of the fact that refugees are generally representative of the population as a whole of high fertility countries...' (United Nations, 1994, p. 78). The UN suggests that these numbers actually will vary across countries and regions (United Nations, 1994, pp. 79-80). Clearly, the collection of complete and accurate data on the sex composition of refugee flows are an important area for research on women and international migration.

While collecting accurate data on the absolute numbers of men and women in refugee flows represents an important preliminary step for further migration research in this area, it is even more crucial that migration scholars reflect on how gender stereotypes shape state refugee policies and, in this way, may work to the detriment of women. The United Nations notes that women have been underrepresented in the numbers of refugees admitted for resettlement and among asylum-seekers in developed countries. The under-representation of women in refugee flows reflects, in part, the legal criteria for granting refugee status (United Nations, 1994, p. 80). Under the 1951 Convention Relating to the Status of Refugees and the 1967 Protocol to this convention, refugees can be defined as any person outside of his or her country of persecution who is unwilling to return to this country because of a 'well-founded fear' of persecution 'for reasons of race, religion, nationality, membership of a particular social group or political opinion'. Note that this definition does not include gender persecution as grounds for receiving refugee status. As a result, women who are trying to escape violence or persecution that they suffer specifically because they are women, which might range from domestic violence, to genital mutilation, to rape (Slack, 1988; Thomas and Beasley, 1993; Cook, 1993), may not be granted refugee status on these grounds.

Although female international migration has been under-studied in general, the lack of systematic scholarly research on women in international refugee movements is especially acute. A great deal of research has been completed on the particular forms of persecution against women; more work needs to be done on the extent to which such persecution leads women to seek refugee status abroad. At the same time, further research on how the existing international legal definition of refugee shapes female migration flows is necessary. Similarly, more research on how states' interpretation and application of this definition shapes female migration flows would be very valuable. For example, an investigation of whether the failure of refugee policies to adequately address gender persecution leads women to attempt to migrate illegally in large numbers would add significantly to migration scholars' understanding of the determinants of international migration flows in general. Finally, investigations of how gender roles shape women's inability or unwillingness to view migration as an outlet for escaping persecution will be useful.

III. OVERVIEW OF VOLUME

The chapters in Part I of this volume examine the economic status of migrant women in their host societies.[8] To date, studies of the economic status of migrant women have focused on the exploitation of women who migrate to work in the low-wage labor sector. Two of the chapters in this section address women in these vulnerable economic positions. Kathleen Staudt examines the case of women who work in the 'informal economy' along the US–Mexico border, specifically in the border cities of El Paso–Juárez. Staudt argues that US immigration policy discourages women's self-sufficiency by cracking down on work in the informal sector, including domestic service, street vending, and home-based contracting, which is widely accepted in Mexico and which often enables women to be self-employed. As a solution to this problem, Staudt looks at the activities of FEMAP, a Mexican non-governmental organization which uses a community bank model to promote women's businesses in an effort to plant the seeds of their self-sufficiency, and the obstacles to applying this model in the US. Finally, Staudt explores policy proposals designed to balance dual concerns: promoting women's self-sufficiency while ensuring that they are not exploited in the informal labor sector.

Shu-Ju Ada Cheng also looks at the status of women in the low-wage sector of in the international economy through a case study of women domestic workers in East Asia. She argues that the international sexual division of labor has been reinforced and perpetuated through labor migration. Importantly, she concludes that pre-existing gender inequality is reinforced not only by the position of women in a capitalist global economy but also by state policies on development.

The remaining chapters in Part I are unique in that they look at women in other sectors of the global economy. The chapter by David Ip and Constance Lever-Tracy focuses on migrant women from Asia who work in business in Australia. Looking at the cases of 138 businesses owned by people of Chinese and Indian ethnicity in Brisbane and Sydney, the authors find that women play an important role in nearly two-fifths of these businesses. In fact, women play important management roles in many cases, and in some cases have the primary responsibility for running the business. Ip and Lever-Tracy conclude that these findings challenge the notion that women are underrepresented in migrant businesses and that they are in subordinate positions in a patriarchal system.

The chapter by Nandini Assar also looks at the role of women in family-owned business among migrants in the case of Indian-American motel owners in the US. She finds that women's labor substantially contributes to the economic success of these families. At the same time, she argues that US immigration policy, in particular with its emphasis on family reunification, reinforces traditional gender roles within Indian families.

Cecilia G. Manrique and Gabriel G. Manrique look at the case of 'third world' migrant women in higher education in the US. Relying on both analyses of a nationwide survey as well as in-depth interviews of immigrant women faculty, Manrique and Manrique show that a variety of factors, not only economic ones, drive the migration of women. These factors include a desire to improve their social status, to find new opportunities for professional advancement, and to escape traditional gender roles. Although many of the immigrant women interviewed by Manrique and Manrique say that these goals have been satisfied, this chapter also documents the multiple forms of discrimination that third world migrant women face in higher education in the US.

Part II of this volume addresses the social status of migrant women in their host societies. The chapter by Lisa Simons discusses the mail order bride industry with a specific focus on the case of Filipina women migrating to the US. Simons, relying especially on advertisements posted on the Internet, documents the way in which mail order brides are marketed. She also explores the way in which cultural changes in the US have helped to create a 'niche' of men who need to look abroad for women who will fulfill their wishes for a 'traditional' (read submissive) wife. Simons concludes by arguing that the status of mail order brides could be improved through a shift in the legal understanding of women's rights as international migrants.

The chapter by Lynn Morrison, Sepali Guruge, and Kym Snarr also addresses the issue of migrant women and marriage in the host societies. Their study of Sri Lankan Tamils in Toronto considers the ways in which migration has shaped gender relations, with a particular focus on the issues of marriage, dating, premarital sex, and 'sexual decision-making'. The authors note that certain behavioral changes are evident, with some increase in the acceptance of dating and premarital sex as well as a significant increase in divorce rates and separations. Additionally, the authors found evidence of an alarming increase in reports of domestic abuse, perhaps attributable to the profound transformation of gender roles in Canada. The authors also point out that many Tamil men prefer to marry women who are still residing in Sri Lanka and who have not yet been immersed in Canadian culture. In spite of these changes, the authors conclude that it is too early to know the extent to which traditional values will be maintained among Tamils in Canada.

The chapter by Larissa I. Remennick examines the experience of women from the former Soviet Union who have resettled in Israel. Remennick's chapter focuses on the downward social-occupational ability of these women and their exposure to sexual harassment due to their vulnerable economic status. The chapter also discusses changes in family and child-bearing practices among these women. It concludes by exploring the health problems faced by these women in Israel.

In the final chapter in this section, Brigitte Bechtold and Ludmila Dziewięcka-Bokun examine social services for immigrant women in Europe. The authors provide an overview of the status of female immigrants in the traditional and the new receiving countries in Europe and explore the relevant European Union regulations that affect women migrants. They also examine the impact of European integration and the move to the common currency, which they argue is reducing the economic commitments to social protection programs. Finally, they look at the Council of Europe's Project on Human Dignity and Social Exclusion as potential mechanisms for improving the well-being of immigrant women. Unfortunately, they conclude that, to date, women remain invisible in official statistics on the social well-being of Europeans in general. The invisibility of women in official statistics, in turn, hinders the access of women to social services and, hence, is an obstacle to the improvement of migrant women's social status in the host societies.

The chapters in this volume represent a diversity of views regarding the status of migrant women in host societies. They illustrate that migrant women do not represent a homogenous category. Migrant women come from a variety of places and are shaped by divergent cultures and class experiences. Moreover, their reasons for leaving their countries of origin range from political persecution, to economic vulnerability, to a desire for professional opportunities and liberation. The chapters in this volume recognize the diversity of migrant women by looking not only at the cases of women who migrate to participate in low-wage sectors of the global economy but also women who have managerial positions in business as well as women in academics. By highlighting the experiences of diverse women who have various motivations for migrating and who experience migration in different ways, this volume challenges simplistic assumptions about the status of migrant women in host societies. It is too simple to conclude that migrant women constitute only a vulnerable, exploited class. At the same time, it is just as simplistic to assume that migrant women are necessarily liberated from restrictive gender roles in their host societies. As this volume illustrates, international female migration is a multifaceted experience, characterized simultaneously in many cases by liberation, discrimination, and exploitation.

IV. CONCLUSION: MAKING WOMEN VISIBLE IN SCHOLARSHIP ON INTERNATIONAL MIGRATION

The invisibility of women in international migration scholarship does not correspond to the reality of international migration. Women migrate across international boundaries at approximately the same rate as men, and the multiple causes of female international migration challenge uni-dimensional analyses of international migration. Existing studies suggest that women migrate across international borders for a variety of complex reasons, including economic incentives, family reunification, the possibility of greater autonomy, opportunities for their children, or the hope that they can escape gender-based prosecution. Moreover, the unique experiences of women migrants in adjusting to host societies also challenge migration scholarship which would treat males as the norm. Thus, making women visible in the study of international migration is likely to complicate rather than simplify the scholarly effort to explain international migration.

By making women visible, a fundamental purpose of this volume is to contribute to a more accurate and complete picture of international migration. Yet, the research in this volume represents only one step towards raising the visibility of women in international migration research. In the future, migration scholars also should examine several issues related to female international migration in order to enhance our understanding of international migration in general. First, scholars should explore the ways in which prescribed gender roles shape immigration policies in receiving countries and affect migration choices in countries of origin. By examining these issues, scholars will contribute to a greater understanding of the dynamics of family migration, which likely will continue to be the primary avenue for female migration in the years to come. Second, scholars should continue to investigate the employment-based migration of women under a variety of occupational categories. Studies of female labor migration, to date, typically have focused on the migration of unskilled female labor. The studies of women in diverse occupations, such as those included in Part I of this volume, will enhance our understanding of international labor migration. Specifically, greater attention to the migration of skilled female labor and the migration of female managers and professionals will provide a more complete and accurate picture of employment-based international migration. Third, additional studies on the determinants of the illegal migration of women across international borders are necessary in order to contribute to our understanding of the causes of international migration in general as well as our ability to answer the question of whether states can control illegal immigration or not. The ability of states to control illegal migration depends, to a great extent, on the extent to which the state can affect the forces driving illegal migration. Thus, it is crucial to learn more about what drives the illegal migration of women as well as men. Finally, additional research on how gender roles shape both state refugee policies and women's migration decisions will contribute greatly to our understanding of the causes of international migration. In sum, migration scholars need to concentrate on making women visible in the study of international migration in order to enhance our understanding of this complex phenomenon. This volume represents a preliminary effort to move towards this goal.

NOTES

1. A significant proportion of the feminist literature on international relations draws on the idea that gender, viewed as the socially or culturally constructed ideals of masculinity and femininity, tells us more about male and female behavior than biological differences between men and women (Peterson and Runyan, 1993, pp. 5, 120–1; Tickner, 1992, p. 7).
2. It is necessary to distinguish between the stock and flow of immigrants. The flow of immigrants refers to the number of individuals entering a country during a particular period of time. The stock of immigrants refers to the number of individuals residing in a country at a specific time. Migration

flows into a country do not provide any evidence about net migration because they do not incorporate flows out of the country. Thus, the stock of international migrants provides a better picture of permanent migration.

3. Note that the proportion of women admitted under the occupational preference categories would be even higher than one-third because visas are allocated under the occupational preference categories in US immigration law to the dependents of migrant workers as well. Thus, spouses and children of workers admitted under occupational preferences are also counted as occupational migrants even if they are not admitted to work. A higher proportion of the dependents admitted under the occupational preference categories have been women.

4. Immigration scholars increasingly use the term 'undocumented' to describe illegal immigrants because the term 'illegal' negatively characterizes immigrants who enter and/or reside in a country without legal documentation, and the same term is not used to describe the employers of these individuals. However, the term undocumented has problems as well. Technically it does not accurately describe those immigrants who enter or reside in a country with fraudulent documents, and it downplays the fact that these immigrants have violated immigration laws in the 'receiving country,' regardless of what one thinks about these laws. In spite of their shortcomings, both terms will be used because of the lack of consensus on a more appropriate term.

5. Another dimension of illegal female migration in the US case involves 'commuter workers'. Many Mexican women commute across the US–Mexican border daily, using short-term crossing cards issued to allow tourism and shopping, to work in the US as domestic workers (Fernández-Kelly, 1983, pp. 213–14).

6. Only 18 percent of these women were legalized under the Seasonal Agricultural Program, which suggests that a small, though still noteworthy, number of women participate in illegal agricultural labor.

7. The importance of economic motivations for the undocumented women contrasted with the response of legal female immigrants in the same survey who cited family unity as the most important reason for migrating. Nevertheless, even the legal female migrants cited economic incentives, personal benefits, and opportunities for their children as key motivations (Simon and DeLey, 1984, p. 1214).

8. There is some overlap among the categories in this volume. For example, some of the papers included in the section on economic status also address the social status of migrant women and vice versa. Nevertheless, papers were categorized according to their primary focus.

REFERENCES

Boyd, Monica. 1995. 'Migration Regulations and Sex Selective Outcomes in Developed Countries'. In *International Migration Policies and the Status of Female Migrants*. Proceedings of the United Nations Expert Group Meeting on International Migration Policies and the Status of Female Migrants. San Miniato, Italy, 28–31 March 1990.

——. 1989. 'Family and Personal Networks In International Migration: Recent Developments and New Agendas'. *International Migration Review*. 23(3): 638–69.

Brettell, Caroline B. and Rita James Simon. 1986. 'Immigrant Women: An Introduction'. In Rita James Simon and Caroline B. Brettell, eds. *International Migration: The Female Experience*. Totowa, New Jersey: Rowman and Allanheld.

Cook, Rebecca J. 1993. 'Women's International Human Rights Law: The Way Forward'. *Human Rights Quarterly*. 15: 230–61.

DeLaet, Debra L. 1995. *Domestic Politics, Interdependence, and the Regulation of International Migration: a Case Study of Current Immigration Policy*. Dissertation. Department of Government and International Studies, University of Notre Dame.

De Wenden, Catherine Wihtol and Margo Corona DeLey. 1986. 'French Immigration Policy Reform 1981–1982 and the Female Migrant'. In Rita James Simon and Caroline B. Brettell, eds. *International Migration: The Female Experience*. Totowa, New Jersey: Rowman and Allanheld, pp. 197–212.

Fernández-Kelly, María Patricia. 1983. 'Mexican Border Industrialization, Female Labor Force Participation and Migration'. In June Nash and María Patricia Fernández-Kelly, eds. *Women, Men, and the International Division of Labor*. Albany: State University of New York Press.

Goodman, Charity. 1987. 'Immigration and Class Mobility: the Case of Family Reunification Wives in West Germany'. *Women's Studies*. 13(3): 235–48.

Halliday, Fred. 1994. *Rethinking International Relations*. Vancouver: University of British Columbia Press.

Houstoun, Marion F., Roger G. Kramer, and Joan Mackin Barrett. 1984. 'Female Predominance in Immigration to the United States Since 1930: A First Look'. *International Migration Review*. 18(4): 908–63.

Lim, Lin Lean. 1995. 'The Status of Women and International Migration'. In *International Migration Policies and the Status of Female Migrants*. Proceedings of the United Nations Expert Group Meeting on International Migration Policies and the Status of Female Migrants. San Miniato, Italy, 28–31 March 1990.

Morokvasic, Mirjana. 1984. 'Birds of Passage are also Women...'. *International Migration Review*. 18(4): 886–907.

——. 1983. 'Women in migration: beyond the reductionist outlook'. In Annie Phizacklea, ed. *One Way Ticket: Migration and Female Labour*. London: Routledge & Kegan Paul.

Peterson, V. Spike and Anne Sisson Runyan. 1993. *Global Gender Issues*. Boulder: Westview Press.

Phizacklea, Annie. 1983. *One-Way Ticket: Migration and Female Labour*. London: Routledge & Kegan Paul.

Ravensten, E.G. 1885. 'The Laws of Migration'. *Journal of the Royal Statistical Society*. 48(2): 167–235.

Sassen-Koob, Saskia. 1984. 'Notes on the Incorporation of Third World Women into Wage-Labor Through Immigration and Off-Shore Production'. *International Migration Review*. 18(4): 1144–67.

Simon, Rita J. and C.B. Brettell, eds. 1986. *International Migration: the Female Experience*. Totowa, NJ: Rowman and Allanheld.

Simon, Rita J. and Margo DeLey. 1984. 'The Work Experience of Undocumented Mexican Women in Los Angeles'. *International Migration Review*. 18(4): 1212–29.

Slack, Alison T. 1988. 'Female Circumcision: A Critical Appraisal'. *Human Rights Quarterly*. 10: 438–86.

Tickner, J. Ann. 1992. *Gender in International Relations*. New York: Columbia University Press.

Thomas, Dorothy Q. and Michele E. Beasley, Esq. 1993. 'Domestic Violence as a Human Rights Issue'. *Human Rights Quarterly*. 15: 36–62.

Tyree, Andrea and Katharine M. Donato. 1986. 'A Demographic Overview of the International Migration of Women'. In Rita James Simon and Caroline B. Brettell, eds. *International Migration: the Female Experience*. Totowa, New Jersey: Rowman and Allanheld.

United Nations. 1995. *International Migration Policies and the Status of Female Migrants*. Proceedings of the United Nations Expert Group Meeting on International Migration Policies and the Status of Female Migrants. San Miniato, Italy, 28–31 March 1990.

——. 1994. *The Migration of Women: Methodological Issues in the Measurement and Analysis of Internal and International Migration*. Santo Domingo, Dominican Republic: International Research and Training Institute for the Advancement of Women.

Zlotnik, Hania. 1995. 'The South-to-North Migration of Women'. *International Migration Review*. 29(1): 229–54.

Part I
The Economic Status of International Female Migrants

2 Seeds for Self-Sufficiency? Policy Contradictions at the US–Mexico Border

Kathleen Staudt

Women at the US–Mexico border frequently work in the informal economy, earning relatively meager sums. On the US side of the border, just as in many 'southern' countries from which migrants come, poverty is widespread: official unemployment rates are in the double-digits; a fourth of households fall below the official poverty line; and approximately a quarter of formal jobs offer poverty-level (that is, minimum-wage) salaries.[1]

Why focus on the international border? The border itself is a special locale, creating opportunities for informal exchanges that use comparative advantages in trade and wages. US residents shop for cheaper goods and services on the Mexico side. Likewise, shoppers and day workers seek US wages and consumer goods for resale on their side. From a distance, borders seemingly *contain* people and corporations who identify with their nations, yet space along the US–Mexico border belies these myths with a porous border as part of everyday reality. Perhaps observers could have looked to the border before waiting for Saskia Sassen's analysis of 'global cities' like New York and Miami which respect few borders both for telecommunication among global elites and for the poor who often work in immigrant enclaves.[2] Robert Reich and others before him have warned about the disconnection between corporate loyalty and nation; what counts are the *people* who live, work, and pay taxes within national lines.[3] Borders and global cities remind us just how much the US economy is globalized. Perhaps US public policy ought to take that into account more fully.

To imagine border connections more metaphorically, then, are borders moving north? In this chapter, we analyze El Paso-Juárez landscape, a metropolitan area of two million people, as the lighthouse for the future. Besides borders, the immigration experience also provides a handle around which we can examine the US in the global political economy. Migrants from the south – Latin America, Africa, and Asia – come from countries with extensively informalized economies, as noted below. Migrants bring everyday experience in informal work, such as home-based contracting, domestic service, open-air markets, and street vending, from their homelands to their US destinations. US immigration policy assumes that migrants will be economically self-sufficient. In US historical experience, many immigrants have climbed the economic ladder through self-sufficiency and self-employment. Policy assumptions about self-sufficiency are painfully and obviously evident with changes in welfare policy, even as US free trade policies encourage capital flight. Nowhere are these contractions clearer than at the border itself, frontlines for the North American Free Trade Agreement (NAFTA).

In this chapter, I analyze public policies at the local, state, and national levels that constrain women's ability to work freely and profitably at self-employment in the informal economy. This chapter first introduces the conceptual lens of informal work to demonstrate the relevance of international development models for application within the United States. It then reports on research at the border which demonstrates the extensiveness of informality – no surprise for Mexico, but perhaps a shock for the United States. The chapter goes on to analyze good and bad news about informal work, including the efforts of a Mexican non-government organization (NGO) to transfer a successful model of women's community banks for micro-enterprise 'northward' to El Paso. What this analysis reveals is a set of contradictory and ineffective policies: *public policies frequently discourage, rather than encourage, women's self-sufficiency, whether the grand surveillance policies of immigration control or the petty surveillance policy of local commerce regulators who generate revenue for the city and county governments.* The chapter concludes with policy recommendations.

INFORMAL, SELF-EMPLOYMENT

To understand and address cheapened labor in a global economy, and specifically women's labor within that global economy, we look southward to the research on women and gender in development. A basic tenet of that research is that much of women's work goes unrecognized, unvalued, and undercounted.[4] This chapter focuses specifically on women's informal work, also known as self-employment. According to Portes, *et al.*, informal labor involves all income-producing activities, except for that 'income from contractual and legally regulated employment'.[5]

The terminology of informal labor was born in Africa and legitimized with studies sponsored by the International Labour Organization (ILO), affiliated with the United Nations. Researchers sought to understand how

people supported themselves with income-generating activities in economies with limited formal, wage-earning opportunities. In many southern
countries, informal workers make up a third or more of economically
active people. Early ILO studies counted, among definitive characteristics
of informality, small-scale, low-capital, simple technology activities that
governments did not count or extract revenue from. From those studies,
policy analysts frequently recommended the simplification of regulations
and the provision of credit in order that 'microenterpreneurs' be able to
upgrade and expand their businesses. The early studies assumed that informality would diminish with modernization and industrialization.[6]

Analysts soon dispelled these assumptions, documenting the connections between a so-called modern global economy and informality.[7] First,
corporations seeking to reduce costs have established 'offshore' operations
in countries of the south. Corporations divide parts of the fragmented
production process to subcontractors who pay low wages and limited
benefits to a temporary workforce. Free trade and regional trading block
policies like NAFTA help foster a global economy with these wage and
consumption links.

Second, structural adjustment programs promulgated by the World Bank
and International Monetary Fund encourage (even force) southern countries
to cut back subsidies, social programs, and government jobs. With less
government support (amid already meager public subsidies), people turn
to multiple income-generating activities, some of them through home-
based and self-employment. Such policies also encourage people to migrate
in search of better income-generating opportunities.

ILO affiliates in the Americas and others have documented women's
sizeable participation among informal, self-employed workers. Women
number nearly half of informals, not surprising when one counts paid
domestic workers in this category.[8] Among informal workers, gender
hierarchy often prevails, with men assuming higher skill, more profitable
activities.[9] And women face even greater squeezes than men from formal
credit programs, whether commercial bank or government sponsored.
According to the United Nations Development Programme (UNDP),
women receive proportionally smaller loan amounts than their numbers
among the self-employed would seem to warrant. Furthermore, '[i]n 1990,
multilateral banks allocated about $6 billion for rural credit to developing
countries, but only 5% reached rural women.'[10]

Governments in Latin America, all too keenly aware of informality, often
document this sizeable group as well through their own studies. Mexico, for
example, began these studies in 1977 and periodically count informals in
quarterly labor surveys. In so doing, the government legitimizes informality

as work, but according to some critics, the government also mystifies poverty therein.[11] Mexico's economic crises of the 1980s, due to international debt and downturns in oil demand, are associated with the increased women among economically active workers.[12]

Yet we cannot assume that self-employment or informality is automatically associated with poverty. Mexico's official minimum wage is below its poverty line, so workers cannot always 'afford' to earn such low wages in export-processing factories and other jobs. Before Mexico's peso devaluation of late 1994, weekly minimum wages amounted to $30, while after devaluation they amounted to half that figure, or $15. Moreover, the international border offers crossing opportunities in sales and service work that reap more than the Mexican minimum wage.[13] Workers turn to self-employment instead.

The political culture in Mexico, like other southern countries in the Americas, fosters collective organization among residents. Some informal workers belong to such organizations, affiliated with political parties. Thus, they gain some political leverage unavailable to illegitimate, hidden informal workers. Even paid domestic workers organize themselves collectively in many Latin American countries, unlike the United States.[14]

In the United States, informality is neither well recognized nor fully counted. The census counts people's primary jobs, undercounting second and casual income-earning work and resulting in self-employment figures around 10 percent since the 1950s.[15] Sociologists have documented the existence of ethnic and immigrant enclaves in which informality flourishes.[16] Yet the stigmatization of both this work and its study[17] may reduce our ability to understand the full scope of informality in the US economy.

All too often, research and official studies of the US treat informal work as crime or tax evasion.[18] For people who depend on needs-based assistance, such as welfare, food stamps or subsidized housing, additional income-earning results in penalties (reduced benefits) and fines (for 'coverups'). Mid-1990s changes in social programs may change penalties associated with work; most certainly, though, budgetary reductions will diminish the number of recipients, thereby increasing their needs to earn income.

RESEARCH: LOCALE, RESULTS

The US–Mexico border serves as a lens through which to examine policies that support or undermine women's ability to support themselves through informal labor. The use of multiple research methods allowed a comprehensive understanding of spatial, income, and migrant characteristics associated with informal labor and its profitability. The use of a border laboratory-like social setting allowed a comparison of the policy and political context in which informals work. Specifically, what does the Mexico experience have to say to the United States? El Paso-Juárez is a gateway in the Americas, a magnet for different kinds of migrants. 1990 Census data from both countries are revealing. In El Paso, a quarter of the population is what the census calls 'foreign born'. Its population is a 'majority minority group'; 70 percent of El Pasoans are Spanish speakers whom the census calls 'Hispanic', but who identify themselves largely as Mexican-American, Mexican, and Mexicano. A full half of the Juárez population was born elsewhere in Mexico. The largely US-based maquiladoras offer mostly minimum-wage salaries to between 130,000 and 150,000 workers in the early 1990s, a majority of them female. Job availability attracts migrants from the interior.[19] (The 1994 peso devaluation reduced labor costs in US dollar terms, thereby accounting for the increased numbers.) The El Paso-Juárez gateway locale, hopefully, is also a gateway of insights on policies and political strategies involving the self-employed, insights applicable to other cities increasingly part of the global economy.

The data came from several samples. First and foremost, in a National Science Foundation-supported faculty-student research team, we drew random samples of households from six neighborhoods in El Paso and Ciudad Juárez. The sample numbered 465 households, representing 2031 individuals with 131 informal businesses. Our response rate was 77 percent.[20] These spatially distinctive neighborhoods comprised core, old periphery and new periphery areas of both cities. While core, downtown neighborhoods are old, with high numbers of renters, the periphery neighborhoods of the US southwest and of Mexico draw settlers to these unplanned, underserviced areas in which considerable housing is built through self-help.

The survey research is supplemented with several smaller purposive samples of street vendors, cross-border traders (*fayuqueras*), and community bankers (*banqueras*). Since 1993, I have provided service for the Seeds Across the Border Initiative, spearheaded by the Federación Mexicana de Asociaciones Privadas (FEMAP), a Mexican NGO devoted to health and community development. Additionally, we in the research team interviewed officials and leaders in both cities.

THE PREVALENCE OF INFORMAL WORK

In this study, we defined informality in inclusive ways, drawing on approaches used in various countries. In Mexico, work without social security payments indicates informality as does people's self-identification of work and business out of their homes and on the streets. We also tapped routine and occasional informality. With this inclusive approach, we documented informal work in at least one in three households, on both sides of the border. This is a conservative estimate, for one should assume a certain reluctance among people to reveal income generation, even in face-to-face interviews that guarantee anonymity and disconnection with officialdom. We deliberately excluded illegal goods and services from our study, such as drugs, gambling, and sex work.

Women and men work in nearly equal numbers at informal work, but often in sex-typed activities. Women worked as maids, traders, and childcare attendants. Some did home-based catering for parties or provided beauty services. Several, trained as practical nurses, gave injections to neighbors, for pharmaceutical goods are easily and cheaply available without prescription in Juárez. Men worked as gardeners and in house and auto repair. Some bought, fixed up, and resold cars. Still others worked in construction and brick masonry.

Both men and women, especially in Juárez, bought goods on one side of the border (El Paso) and resold them to Mexican consumers hungry for US goods. Together, men and women sell goods out of their homes (*tienditas*, or little stores for snacks and sodas), and at garage, neighborhood and flea markets where used goods are an important stock in trade. Street vending, high-visibility work in Juárez, draws both men and women who sell prepared food, cigarettes, balloons, and seasonal gifts. Men who sell food visibly are often assisted by women, who work less visibly to prepare the food.

Informals' earnings were modest, even meager from the perspective of the US side of the border. Men and women informals in Juárez earned the equivalent of $60 weekly, which represented earnings of double the minimum wage. Some of them, especially the border crossers, capitalized on the comparative advantage of US wages for part-time work in El Paso and of high-demand US goods and prices for small electronics, jewelry, clothing, and household goods (before the Border Patrol instituted its blockade, discussed below). Juárez women who didn't cross the border reaped pitiful wages, working as maids or taking in ironing. US-resident women also earned an average of $60, most of them working in a home base (child care, domestic work); cross-border shopping for goods produces no advantage for them as for Juárez women. Only one group emerged as relatively privileged among informals: US-resident men, who enjoy comparable advantages in work with machines (for cars and home repair) versus work with people (cleaning, children). Yet their average earnings of

$120 weekly, double that of Juárez men and women in both Juárez and El Paso, still is less than the poverty-level US minimum wage in multiple-person households.

MIGRATION AND POVERTY IN EL PASO

Border residents are a mix of citizens and immigrants, most of them legal permanent residents but some of them undocumented immigrants. Frequently, households are migration mosaics containing people who range from native born to naturalized and citizen children to permanent residents (including those amnestied from the 1986 Immigration Reform and Control Act) and those without 'papers' (the colloquial term for undocumented). On the El Paso side, two neighborhood samples had particularly high percentages of households with the 'foreign born' (in census terms): the core downtown, and the new periphery outside the city limits in one of many unplanned settlements known as *colonias*.

Presumably, immigrant heritage provides baggage with connections to informal work. While some immigrants live in a kind of citizenship limbo, others shed the heritage, exposed as they are to hegemonic institutions (in Gramscian terms) that seek to embrace them, even with homelands (Mexico) so close to their new homes. Almost the entire sample of those surveyed consisted of self-defined ethnics (Mexican Americans, Hispanics) or Mexicans (Mexicanos), but it would be a mistake to assume that ethnics necessarily share immigrant characteristics.

No clear relationship exists between immigration and informality. Looking at the El Paso subsample, and the informal subsample within that, households with all adults born in the US were just as likely to work informally as those households with immigrant/naturalized adults. Yet readers should exercise caution with this small sample size. Moreover, household samples cast wider nets than samples targeted at informal workers. A study of El Paso street vendors – based on face-to-face interviews and on a universe of those issued tickets in a street vendor sweep of 1992 – found about half of them non-US citizens.[21]

Similarly, no clear relationship existed between poverty and informality. If, in a neighborhood-contextualized definition, we understand poverty as above or below the income mean, informality was just as likely to be pursued by the relatively well off as the not-so-well off. Informal work requires some start-up capital, and even money for transportation. Virtually all informals in our sample – whichever side of the border on which they lived – used their own savings or help from family and friends for start-up costs. They did not rely on commercial banks and government loans. Those people in absolutely dire circumstances lack savings or friends for loans.

Those well-off households maintained their status through multiple jobs among household members. Three and four earners created the highest household earnings (sometimes all earning the minimum wage), and informality is another earning source. These residents rely on what Henry Selby *et al.* call the 'Mexican Solution', of multiple earners in households.[22] But it is a solution also used among US citizens in a globalized economy.

The household migration mosaic creates a disposition to avoid rather than engage government for needs-based assistance. One of the most surprising findings from the worst-off neighborhood – the El Paso core – was that just a third of those households received food stamps, despite probable need and qualification in all those households. According to the 1990 census, the household income in this census track can be rounded off to a mere $7,100 compared to El Paso's household median of $22,600.

Even worse for those residents, an atmosphere of surveillance pervades the area whether from the immigration authorities or from gangs. Amid fearfulness and disgust about drugs and public drunkenness, residents have few to call on save the police. Yet many respondents offered complaints about those same police, from delays to abuse. Although residents often conveyed the sentiment that police are never there when needed, they offered no parallel sentiments about the ubiquitous Border Patrol agents driving around in their green vans. Even though our questionnaire contained no specific questions about these street-level bureaucrats – Border Patrol agents whose actions make public policies real for residents[23] – many respondents offered unsolicited comments. 'They're always around, but they don't do anything for the community'; 'He stopped me for no reason.'

PUBLIC POLICY IN PRACTICE: PEOPLE'S EVERYDAY EXPERIENCES

A myriad of public policies are designed to regulate informal work and cross-border movements of people and goods. Those policies require permits or licenses as well as fees and taxes to be paid. For some types of work, policies require goods and services to be provided in particular ways – ways that on the one hand enhance public health and safety as well as on the other, cover the costs of enforcement staff, satisfy past bureaucratic whims, and prove compliance. What matters here is how those policies are enforced.

Policies, of course, change constantly – not the least reasons for which are prevailing political winds. Local and state governments extract revenue from commerce, including the more difficult to monitor informal commerce. They do so with more (Juárez) or less (El Paso) plentiful staff. Three factors are addressed in this chapter which set Juárez informals apart from the counterparts in El Paso. First, informal commerce is a legitimate and recognized form of labor in Mexico. In the US, prevailing views assume that informality is not job creation, but rather crime or tax evasion. Second, policies about informal commerce in the Municipality of Juárez are enforced flexibly, sometimes subject to negotiation, revenue extraction, and side payments. In contrast, El Paso policies about informal commerce often go unenforced, partly due to insufficient staff for implementing complex regulations. But when those rules are enforced, staff do so with a virulence and momentum that envelops informals in a costly criminal justice system. Third, informals in Juárez are a large, visible group who occasionally organize and protest publicly when they perceive their interests are threatened. El Paso informals operate alone, using enforcement cracks to their advantage (meager as that advantage is for most).

In the household sample, respondents say they are able to ignore regulations on the whole. On questions about the need for permits, approximately a quarter claimed these were necessary and fewer still held permits on both sides of the border. Few informals in the household sample had problems with authorities, one in ten or less on both sides of the border. We must understand this 'noncompliance' in terms of modest businesses which operate unexposed in the public world on the whole.

In contrast, in the special samples of informals who operate in public and visible ways, problems with authorities were far more common. Two brief cases illustrate this process.

Cross-border traders, known as *fayuqueras*, shopped in El Paso for new and used goods they would resell in Juárez. Many have Border Crossing Cards that permit up to 72 hours presence in the US for shopping and visiting relatives. The term sounds ominous (contrabandists) for these informal small-scale businesses which generally fit stock in trade in shopping bags. However, *fayuqueras* avoid the complexities of customs brokers, import–export trade regulations, sales tax in Mexico (they pay in the US), and duty-free caps. Moreover, they even deal in 'prohibited' goods such as used clothing. In the 1992 sample, 21 of the 36 women had been harassed by authorities, most of them Mexican customs agents at the international border bridges. Yet the negotiations and payments they made could be absorbed in the costs of doing business. However, NAFTA was put in place on 1 January 1994. Once 'free trade' was in place, procedures tightened up in the name of efficiency, a likely blow to most informals for whom accountants, lawyers, customs brokers would undermine their operations. In 1992, street vendors, downtown merchants, and urban authorities underwent conflicts over the use of public space. The course of resolving these conflicts varied widely in Juárez and El Paso, due to their political institutions and vendor voices in those institutions. In Juárez, the authorities offered hundreds of spaces in some of the many public markets in the city wherein vendors pay rent and are more easily policed for sales tax payments; to ease the move, officials offered discounts and forgiveness for permits and fines. Still, vendors unhappy with spots in outlying markets simply moved back. In large numbers, and with their willingness to protest publicly, vendors became a thorn in the side of authorities, too costly politically to eliminate. Downtown vendors simply absorbed the fines, side payments, and confiscation of their goods as part of doing business.

The course of action in El Paso was quite different. During the 1992 conflict with merchants, vendors were ticketed, fined, and for those who did not appear, issued warrants for their arrest. A small group organized a vendors' association through which they negotiated with better organized downtown merchants and city officials. City councilmen passed an ordinance that legitimized 32 authorized public spaces with high permit, insurance, storage, and surveillance costs. Women and men vendors used kinship connections to secure spots in the official, public draw. For example, the husband (president of the vendors' organization) picked a low number, but the wife (treasurer) and daughter picked numbers high enough in the draw to secure spots.

Petty regulations range from those absorbable in business costs to others that put people out of business. People are often willing to take risks that bank on uneven enforcement, and if netted, negotiate individually or collectively with street-level bureaucrats or local government officials.

In great contrast, grand regulations imposed from above or from national officials in distant capital cities, are far more difficult to manage for informals. NAFTA is one such example, supposedly streamlining procedures to make it easier for established businesses to engage in cross-border trade. No NAFTA side agreements got negotiated for informals.

Another example of grand regulations comes from Border Patrol surveillance. On 19 September 1993, a border blockade was installed, linking agents close to one another along the border within city limits. This operation was subsequently renamed Operation Hold the Line, and Congress authorized many more positions for policy enforcement. The blockade intimidated, even eliminated some daywork crossers such as vendors, maids, and gardeners. Even shoppers with Border Crossing Cards worried, for cards got confiscated. Of course, the Blockade eased some of the street surveillance that downtown residents faced on an everyday basis.

The biggest blow, however, to Juárez crossers came in the form of the 1994 peso devaluation. Within months, pesos diminished to half their value in US currency terms. With most food and housing prices continuing at pre-devaluation levels, Juárez workers and shoppers had less surplus and savings to trade or to buy. Fiscal austerity measures pulled people in line, containing them within their own borderline at the same time.

What, then, should be done in political and policy enforcement terms to allow people to work toward self-sufficiency? Self-employment is the essence of informal labor. And how can modest earnings be expanded into more profitable labors with the capacity to generate employment for others? To upgrade informality is to legitimize it, make it visible, and give it public voice in politics and policymaking. To these topics we now turn.

POLICY IMPLICATIONS

Researchers often avoid taking research results and applying them to action, for the solutions are inevitably flawed. Twenty years ago, it was easier to conclude studies with a call for a new kind of economy which put people's interests first. More recently though, to use Robert Heilbroner's words, capitalism has triumphed[24] and the challenge is to make capitalism work better, amid policies that prize self-sufficiency in political systems that give voices to people. For the purposes of this chapter, the distinction between 'petty' and 'grand' policy regulation makes the analysis more manageable, more tractable.

At the bottom line, the fundamental issue discussed herein is a set of contradictory policies that seem to assume and value self-sufficiency but that actually make it difficult for those with limited resources – immigrants among them – to work and organize in open and collective ways. Paradoxically, in this US land of freedom, democracy, and opportunity, people operate within a somewhat hostile and intimidating climate wherein public officials care little about those with meager resources.

SEEDS ACROSS THE BORDER

I will illustrate this policy argument with an analysis of an initiative known as Semillas a traves de la Frontera/Seeds Across the Border. Semillas grew out of a cross-border community of people who recognize the common interests, cultures, and economies of people on both sides of the border.[25] In this community, leaders and members of the Mexican Federation of Private Health and Community Development Associations (FEMAP), a Mexican non-government organization, sought to apply FEMAP's community bank model in Juárez to the US side.

FEMAP's two-decade track record in Mexico involves working through community-based *promotoras* (promoters, fem.) on maternal and reproductive health. In the late 1980s, FEMAP worked with its existing network to build community bank groups wherein mostly women (*banqueras*) would obtain up to nine cycles of small loans (around $100 each) to develop their businesses. Peer pressure was the loan guarantee, somewhat like the Asian Grameen Bank model, and in the context of these relations of trust, the guarantee worked; repayment rates always exceed ninety percent.

Banqueras have been able to identify market niches and upgrade tiny businesses into viable income-generating activities that reap more than the official Mexican minimum wage. At a conference in 1995,[26] *banqueras* gave testimony about their neighborhood grocery stands, used clothing businesses, and butcher shops among others. Outside the downtown area, which inspectors monitor for street vendors, the surveillance net is minimal. Moreover, without major grocery store chains in Juárez's many neighborhoods, consumer demand exists for the goods women sell. At this conference, *banqueras* engaged in dialogue with government and private-sector business officials.

At that time, three community banks operated on the US side. Although they provided opportunity in outlying areas (known as *colonias*), with heavy representation of immigrants (permanent residents, naturalized citizens, and others), women earned meager incomes. The average earnings amounted to $40 weekly, hardly enough to sustain households especially when other earnings bring in minimum wages. Why the difference?

First, market niches are not so plentiful and obvious. For example, large grocery chains buy in large volumes and sell for lower prices than women could offer even for fresh, thick, homemade tortillas. Second, US-based *banqueras* perceive high levels of surveillance. For those receiving needs-based assistance such as food stamps, they worry that discovery of income supplements will result in reduced benefits or even penalties. A myriad of regulations, even if unevenly enforced, sends a chill over people's sense of possibilities. Everyone has heard horror stories of court appearances and fines (as a visit to the mundane Municipal Court would testify). In immigrants' checkerboard households, discussed above, women worry that they will put loved ones at risk. Even setting up bank accounts brings anxiety. FEMAP requires that *banqueras* save simultaneously, and bank accounts require social security numbers that – people worry – busy bureaucrats can track. Third, residents' monolingual Spanish capabilities, along with limited education, limit their ability to qualify for training and/or licensing for higher pay alternatives. Home health-care aids are in demand, but many women must first acquire more basic skills to begin the process. Fourth, known and trusted community organizations like FEMAP are lacking on the US side. Poverty is more than a lack of financial capital; social capital[27] is also thin in the area. Social capital would provide thick networks that bind community members together in organizations. In such contexts, the sort of volunteerism that sustains FEMAP in Juárez could flourish in El Paso. The US is a land that was once blessed with Tocquevillian community but is now characterized by Madisonian individual self-interest. But even self-interest needs some social capital to grow.

Immigration law has long assumed self-sufficiency rather than dependence, an assumption now brutally enforced with mid-1990s welfare changes. Yet precious little happens to build on the baggage of informal, risk-taking self-sufficiency that many new residents bring to the country. Informal self-employment is treated as suspect, and regulations hinder its ability to flourish rather than nourish that ability. Political officials routinely treat nonvoting people with meager resources as unimportant. Occasionally service providers engage with new residents with help.[28] But it is help that assumes need rather than *also* assumes grit, determination, informal skills, and willingness to work that propelled many immigrants to take the risks to move in the first place. Policy should build on those strengths. Immigrants are not all pathetic victims, as those in some helping professions (AND those with anti-immigrant sentiments) would have us believe.

POLICY RECOMMENDATIONS, PETTY AND GRAND

Let us begin with the petty regulations, tractable and more amenable to reform. Let us also recognize that amid many many policy goals, trade-offs may be necessary, for some goals contradict others. In our global economy, job creation is an important and worthy goal for, more and more, people work like temporary contractors when they once had stable and secure lifetime jobs. As such, their work begins to resemble informality. The risk-taking, self-sufficient skills of informals should be legitimized and prized. At the same time, public health and safety measures must be put in place to protect against abuses in noncontractual employment. After all, one woman's home-based shop could be another woman's sweatshop.

Informal business incubation needs to include credit and training. The Small Business Administration is probably too big in this effort, for most of its loans involve lengthy forms that require consultation with accountants and lawyers. NGOs have a place in mediating relationships with lenders and microenterpreneurs. After incubation, free of petty regulations and fee extractions, informality should be public and recognized both for its growth potentials and for open exposure of potential abuse. Informals eventually need to shoulder their share of the public support burden through tax contributions. Many informals in this study earn poverty-level amounts, too meager for tax collection and too costly for the bureaucratic machinery of tax collection. The criminalization of noncompliance, however, is an intimidating threat that chills the growth of informality. No groups are frozen through that chill more than recent immigrants who endanger themselves in other ways by exposing their work and profit to public gaze. Value-added regulation, basic on civil rather than criminal penalties, should increase voluntary compliance in larger, publicly visible workplaces. Local governments can support public markets in which vendors rent space.

Grand regulations operate from on high, distant from ordinary people and, often, behind the closed doors of bureaucracy. Several grand efforts undermined informals' ability to earn income above poverty levels. First, NAFTA (and similar regional trade blocs) do little for informal entrepreneurs who get caught in, paradoxically, this increasingly bureaucratized machinery for 'efficient' markets that ordinary businesses can manage far more than informals. Free trade should also work for the quintessential free traders – the informals.

Second, people's movement across the border should be facilitated, especially among free trade partners like the NAFTA 'citizens', be they Mexicans, Americans, or Canadians. Once on US soil, people spend money and pay property and sales taxes. If NAFTA were more like the European Union, people movement would be as easy as capital movement within those larger borders.

Third, global causes of migration and poverty require national policy action. With different levels of capital 'migration', the stimulus to informality would diminish and the migration of people might change. Currently US capital migrates to Mexico, not for wage creation above poverty levels, but for jobs that pay $15–20 weekly. As long as capital migration cheapens labor in these ways, people will migrate northward and US residents will increasing operate like informal contractors.

NOTES

1. Much of this condensed analysis comes out of, in slightly updated form, *Free Trade? Informal Economies at the US–Mexico Border*, Kathleen Staudt (Philadelphia: Temple University Press, 1998).
2. Saskia Sassen, *Cities in a World Economy* (Thousand Oaks: Pine Forge Press of Sage, 1995), pp. 106–7.
3. Robert Reich, *The Work of Nations: Preparing Ourselves for 21st Century Capitalism* (New York: Alfred A. Knopf, 1992).
4. The Women in Development/Gender and Development (WID/GAD) literatures are voluminous. On numbers, the classic work is by Lourdes Benería (the latest iteration being) '*Accounting for Women's Work*: The Progress of Two Decades,' *World Development*, 20, 11 (1992). For reviews, see Staudt's *Managing Development* (Newbury Park, CA: Sage, 1991), ch. 4 especially, and *Policy, Politics, and Gender: Women Gaining Ground* (West Hartford, CT: Kumarian Press, 1998).
5. Alejandro Portes, *et al.*, eds. *The Informal Economy: Studies in Advanced and Less Developed Countries* (Baltimore: Johns Hopkins University Press, 1989).
6. The early and later literatures are reviewed well in Cathy Rakowski, ed., *Contrapunto: The Informal Sector Debate in Latin America* (SUNY/Albany Press, 1994). Ironically, Portes initially suggested diminishing informality with his historical review of Latin American countries in 'Latin American Class Structures: Their Composition and Change During the Last Decades,' *Latin American Research Review*, 20 (1985), pp. 7–39.
7. Portes *et al.*, 1989.
8. Marguerite Berger and Mayra Buvinic, eds. *Women's Ventures: Assistance to the Informal Economy in Latin America* (West Hartford, CT: Kumarian Press, 1989); InterAmerican Development Bank; selections in Rakowski, 1994.
9. Alison MacEwen Scott, 'Informal Sector or Female Sector? Gender Bias in Urban Labour Market Models,' *Male Bias in the Development Process* (Manchester: Manchester University Press, 1991); Caroline O.N. Moser, *Confronting Crisis: A Comparative Study on Household Responses to Poverty and Vulnerability in Four Poor Urban Communities* (Washington, DC: World Bank Environmental Sustainability Development Studies No. 8, 1996), pp. 4, 17, 33.
10. UNDP, *Human Development Report* (New York: Oxford University Press, 1996), p. 98.
11. Among the first, see Secretaria de Programacíon y Presupuestó, *La Ocupación Informal en Areas Urbanas* (Mexico City: SPP, 1976); Secretaría del Trabajo y Previsión Social and US Department of Labor, *The Informal Sector in Mexico* (Washington, DC and Mexico City: STPS and USDL, 1992). See various work by Bryan Roberts, the latest of which is in a special issue of the *International Journal of Urban and Regional Research* 1994. Priscilla Connolly used the poverty mystification terms in 'The Politics of the Informal Sector: A Critique', in *Beyond Employment: Household, Gender and Subsistence*, N. Redcliff and E. Mingione, eds. (Oxford: Blackwell, 1985).

12. Sylvia Chant, *Women and Survival in Mexican Cities* (Manchester: Manchester University Press, 1991); Mercedes González de la Rocha, 'Economic Crisis, Domestic Reorganisation and Women's Work in Guadalajara, Mexico,' *Bulletin of Latin American Research* 7, 2 (1988), pp. 207–23.

13. On delinking absolute poverty and informality, see Vanessa Cartaya, 'Informality and Poverty: Causal Relationship or Coincidence?' in Rakowski 1994, pp. 223–51; selected profiles in Judith Hellman, *Mexican Lives* (New York: New Press, 1994); Bryan Roberts, 'Enterprise and Labor Markets: The Border and the Metropolitan Areas,' *Frontera Norte*, 5, 9 (1993); Kathleen Staudt, 'Struggles in Urban Space: Street Vendors in El Paso and Juárez,' *Urban Affairs Review*, 31, 4 (1996); and comparisons made in Staudt 1998, *Free Trade?*

14. Elsa Chaney and Mary Garcia Castro, eds., *Muchachas No More: Household Workers in Latin America and the Caribbean* (Philadelphia: Temple University Press, 1989); on the US see Mary Romero, *Maid in the USA* (London: Routledge, 1992) and Vicki Ruiz, 'By the Day or the Week: Mexicana Domestic Workers in El Paso,' in V. Ruiz and S. Tiano, *Women on the US–Mexico Border* (Boston: Allen & Unwin, 1987), pp. 61–76.

15. Eugene Becker, 'Self-Employed Workers: An Update to 1983,' *Monthly Labor Review*, July 1984, pp. 14–15. On Current Population Survey data, though, see Harriet B. Presser and Elizabeth Bamberger, 'American Women Who Work at Home for Pay: Distinctions and Determinants', *Social Science Quarterly*, 74, 4 (1993), pp. 823–4.

16. Alejandro Portes, *The Economic Sociology of Immigration: Essays on Networks, Ethnicity, and Entrepreneurship* (New York: Russell Sage, 1995); Howard Aldrich and Robin Ward, *Immigrant Business in Industrial Societies* (Newbury Park, CA: Sage, 1990); selections in Ivan Light and P. Bhachu, eds., *Immigration and Entrepreneurship: Cultures, Capital, and Ethnic Networks* (New Brunswick: Transaction Books, 1993); M. Patricia Fernández-Kelly and Anna M. Garcia, 'Informalization at the Core: Hispanic Women, Homework, and the Advanced Capitalist State', in Portes *et al.*, 1989, pp. 247–64.

17. Joan Moore and Raquel Pinderhughes, eds. in their introduction to *In the Barrios: Latinos and the Underclass Debate* (New York: Russell Sage, 1993), pp. xxvii.

18. Edgar L. Feige, *The Underground Economies: Tax Evasion and Information Distortion* (Cambridge: Cambridge University Press, 1989); Susan Pozo *et al.*, eds., *Exploring the Underground Economy: Studies of Illegal and Unreported Economic Activity* (Kalamazoo, MI: W.E. Upjohn Institute, 1996); though for commendable recognition, see Steve Balkin, *Self-Employment for Low-Income People* (New York: Praeger, 1989).

19. Enrique Suárez and Octavio Chávez, *Profile of the United States–Mexico Border* (Juárez: FEMAP, 1996).

20. Thanks to the National Science Foundation (no. HRD 9253027) and to participating team members, including faculty Cheryl Howard, Gregory Rocha, and Alejandro Lugo and twelve students. The interviews were conducted in 1992. Staudt 1998 contains full analysis of sample selection and output.

21. Staudt, 1996.

22. Henry Selby *et al.*, *The Mexican Urban Household: Organizing for Self-Defense* (Austin: University of Texas Press, 1990), p. 71.
23. Michael Lipsky, *Street-Level Bureaucracy* (New York: Russell Sage, 1980).
24. Robert Heilbroner, 'The Triumph of Capitalism,' *New Yorker*, 1989.
25. See the conference *memoria*, 'Women and Development at the US–Mexico Border' (Juárez: FEMAP, 1995). Many thanks to counterparts in Seeds, including FEMAP President Guadalupe de la Vega, Enrique Suárez, Helenmarie Zachritz, Kym Hemley, and Margaret Schellenberg. This material is fully discussed in Staudt, 1998, ch. 7.
26. See note 25.
27. The best-known work on social capital has been done by James Coleman, Robert Putnam, and Robert Bellah *et al.*, who draw on Alexis de Tocqueville in *Habits of the Heart* (1987) and *The Good Society* (1992). See a special issue of *American Behavioral Scientist*, 40, 5 (1997) for the uses and abuses of this work.
28. Helping profession comments can be found in proceedings from a LBJ School/University of Texas conference on *colonias*, May 1996. At the FEMAP conference, only one El Paso official attended (not even a political 'wife'). The community development director could see no relevance in her or a member of her staff attending. As a Seeds collaborator, I was heavily involved in planning and implementing the 1995 conference (see note 25).

3 Labor Migration and International Sexual Division of Labor: A Feminist Perspective

Shu-Ju Ada Cheng

INTRODUCTION

For the past two decades, gender has emerged as an important variable for the study of development. Feminist scholars have argued that the development process has had different impact on men and women in developing nations (Beneria, 1981; Boserup, 1970; Brydon and Chant, 1989; Charlton, 1984; Rogers, 1980; Sen and Grown, 1988; Tinker, 1990). The differential impact of development is in fact reflective of the pre-existing gender inequality within the developing world, and, in turn, reinforces its gender stratification through this process. The existing feminist literature on development has pointed out that the increasing globalization of economy has created the division of labor by gender at the international level (Leacock and Safa, 1986; Mies, 1986; Nash and Fernandez-Kelly, 1983; Ward, 1990; Young *et al.*, 1981). For example, while the third world occupies the bottom end of the global production linkage, women in the third world provide the source of cheap labor for this production process as a result of the gender and racial ideologies (Enloe, 1989; Leacock and Safa, 1986; Mies, 1986; Young *et al.*, 1981). In short, gender has always been an essential principle organizing the political economy of international development (Pettman, 1996).

Labor migration, both internal and international, has been an inevitable part of the global development process. Particularly for the past two decades, the process of the movement of people across national borders for employment has not only been accelerating in its scale but has also been expanding in its territorial implications. Along with such traditional nations of immigrants as the United States, Canada, Australia, New Zealand and Western Europe, countries of destination have grown to include both the Middle East and the East Asian region. Advanced economies in East and Southeast Asia, for example, Hong Kong, Singapore, South Korea and Taiwan, have become major labor receiving countries in the region.

This chapter argues that gender as an organizing principle of social relationships of power should be a fundamental analytical element within the comprehensive approach of theoretical conceptualization in the field of international migration. Drawing from the contributions of the feminist critiques in various academic disciplines, this paper elaborates how gender ideology has functioned and been utilized by the state within the global capitalist system to structure the particular contours of the process of international migration and to construct the particular outlook of global labor market. Using migrant women domestic workers in East and Southeast Asia as a case study, this paper attempts to show that the issue of power in relation to gender is pervasive in shaping the dynamics of migration, ranging from the micro to the macro level, extending from the socio-economic forces to state policies, in structuring a gendered global labor market. It contends that an international sexual division of labor has been structured through the adoption of state policies and further perpetuated through the process of international migration.

FEMINIST STANDPOINT IN INTERNATIONAL MIGRATION

The existing theoretical frameworks, including neoclassical migration theory with both micro and macro level variants, world system theory, new economics of migration, dual labor market theory, network theory, cumulative theory, institutional theory, system theory and structuration theory, explain the process of international migration in divergent ways (Massey *et al.*, 1993 and 1994). For example, the macro level variant of neoclassical theory perceives the process of international migration as a result of wage differentials and disequilibrium in labor supply and demand among competing economies. World system theory postulates that the process of international migration exists as a result of the unequal impact of global capitalism. Network theory examines social networking as a major force sustaining the flow of population movement across national borders. All theories have their own strengths and weaknesses from their particular vantage points and are capable of capturing a particular dimension of the contours of international migration. The complexity of the migration process and its multidimensional impact on political, social, economic, cultural and demographic aspects, has rendered no one single theoretical framework adequate to explain this dynamic process. Recently, scholars in the field of migration have recognized the importance of adopting a more comprehensive and integrative approach toward the study of population movement.

Feminist literature in the field of migration has pointed out that the existing theoretical frameworks have largely ignored the element of gender and its implications for the impact of unequal power dynamics in the analysis of international migration. Before the 1970s, gender as an analytical approach was largely missing from the literature of migration (Boyd, 1989; Chant and Radcliffe, 1992; Lee, 1996). Women were either invisible or treated as dependents of male migrants without individual identities; the experiences, contributions and roles specific to their particular social locations were not distinguished conceptually from those of male migrants. Not until the late 1970s did female migrants and their particular experiences in migration begin to be recognized in the field. The importance accorded to the question of gender in migration, in fact, reflected the overall political, socio-economic and intellectual climates of that particular era. The integration of gender in the study of migration paralleled the increasing importance of women in the field of international development, and the introduction of a gendered analysis in migration has led to a change of perception toward migrant women and to a distinct conceptualization of the differential impact on men and women during the migration process.

Gender is important in that it exists as a major principle shaping the unequal power dynamics of the social world. Gender affects the dynamics within the family; it determines who migrates and who stays behind. It helps construct the social purposes for overseas employment for individual migrants and dictate how the remittances should be spent. Gender ideology shapes the differential experiences of male and female migrants in terms of what kind of work they are channeled to take on and within what contexts they are employed. Gender relationships shape the particular roles of male and female members for productive and reproductive work within the same household throughout the whole process. Gender dynamics within the household also dictate that negotiations occur constantly among members of different sexes and generations. In short, this important organizing principle of power shapes the particular contours of the migration process as well as the diverse experiences particular to people situated in different locations along social hierarchies. Besides, it also interacts with other systems of stratification, such as race and class, and with the larger socioeconomic and political contexts.

The movement of labor, along with the movement of capital, responds to the needs of the existing stratified global economy, facilitated and constrained by the states. Women in international migration have existed to perform certain functions that have been built on the existing gender stratification and that have further reinforced the hierarchical gender structure. Their experiences of migration have differed from those of male migrants as a result of their differential social locations that determine their distinct roles and particular contexts of employment in the process. Therefore, in studying international migration, it is important to look at how the stratification of development intersects with the gender hierarchy that extends the sexual division of labor from national to international level, and how their interlocking impact has perpetuated the inferior status of women both nationally and internationally.

INTERNATIONAL SEXUAL DIVISION OF LABOR: INTERTWINED SYSTEMS OF STRATIFICATION

World system theory has argued that capitalism has been the dominant force shaping world development for the past 500 years (Chirot and Hall, 1982; Shannon, 1989; Wallerstein, 1979). With the spatial expansion of capitalism, nations have been integrated within the global economic system, in which the division of labor determines the relative position of individual states. The globalization of economy has shaped the unequal trade relationships among nations as well as regions, and it has dictated the hierarchical structure between the first and the third world. The interaction and dynamics of the core, semi-periphery and periphery have structured the world politics in which all nations are subject to the sweeping forces of the global capitalist system.

The focus on global capitalism as the single determinant of stratification in development has been criticized by feminist scholars as gender-blind (Eviota, 1992; Leacock and Safa, 1986; Mies, 1983; Nash and Fernandez-Kelly, 1983; Sen and Grown, 1988; Smith *et al.*, 1988; Young *et al.*, 1981). The development theory with its historical-structural and systemic orientation has failed to examine how the globalization of economy has differential impact on people in the process depending on their respective positions and identities under the larger political and socio-economic contexts. The process in which gender interacts with other identities as well as with the capitalist force has been ignored as an important analytical approach in understanding the complexity of development. The lack of analysis in the intersection among gender, class, ethnicity and race has been proven insufficient to account for the multiple identities of people and the complexity of human societies. To advance the analysis of development from a gender-centered approach, feminist scholars have argued the importance of examining the interaction between patriarchy, racism, capitalism and the state in reinforcing gender stratification through the development process (Pettman, 1996).

Although there is an agreement among feminist scholars concerning the intersection between patriarchy and capitalism, the conceptualization concerning them has been the focus of contention (Acker, 1988 and 1989; Barrett, 1980; Mies, 1986). Some feminist scholars assert that capitalism and patriarchy are two separate structures, with independent yet interconnected historical development. Others look at them as an intertwined system; that is, capitalism is the manifestation of a temporal formation of patriarchy as an historical system. For example, Mies (1986) uses the concept of capitalist-patriarchy to argue their interconnection, with capitalism being the contemporary form and the latest development of the historical patriarchal system. Therefore, capitalism is patriarchal by its own nature. Through the expansion of the capitalist-patriarchal system globally, women as a collective are relegated to perform certain functions within the international division of labor. Mies argues that:

> The strategy of the new international division of labor can work only if two conditions are fulfilled. First, the relocated industries, agro-business and other export-oriented enterprises must be able to find the cheapest, most docile and most manipulatable workers in the underdeveloped countries in order to lower production costs as far as possible. Second, these corporations must mobilize the consumers in the rich countries to buy all the items produced in third world countries. In both strategies the mobilization of women plays an essential role. (1986, p. 114)

While the debates concerning the relationship between capitalism and patriarchy remain unresolved among feminist scholars, these debates serve as important conceptual tools in understanding the dynamics among structures of stratification in shaping the development process. They alert us to transcend the monolith of the systemic approach and to contextualize the analysis of development. The intervention of capitalism has resulted in the overall restructuring of the political, socio-economic and cultural systems in developing nations. However, the patriarchal system, which dictates the unequal power relationship between men and women, has interacted with the process of capitalist intervention and determined the differential impact on the sexes depending on their relative positions and power within the larger socio-economic contexts.

The reviving interest in the 1980s toward the study of the state has prompted feminist scholars to examine its role in shaping women's experiences in the development process (Charlton *et al.*, 1989; Yuval-Davis and Anthias, 1989). It is argued that the state has been a major force in negotiating the collective impact on society of gender hierarchy and capitalism. The intervention of the state in the development process has helped either rearrange the political and socio-economic systems for more equitable distribution or strengthen the existing unequal political and socio-economic structures. It has thus played a major role in shaping gender relationships and changing the relative status of the sexes through the process of restructuring.

Although gender is an important element in arranging social relations and organizations, it is also always racialized, with distinct class implications (Collins, 1990; Glenn, 1992; Mohanty *et al.*, 1991; Romero, 1992). Minority and third world feminists have maintained that gender should not be treated as an autonomous system independent of other systems of stratification, such as ethnicity, race and class; they have criticized the additive model of the conceptualization of gender. Instead, the attention should be given as to how gender, race, class and global inequality interact with one another and how the interconnection of these dynamics form the interlocking hierarchical and stratified system that shapes the different experiences of people in relation to their multiple identities. With the embeddedness of racial and ethnic implications in gender hierarchy, women of diverse ethnic and racial identities have encountered the development process differently as a result of their specific locations in the political and socio-economic systems. This is particularly true with the maintenance of the modern nation-state, which is based on the hegemony of the dominant racial ideology, the idealized construction of nationalism and racial homogeneity, and the consistently overt and subtle suppression of ethnic and racial minorities. It is thus important to examine how the state maintains the homogenization and harmonization of the nation-state through the articulation of a particular gender ideology with its racial implications in the development process.

When looking at the reinforcement and perpetuation of international sexual division of labor, we need to examine how the state intervenes in the development process and interacts with the forces of capitalism, racism and patriarchy in order to better grasp the particular implications to women of social changes. Only through the understanding of the interaction among patriarchy, racism, capitalism and the state can we comprehend the differential impact on the sexes of the complex dynamics of development.

THE CASE OF FILIPINO MIGRANT WOMEN
DOMESTIC WORKERS IN EAST ASIA

Both the movement of capital and that of labor have reinforced and perpetuated the international sexual division of labor. The majority of the feminist literature in the development field has dealt with the former, examining how the investment of foreign capital in developing nations has created and strengthened the international sexual division of labor through the exploitation of the female labor force in the third world. However, the question as to how the movement of labor has contributed to the reinforcement and perpetuation of the sexual division of labor at the international level has not drawn comparable attention.

Beside the continuous dynamic economic growth, the massive movement of labor has been another major development characterizing the miraculous economic growth of East Asia during the past ten years. As a result of the regional unequal development, advanced economies in this region have emerged as the major labor receiving countries, importing migrant labor from less developed areas. Two major features characterize this migration flow in Asia. First, the percentage of women in the overall migration flow as well as in the migrant labor population has been increasing (Abella, 1992 and 1991; Barsotti and Lecchini, 1991; Battistella, 1994 and 1992; Lane, 1992). Between 1976 and 1987, the percentage of women in the labor migration flow expanded from 15 to 27 percent (Lin and Oishi, 1996, p. 87). Secondly, migrant women are mainly concentrated in certain occupations, such as the service industry, manufacturing industry, sex industry and domestic service (Chant and Mcilwaine, 1995; Heyzer *et al.*, 1994; Lee, 1996). These gendered occupations are traditionally reserved for local women of labor receiving countries. Therefore, the concentration of women in certain female-dominated occupations in the migration process is an extension of the sexual division of labor that has already existed at the national level of both labor sending and receiving countries. The sexual segregation in the global labor market among the migrant population has served to reinforce the division of labor by gender at the international level through the migration process.

The Interaction between Capitalism and the State

Before the mid-1980s, the majority of migrant labor from South and Southeast Asia went to the Middle East for overseas work. Since the mid-1980s, while the Middle East remains the main destination for migrant labor, the newly industrialized countries (NICs) have become the second largest concentration for overseas employment in the Asian region. Hong Kong, Singapore, Taiwan and South Korea have emerged as the major labor receiving countries with their advanced economies while the Philippines, Indonesia, Thailand and Malaysia are the major labor sending countries.[1] Recently, Vietnam and China are also catching up to join the group of the labor-export nations.

In 1994, 64.20 percent of Filipino migrant workers went to the Middle East while 34.42 percent of them went to newly industrialized countries (Source: Philippine Overseas Employment Administration). During the same year, Hong Kong ranked second after Saudi Arabia of the top ten countries of destination for Filipino migrant workers. On the same list, Taiwan was placed as the fourth while Singapore was ranked eighth for Filipino migrant labor.[2] Between 1984 and 1994, Indonesian migrant workers were mainly deployed in Saudi Arabia, Malaysia and Singapore (Asian Migrant, 1993). In 1992, migrant workers from Thailand were mainly concentrated in the following countries, Brunei, Singapore, Taiwan, and Saudi Arabia (Asian Migrant, 1993).

Both push and pull factors have played an important role in this migration trend since the mid-1980s. The pull factors in the labor receiving countries include the continuous economic development, the initiation of development projects, the higher standards of living, the better wage structure, and the opening of the labor market for migrant labor. Push factors vary for labor sending countries. For the Philippines, the largest labor sending country in this region, push factors include prevalent poverty, deteriorating standards of living, and worsening unemployment and underemployment.

In addition to push and pull factors, the state has also played a crucial role in the process of labor migration in this region. Both labor sending and receiving countries are actively involved in facilitating the movement of labor to maximize the benefits of labor export. The severe labor shortage experienced by the advanced economies in this region has compelled them to import migrant labor on a large scale to meet the demands of the economic growth. For labor receiving countries, migrant workers have served as a source of cheap labor to subsidize their economic development. These labor receiving countries have invested little to enhance the social and physical infrastructure for maintaining the migrant labor force. Besides, migrant workers can also serve as the buffer for the fluctuation of the economy (Stalker, 1994, p. 255).[3] The potential negative impact on society and the pressure on the socio-economic resources with the importation of migrant labor can be minimized with the imposition of strict regulations to control their employment and stay. The regulation and intervention of a strong state in the labor-import process has ensured that the labor receiving countries will exact maximum benefits from this process.

For labor sending countries, the exportation of labor has become an important solution for their internal unemployment and underemployment. Remittances from migrant labor have also become a significant source of foreign exchange earnings that can be utilized for development. Therefore, labor sending countries, such as the Philippines and Indonesia, integrate the export of labor as part of their development strategies. In fact, labor has become parallel to commodities and constituted one of the major export products for them.

The Philippine government has pursued an aggressive labor export policy for more than three decades. By 1995, there were more than two million documented Filipino migrant workers in more than 130 countries (source: Philippine Overseas Employment Administration). If undocumented migrant workers are included, the number would reach between four and seven million (source: Department of Overseas Labor and Employment). In terms of remittances, the amount of money remitted home by Filipino migrant workers amounted to US$2.90 billion in 1994. Between 1975 and 1994, the total amount of remittances to the Philippines accumulated to US$18 billion (source: Bangko Sentral, the Philippines). This figure does not include remittances through unofficial channels, such as private agents and acquaintances.

Although the export of labor has helped alleviate unemployment and underemployment in the Philippines, the extent of its relief is still questionable. Doubt has also been raised as to whether remittances have contributed to development of the Philippines if they have largely been used for consumption (Abella, 1992; Heyzer *et al.*, 1994, p. 105; Vasquez, 1992). Furthermore, with the unskilled nature of the overseas employment, the transfer of skills and technology from advanced to less developed economies through labor migration has proven to be unrealistic. What is detrimental to the future development of the Philippines is the loss of human capital through this process, since the labor migration flow from the Philippines is selective of the highly educated and the professional (Carino, 1992). For example, between 1975 and 1977, about 80 percent of Filipino migrant workers were high school graduates. Furthermore, according to a study done in 1983, over 50 percent of migrant workers under survey had completed college or had taken some college courses (Carino, 1992, p. 13). Through the labor export policy, the Philippines is in fact sustaining the economic development of the advanced economies in the region with its own labor force.

The Dynamics between Patriarchy and Capitalism

Feminization of migration has become one of the major characteristics of this migration trend. For the past two decades, the percentage of women in migration in this region has been increasing. For example, throughout the 1980s, Filipino women constituted the majority of the migration flow. The average percentage of women among all Filipinos leaving the Philippines amounted to 58 percent (source: Commission for Filipinos Overseas, the

Philippines). According to the Philippine Overseas Employment Administration, 60 percent of Filipino migrant workers in 1994 were women. Furthermore, Filipino women currently make up 49 percent of all overseas contract workers (source: Philippine Overseas Employment Administration, the Philippines).

One feature accompanying the feminization of labor migration in this region is the concentration of women in gendered occupations. Migrant women are usually concentrated in the service sector, manufacturing industry, sex industry and domestic service. Among these occupations, domestic service is the main category of overseas employment. Based on 1994 statistics, 44.5 percent of the newly employed Filipino migrant workers were in vulnerable occupations, 95 percent of them being women. Two major occupations for Filipino women workers were domestic workers and entertainers. Among the 44.5 percent, domestic workers made up 26.34 percent while the entertainers made up 18.17 percent of all women workers (source: Philippine Overseas Employment Administration, the Philippines).

The concentration of women in gendered occupations is closely related to the stereotypical perception of women's place in society as well as in employment. Feminist scholars have argued that gendered occupations exist as a result of social construction and that the feminization of certain occupations have often been accompanied by the forces of cultural ideologies (Reskin and Padavic, 1994; Williams, 1995). Women have traditionally dominated the service industry and the domestic service. They tend to be relegated to and segregated in occupations that require submission, dexterity, orientation to detail and sensitivity. It is largely because of their reproductive function that women are perceived to be naturally fit for nurturing, caring and secretarial roles in employment. The concentration of women in gendered occupations in the migration process also implies the sexual segregation of the migrant labor force at the international level. Male migrants usually migrate to work at industries and sectors that are traditionally dominated by men, such as the construction and fishing industries.

The sexual division of labor in the migration process renders the contexts of employment for male and female migrant workers completely different, thus shaping their distinct experiences of migration. Particularly important are the questions as to how the capitalist economic system has shaped the contexts of their employment, and how the interaction between gender stratification and global capitalism has dictated their particular experiences.

In the case of migrant women domestic workers, the political economy of housework in the capitalist system has important implications. In the capitalist system, work is defined as a process of production that can contribute to the capital accumulation and exchange (Eviota, 1992; Malos, 1995;

Waring, 1988). It excludes any process of production that does not have the ultimate exchange value. Therefore, housework is not considered as productive work. It is regarded as a process of reproduction since its result mainly contains the use value for the maintenance of the family. The capitalist system has resulted in the devaluation of housework. With the relegation of women in the household sphere, women as a group are thus excluded from the category of workers even though they perform household responsibilities that are crucial to the maintenance of the family and to the continuation of society. Furthermore, with the exclusion of housework from the category of the productive work, the contribution of women to sustain the capitalist system through the reproduction of its future labor force has been rendered invisible. Not only has the labor of women in the private sphere been regarded as 'free' but women as a group have also been categorized as the reserve labor force contingent upon the changing need of the capitalist system.

The political economy of housework has rendered the status of paid housework ambiguous. The particular status of the work performed by migrant workers has significant implications, especially in relation to the legal aspects. Although migrant workers are all vulnerable to exploitation due to their status as migrant labor, male migrant workers are still able to retain their status as workers, thus protected by the labor law. For migrant women domestic workers, since housework is usually not considered as work, they are often denied their status as workers. As a result of their non-labor status, they are often deprived of legal protection in the labor receiving countries.[4]

The Intervention of the Patriarchal State

As mentioned earlier, both labor sending and receiving countries in this region are actively involved in facilitating the process of labor migration. Both labor sending and receiving governments benefit from the massive movement of labor. However, since the role and status of both sexes have been determined by the existing gender stratification in both labor sending and receiving countries, the impact on local societies of the migration of men and women has been different. What, therefore, are the implications of the migration of women for both sides and how has the individual state responded to these implications?

One major element distinguishes Filipino migrant women domestic workers from migrant domestic workers of other nationalities in this region. That is, the average educational level of Filipino migrant women domestic workers is higher than that of women from other countries. According to a

1989 survey done by Asian Migrant Workers Centre, a regional NGO based in Hong Kong, Filipino migrant women domestic workers reported the highest educational level. Among the surveyed, 31.7 percent reached tertiary level of education while 28.7 percent completed this level of education (Asian Migrant Workers Centre, 1991, p. 15). In addition to the college degree holders, many Filipino migrant domestic workers worked as professionals in the Philippines before migration, with skills in nursing and teaching. The main reason for these professionals to migrate abroad for work to support their families is that they earn more employed as migrant domestic workers.

The massive exportation of Filipino women has had a tremendous impact on the Philippine society. The migration of Filipino women has signified the loss of a certain portion of skilled labor for the Philippines. The investment by the Philippine government on the human capital has not fully benefitted its own national development (Carino, 1992; Battistella, 1992; Vasquez, 1992). Besides, the migration process has not strengthened the skills of migrant workers. It has instead resulted in the de-skilling of its female labor force (Heyzer *et al.*, 1994, p. 80). Furthermore, rather than accepting the responsibility of social reproduction, the Philippine government has transferred it to other female household members remaining in the Philippines since the primary caretakers have migrated. In fact, the Philippines has subsidized the reproduction of the future labor force for other advanced economies with its own labor force and spared the states of these economies from assuming the responsibility of reproduction. The Philippine government has facilitated the migration of its female labor force for the short-term monetary benefits while Filipino women have borne the cost of migration.

For labor receiving countries, the intervention of the patriarchal state has been more complex. The following questions need to be raised in relation to the process of labor importation. How does the patriarchal state control the participation of local women in the labor force by regulating the entry and employment of migrant domestic workers? How does the patriarchal nature of the state manipulate the availability of employment for migrant domestic workers in labor receiving countries to control their entry and establish a mechanism of control with gendered implications?

The miraculous economic development of the newly industrialized countries in East Asia has enhanced the standards of living among people in these advanced economies. These improved standards of living have resulted in their attainment of a higher educational level, particularly among the female population. The increase in the educational level has allowed local women to join the labor force, thus enhancing their economic independence and social status. The increasing participation of women, particularly married women, in the labor force has created the need for domestic workers to perform the housework. The higher standards of living have prompted local people to demand better employment terms and working conditions. Accordingly, they shun certain occupations with low social status and poor working conditions, such as construction and fishing industries as well as domestic services. Therefore, the demand for domestic workers cannot be met by local women even with the increased salaries. The gap is thus filled by migrant women domestic workers. It can be further stated that the possibility of their employment is in fact contingent upon the participation in the labor market of the reserve labor force, married women.

How does the state respond to the need for the importation of migrant women for the function of reproducing its future generation and for the maintenance of households? How does the state manipulate both local women and migrant women to meet its own need? Since married women are usually perceived as the reserve labor force, they are often the first group to be called on to join the labor market by the state to relieve the labor shortage and the first one to be encouraged to return home to take care of their families during an economic depression. When facing labor shortages, states of labor receiving countries have to adopt an open migrant labor policy to allow migrant women entry for employment in order to fully mobilize local women to participate in the labor force. While local women are encouraged to join the labor force, states of these labor receiving countries do not take over the responsibility of reproduction. By allowing the importation of migrant domestic workers, they transfer the responsibility of reproduction to women from less developed countries with less cost.

However, although migrant labor provides a source of cheap labor with little cost for their maintenance, the state also wants to minimize the impact on society of the importation of migrant labor, particularly in relation to the use of services and resources. Besides, it is also a concern of the state to reduce the dependence on migrant workers of local industries since the use of migrant labor slows down the pace for industrial upgrading and automation. This ambivalent attitude is applied to migrant women domestic workers by states of labor receiving countries as well. On one hand, the state encourages the participation of married women in the labor force during periods of rapid economic growth. On the other hand, the state also wants to maintain the impression that their participation in the labor market is temporary and the priority of married women should still be the family. To confine the status of married women to the reserve labor is to ensure that the facilitation of their return to the domestic sphere during economic depressions be a smooth process. Further, the state needs to minimize the over-dependence of local women on migrant domestic workers for the function of reproducing its future generations. Therefore, the state exerts control to regulate the employment and stay of migrant women domestic workers to minimize their overall impact on society.

The dependence on migrant women domestic workers for the function of social reproduction is not the only concern facing labor receiving countries. Labor receiving countries are concerned not only with the importation of labor, but also with the importation of labor of a certain ethnicity and race. Furthermore, they insist that the labor of a certain ethnicity and race be imported to take up a certain kind of work compatible with their status in host societies. That is, the importation of labor is heavily influenced by the existing racial hierarchies and prejudices in societies of labor receiving countries. The racial ideology thus shapes the economic aspect of the process of international labor migration.

Take Singapore and Taiwan for example. These two advanced economies have been the major labor receiving countries in the East Asian region since the mid-1980s. The governments of these two countries have adopted restrictive labor policies concerning the employment of migrant labor. All mechanisms are established to ensure that migrant workers will not stay for permanent settlement and that local industries will not depend on migrant labor for good without being able to move toward the stage of upgrading. For local industries, these two governments have established a quota system to control the flow of migrant labor and a levy system to increase the cost of importing migrant labor. For all migrant workers, unskilled labor in particular, these two governments subject them to strict immigration regulations regarding their employment. For example, migrant workers can only work for a certain period of time. During their stay, they will not be able to change employment irrespective of their skills. They will not be able to bring their families to live with them. In Singapore, migrant workers cannot marry local people without permission from the government; in Taiwan, migrant workers cannot marry either local people or any foreigners. Migrant workers are subject to immediate deportation if found in violation of any immigration regulations. Furthermore, the gendered regulation and control alert us to examine the patriarchal nature of the state. The state usually imposes treatment that is discriminatory toward migrant women workers. In both Singapore and Taiwan, migrant women workers are required to have a pregnancy test every six months. They are deported if found pregnant.

The requirement for mandatory pregnancy tests can be analyzed as a state control of the reproductive function of migrant women to contain the maintenance and reproduction cost of importing migrant labor. However, the regulation of the fertility of migrant women should not be restricted to Marxist analysis. Racial ideology, particularly its connection to population control, is essential to the analysis. The regulation of migrant women's fertility needs to be seen in relation to the larger political context of ethnic-racial stratification and as a mechanism for population control to perpetuate the ethnic and racial composition of labor receiving countries. The Singaporean and Taiwanese governments regulate migrant women's fertility to prevent them from having legitimate grounds to apply for citizenship and in order to minimize the impact on the ethnic and racial composition of their societies. Ultimately, the regulation of migrant women's fertility reflects their construction of the appropriate national identity. As Harris (1995) argues, the 'problem of immigration' is in reality the problem of the state and its exclusive power to decide the distribution of membership:

> The very word 'nation' has been suborned in the process so that it no longer primarily refers to a separate people but is tacked on to the word 'state' as a kind of sociological shadow of political authority. The state reserves the exclusive right to decide who belongs to the nation, and then claims that it is created and sustained by those whom it has so recognized. Thus, in sum, the 'problem of immigration' is wrongly specified. The problem is that of the state and the social foundation of its power. (1995, p. 87)

The movement of labor between nations is thus not simply a response to the market; the control of the stay and employment of migrant labor by labor receiving countries is often the attempt of the state in intervening the function of the market. The level of control and the kind of mechanism established to exercise the control depend on the nature and the history of that particular state as well as the political and socio-economic contexts under which that particular state is situated.

It might seem that local women in these advanced economies have acquired their equality with men through the ability to join the labor force. The fact that states of these advanced economies have played an active role in encouraging their participation in the labor force also gives an impression of their governmental progressiveness. However, the importation of migrant women to take up household responsibilities does not resolve the basis of gender inequality that is rooted in the domain of the family. In fact, the burden of housework is transferred from local women to women from less developed countries. The gender ideology that dictates the place of women in the domestic sphere has not been dismantled; the root of gender inequality that is embedded in the private sphere has not been resolved. Instead, the gender ideology of confining women in the private sphere has continued to be reinforced. The state is thus able to avoid its responsibility of reproduction by exploiting the cheap female labor from less developed nations in the third world.

The Intersection among Capitalism, Racism, Patriarchy and the State

Many questions can be raised in relation to the case of Filipino migrant women domestic workers. Can the function of capitalism fully explain the sexual segregation in employment of a migrant labor force? How does the interaction between capitalism and patriarchy function to relegate women in certain employment during the migration process that is reflective of the existing gender hierarchy in both labor sending and receiving countries? How has the state facilitated the labor migration for its own benefits? How has the patriarchal state facilitated and regulated the labor migration of women to maintain its internal sexual division of labor? How has the state regulate and control the fertility of migrant women to implement the population control for the construction and maintenance of the ideal nation-state?

In response to the international sexual division of labor, Heyzer and Wee (1994) argue that the international labor migration is a cross-national transfer of gendered labor due to the gendered dimension of this process. However, Truong (1996) further argues that the more appropriate term for the movement of migrant women is a transfer of the reproductive labor since it is reproductive work to which migrant women are usually confined. Therefore, instead of the sexual division of labor, there exists an international division of labor in reproduction. While these terms illustrate the gendered dimension of international labor migration, they do not point to the fact the gendered or the reproductive labor is also racialized at the same time. That is, the sexual division of labor intersects with the racial division of labor, and the division of labor in the international arena is organized along both racial and sexual lines.

Glenn (1992) argues that domestic service, as a gendered domain of social reproduction, has long been a racialized division of labor in the history of the United States. Minority and immigrant women have usually taken up domestic service with the participation of middle-class European American women in the labor force. These racial and sexual inequities involved in the domestic service points to the ironic implication with the increasing equality of 'women' in the workplace. This argument is applicable to the same process of transferring the burden of housework from local women to migrant women in the Asian region.

The case of Filipino migrant women domestic workers has shown that the international sexual division of labor is reinforced and perpetuated through the process of sexual segregation in employment among the migrant population. It is a function and extension of the gender stratification and gender ideology that have already existed in societies of both labor sending and receiving countries. Women in migration have served to perform certain functions prescribed by the existing hierarchical gender structure to sustain the international sexual division of labor. This case also shows that the international division of labor is not only gendered but also racialized; the racialized sexual division of labor at the international level is shaped and strengthened through labor migration. As a result, migrant women are subject to state policies that are both gender specific and racial implicated. The case of Filipino migrant women domestic workers cautions us to transcend the single determinant to examine the interaction among capitalism, racism, patriarchy and the state in perpetuating the division of labor at the international level.

CONCLUSION

Through the concentration of women in gendered occupations in the migration process, the international sexual division of labor has been reinforced and perpetuated. In this process, women are relegated and segregated in female-dominated occupations that sustain the division of labor by gender at the international level, and the sexual division of labor is linked at the national and international levels through the migration process. Furthermore, the sexual division of labor both nationally and internationally is also racialized at the same time; the international division of labor is organized along both gender and racial lines.

The case of migrant women domestic workers cautions us to look beyond the class analysis to examine the interaction of capitalism, racism, patriarchy and the state in sustaining the international sexual division of labor and determining the gendered nature of international migration. The feminist approach toward the analysis of migration and the construction of migration theory is essential in order to better understand the experience of women in the migration process.

NOTES

1. Malaysia is a unique case because it is both a labor sending and receiving country. The source of labor in East Asia does not come from Southeast Asia exclusively. Workers from South Asia have also migrated to the East Asian region for overseas work. Sri Lanka, Bangladesh, India and Pakistan are the major labor sending countries in South Asia.
2. Source: Philippine Overseas Employment Administration, the Philippines. The top ten countries for Filipino migrant workers are Saudi Arabia, Hong Kong, Japan, Taiwan, United Arab Emirates, Malaysia, Kuwait, Singapore, Brunei, and Qatar.
3. Peter Stalker, *The Work of Strangers: A Survey of International Labor Migration* (Geneva: ILO, 1994), p. 255. The Singaporean government clearly stated in 1988 that the intention of importing migrant labor is 'to use foreign workers as a buffer to even out the swings in the business cycle. When a temporary export boom increases the demand for foreign workers, the Government can accommodate it by letting in more foreign workers, providing the workers do not stay on after the boom.'
4. In Singapore and Taiwan, both local and migrant domestic workers are excluded from the protection of the labor law. While the labor law in Singapore specifically excludes domestic services from its protection, the labor law in Taiwan excludes the whole service industry, of which women constitute the majority.

REFERENCES

Abella, Manolo I. 1992. 'Issues in Contemporary Migration in the Asian Region,' *Asian Migrant Forum*, 5: 5–11.
——. 1992. 'International Migration and Development'. In *Philippine Labor Migration: Impact and Policy*. Edited by Graziano Battistella and Anthony Paganoni. Quezon City, Philippines: Scalabrini Migration Center.
——. 1991. 'Recent Trends in Asian Labor Migration: A Review of Major Issues,' *Asian Migrant*, 4(3): 72–7.
Acker, Joan. 1989. 'The Problem with Patriarchy,' *Sociology*, 23: 235–40.
——. 1988. 'Class, Gender, and the Relations of Distribution,' *Signs*, 13: 473–97.
Asian Migrant. 1993. 'Trends in Asian Labor Migration, 1992,' *Asian Migrant*, 6(1): 4–16.
Asian Migrant Workers Centre. 1991. *Foreign Domestic Workers in Hong Kong: A Baseline Study*. Hong Kong: AMWC.
Barrett, Michèle. 1980. *Women's Oppression Today: Problems in Marxist Feminist Analysis*. London: Verso.
Barsotti, Odo and Laura Lecchini. 1991. 'The Case of Asian Female Migrants,' *Asian Migrant*, 4(2): 40–5.
Battistella, Graziano. 1994. 'Migration Trends in Asia,' *Asian Migrant*, 7(4): 131–4.

——. 1992. 'Migration in 1991: Consideration from a Review of the Press,' *Asian Migrant*, 5(1): 4–11.

——. 1992. 'Migration: Opportunity or Loss?' pp. 113–34 in *Philippine Labor Migration: Impact and Policy*, eds. Graziano Battistella and Anthony Paganoni. Quezon City, Philippines: Scalabrini Migration Center.

Beneria, Lourdes. 1981. 'Accumulation, Reproduction and Women's Role in Economic Development: Boserup Revisited,' *Signs*, 7: 278–98.

Boserup, Ester. 1970. *Women's Role in Economic Development.* New York: St. Martin's.

Boyd, Monica. 1989. 'Family and Personal Network in International Migration: Recent Development and New Agendas,' *International Migration Review*, 23(3): 638–70.

Brydon, Lynne and Sylvia Chant. 1989. *Women in the third world: Gender Issues in Rural and Urban Areas.* New Brunswick: Rutgers University Press.

Carino, Benjamin V. 1992. 'Migrant Workers from the Philippines,' pp. 4–21 in *Philippine Labor Migration: Impact and Policy*, eds. Graziano Battistella and Anthony Paganoni. Quezon City, Philippines: Scalabrini Migration Center.

Chant, Sylvia. 1992. 'Conclusion: Toward a Framework for the Analysis of Gender-Selective Migration,' pp. 197–206 in *Gender & Migration in Developing Countries*, ed. Sylvia Chant. London: Belhaven Press.

Chant, Sylvia and Cathy McIlwaine. 1995. *Women of a Lesser Cost: Female Labor, Foreign Exchange and Philippine Development.* London: Pluto.

Chant, Sylvia and Sarah A. Radcliffe. 1992. 'Migration and Development: The Importance of Gender,' pp. 1–29 in *Gender & Migration in Developing Countries*, ed. Sylvia Chant. London: Belhaven Press.

Charlton, Sue Ellen M. 1984. *Women in third world Development.* Boulder: Westview.

Charlton, Sue Ellen M., Jana Everett, and Kathleen Staudt, eds. 1989. *Women, the State, and Development.* Albany: SUNY.

Chirot, Daniel and Thomas D. Hall. 1982. 'World-System Theory,' *Annual Review of Sociology*, 8: 81–106.

Collins, Patricia Hill. 1990. *Black Feminist Thought: Knowledge, Consciousness, and the Politics of Empowerment.* New York: Routledge.

Enloe, Cynthia. 1989. *Making Feminist Sense of International Politics: Bananas, Beaches & Bases.* Berkeley, CA: University of California Press.

Eviota, Elizabeth U. 1992. *The Political Economy of Gender: Women and the Sexual Division of Labor in the Philippines.* London: Zed Books.

Glenn, Evelyn Nakana. 1992. 'From Servitude to Service Work: Historical Continuities in the Racial Division of Paid Reproductive Labor,' *Signs*, 18(1): 1–43.

Goss, Jon and Bruce Lindquist. 1995. 'Conceptualizing International Labor Migration: A Structuration Perspective,' *International Migration Review*, 26(2): 623–45.

Harris, Nigel. 1995. *The New Untouchables: Immigration and the New World Worker.* London: I.B. Tauris.

Heisler, Barbara Schmitter. 1992. 'The Future of Immigrant Incorporation: Which Models? Which Concepts?' *International Migration Review*, 29(2): 317–51.

Heyzer, Noeleen, Geertje Lycklama a Nijeholt, and Nedra Weerakoon, eds. 1994. *The Trade in Domestic Workers: Causes, Mechanisms and Consequences of International Migration.* London: Zed Books.

Heyzer, Noeleen and Vivienne Wee. 1994. 'Domestic Workers in Transient Overseas Employment: Who Benefits, Who Profits,' pp. 31–101 in *The Trade in Domestic Workers*: *Causes, Mechanisms and Consequences of International Migration*, eds. Noeleen Heyzer, *et al.* Selected Papers from Regional Policy Dialogue on Foreign Women Domestic Workers, Colombo, Sri Lanka, 10–14 Aug. 1992. Kuala Lumpur: Asian and Pacific Development Center.

Lane, Barbara. 1992. 'Filipino Domestic Workers in Hong Kong,' *Asian Migrant*, 5(1): 24–32.

Leacock, Eleanor and Helen Safa, *et al.* 1986. *Women's Work: Development and the Division of Labor by Gender*. New York: Bergin & Garvey.

Lee, Sharon M. 1996. 'Issues in Research on Women, International Migration and Labor,' *Asian and Pacific Migration Journal*, 5(1): 85–116.

Lin, Lean Lim and Nana Oishi. 1996. 'International Labor Migration of Asian Women: Distinctive Characteristics and Policy Concerns,' *Asian and Pacific Migration Journal*, 5(1): 85–116.

Massey, Douglas S. *et al.* 1993. 'Theories of International Migration: A Review and Appraisal,' *Population and Development Review*, 19(3): 431–65.

——. 1994. 'International Migration Theory: The North American Case,' *Population and Development Review*, 20(4): 699–753.

Mies, Maria. 1986. *Patriarchy and Accumulation on a World Scale: Women in the International Division of Labor*. London: Zed Books.

Mohanty, Chandra Talpade, Ann Russo, and Lourdes Torres, eds. 1991. *Third World Women and the Politics of Feminism*. Bloomington: Indiana University Press.

Malos, Ellen. 1995. *The Politics of Housework*. New edition. Cheltenham, England: New Clarion Press.

Nash, June and Maria Patricia Fernandez-Kelly, eds. 1983. *Women, Men and the International Division of Labor*. Albany: SUNY Press.

Pettman, Jan Jindy. 1996. *Worlding Women: A Feminist International Politics*. London: Routledge.

Piore, Michael, J. 1979. *Birds of Passage: Migrant Labor and Industrial Societies*. New York: Cambridge University Press.

Portes, Alejandro and John Walton. 1981. *Labor, Class, and the International System*. New York: Academic Press.

Reskin, Barbara and Irene Padavic. 1994. *Women and Men at Work*. Thousand Oaks, CA: Pine Forge Press.

Romero, Mary. 1992. *Maid in the USA* New York: Routledge.

Rogers, Barbara. 1980. *The Domestication of Women: Discrimination in Developing Societies*. London: Tavistock.

Sassen, Saskia. 1988. *The Mobility of Labor and Capital: A Study in International Investment and Labor Flow*. New York: Cambridge University Press.

Sen, Gita and Caren Grown. 1987. *Development, Crises and Alternative Visions: Third World Women's Perspectives*. New York: Monthly Review Press.

Shannon, Thomas Richard. 1989. *An Introduction to the World-System Perspective*. Boulder, CO: Westview Press.

Smith, Joan, Jane Collins, Terence K. Hopkins, and Akbar Muhammad, eds. 1988. *Racism, Sexism, and the World-System*. New York: Greenwood Press.

Stalker, Peter. 1994. *The Work of Strangers: A Survey of International Labor Migration*. Geneva: ILO.

Tinker, Irene, ed. 1990. *Persistent Inequalities: Women and World Development.* New York: Oxford University Press.

Truong, Thanh-Dam. 1996. 'Gender, International Migration and Social Reproduction: Implications for Theory, Policy, Research and Networking,' *Asian and Pacific Migration Journal,* 5(1): 27–52.

Vasquez, Noel D. 1992. 'Economic and Social Impact of Labor Migration,' pp. 41–67 in *Philippine Labor Migration: Impact and Policy,* eds. Graziano Battistella and Anthony Paganoni. Quezon City: Scalabrini Migration Center.

Wallerstein, Immanuel. 1979. *The Capitalist World-Economy.* New York: Cambridge University Press.

Ward, Kathryn, ed. 1990. *Women Workers and Global Restructuring.* Ithaca: Cornell University Press.

Waring, Marilyn. 1988. *If Women Counted: A New Feminist Economics.* New York: Harper San Francisco.

Williams, Christine L. 1995. *Still a Man's World: Men Who Do 'Women's Work.'* Berkeley: University of California Press.

Young, Kate, Carol Wolkowitz, and Roslyn McCullagh, eds. 1984. *Of Marriage and the Market: Women's Subordination Internationally and Its Lessons.* London: Routledge.

Yuval-Davis, Nira, and Floya Anthias, eds. 1989. *Woman-Nation-State.* New York: St. Martin's.

Zolberg, Aristotle. 1983. 'International Migration in Political Perspective,' pp. 3–27 in *Global Trends in Migration,* ed. M. Kritz. New York: Center for Migration Studies.

4 Asian Women in Business in Australia

David Ip and Constance Lever-Tracy

1.

Much of the literature on migrants in the work-force, in Australia as overseas, has tended to paint a picture of passive victims – unskilled, weak and lacking the ability to shape their own fate or to defend themselves against exploitation or the marginality of secondary or reserve army of labor status.[1] On the other hand, an alternative emphasis has drawn attention to the resources of many of these workers in skills, industrial and trade union experience and community solidarities not always available to native workers.[2] In the case of migrant women, the first approach has predominated, although there has been some emphasis on ways waged work can provide liberation from traditional patriarchy.[3]

Since the mid 1970s in Britain and America, and in the last few years in Australia, attention has also turned to the increasingly prominent migrant and ethnic small business sector. Significant proportions of the migrant working class of the post-war decades have been turning laboriously acquired savings into a self-employed escape from the factory, while others have been obliged to convert redundancy payments into an alternative to unemployment. Increasingly, too, the patterns of migration are changing, as small (and larger) business people and professionals are also drawn into globalizing currents, while immigration policies increasingly promote such arrivals.[4]

A contrast of perspectives is also to be found in analyses of the ethnic economy. On the one hand is the approach which stresses dependent and marginal conditions, in various forms of outwork and subcontracting, the lack of choices of those driven into the sector by blocked opportunities elsewhere, and the secondary and sweated or 'self exploited' conditions of those working within it, whether owners or employees.[5] On the other hand are those who argue that ethnic small business enclaves are not part of the 'secondary sector' at all, providing ladders through training and mutual aid from unskilled to skilled jobs, from employee to self-employed status and from struggling subsistence firms to larger and more prosperous ones.[6]

To overemphasize their disadvantaged and marginal position can contribute further to the 'victimology' of immigrants, the tendency to portray them as incapable, poverty-stricken and often dependent recipients of social welfare handouts and policy measures. In times of recession immigrants, tend to become scapegoats for social and economic woes and are frequently regarded as liabilities rather than assets, as takers rather than contributors. There is in fact some evidence that businesses owned by the overseas-born have lower failure rates and more sustained growth and some indications that they make a significantly greater contribution to exports and should be seen as part of a solution to Australia's economic ills, pointing a way to regeneration of entrepreneurship and the balance of payments.[7]

Despite an emphasis on the importance of family firms, until recently, few of the writings on ethnic small businesses have focused explicitly on the circumstances and contributions of women. These questions have, however, been placed at the heart of the debate by claims that positive evaluations of ethnic business activity are based on gender blindness. The entrepreneurs in the ethnic enclaves, it has been argued, are men, while the exploited workers are women. The men at the bottom may indeed have access to ladders, but the women remain trapped under a reimposed patriarchal domination. Some ethnic communities do have resources enabling them to flourish, but the greatest of these resources is the culturally enforced submissiveness of their women.[8] These claims have not been supported by substantial evidence to date.

The real position of women in ethnic business may be at last at the heart of the debate, but actual information is as yet very limited. If the theorists of ethnic economic activity based on family and community networks have been gender blind, those who have chosen to focus explicitly on female entrepreneurship have been oblivious to the widespread existence of jointly or collectively owned and managed family firms and, as a result, have largely passed ethnic women by. Scase and Goffee's *Home Life in a Small Business* emphasizes the temporary and part time, although important contribution made by wives in Britain to the initial establishment of their husbands' businesses. There is one passing reference to wives who may be able to pursue their own career within the family business as part and parcel of its diversification, but this is seen as exceptional.[9] When they later set out to write explicitly about 23 female business proprietors, we find that none is in partnership with a husband, and this fact must have been part of the selection criteria, although it is nowhere stated or justified. Yet men are never excluded from studies of male entrepreneurs because their wife is a working partner![10]

Still and Guerin's work on self-employed women in Australia similarly assumes (again without discussion) that its subject is activity by women outside the family context. It is, therefore, not surprising that they acknowledge a bias towards well-educated, middle-class women and little representation of non-Anglophone migrants, including those from Greece and Italy, despite the fact that census data indicate very high proportions of women with employer and self-employed status in these groups.[11] In view of the almost complete exclusion of working partner couples from research on female entrepreneurs (but not from those looking at male entrepreneurs) it is hardly surprising that such studies contrast the family help and support received by men with its absence in the case of women and stress the self assertive and independence-seeking motivations of such women, rather than any part they may have in family strategies.[12]

A less one-sided approach to the study of women's economic activity could involve elements of what has been called the 'new home economics', which argues that analysis of women's workforce activities must first consider their family situation because 'families are really about the production of household commodities; instrumental activities are alive and well in the household and *all* family members are implicated'.[13] Each household should be seen as a unit of production, seeking to maximize its utility. The study of women's participation in the labor market should, therefore, look at the social dynamics of how household decisions are arrived at and at the socio-economic context and the interrelationship between work and home. Recent theoretical discussions of petty commodity production also stress that it involves a contradictory unity of labor and capital and some have spoken of its operation according to a 'kinship logic' or a 'subsistence logic'.[14] Analyses conducted in such a spirit cannot be restricted to surface data on labor force status, pay rates and property rights but must also involve an in depth understanding of power relationships and consumption patterns within the family and of the long term and possibly differential contributions to and benefits from family strategies as they unfold over its life cycle.

The aim of this chapter is first to examine the available Australian data on female entrepreneurship among the overseas-born and to suggest that on the whole they are far more misleading and ambiguous than is generally supposed. The second and main aim is to present material from a study, financed by the Office of Multicultural Affairs, on ethnic small businesses in the Chinese and Indian communities in Brisbane and Sydney.[15] The study, carried out in Brisbane and Sydney in 1989 and 1990, made use of a snowball approach of personal introductions and in-depth, open-ended interviews with 144 small and medium business owners

(104 of Chinese ancestry and 40 of Indian ancestry) in 138 businesses. In nearly two fifths of these cases we found women centrally involved and playing a primary or equal and often innovative and responsible role in management and decision making. In a large majority of cases, this occurred in the context of a family firm, owned and operated jointly with husbands and sometimes other relatives.

2.

It is often stated that migrant women in Australia are significantly under-represented in the owner management of businesses.[16] The source for this belief lies in Williams data base on small business in Australia, derived from exit interviews with 22,034 loan applicants who had approached banks and other financial institutions between 1973 and 1985. Of these applicants, 4,113 were born overseas, and only 6 percent of the overseas-born respondents were women, a figure which has not been questioned. The low proportion seems, however, hardly consistent with other data from the same interviews which show that 42 percent of these migrant owned businesses involved a partnership of husband and wife and another 35 percent involved ownership by 'one or both spouses' plus adult children.[17] Some of these wives may have been inactive partners, but ABS data (1988) show that, in 1987, of all the overseas born classified as employers, 28 percent were women. This is a figure nearly five times higher than that indicated by the Williams data, and one not very different from the 31 percent of females among native born employers. Among the self-employed, native and immigrant women constituted the same proportion of 30 percent.[18]

The discrepancy with census data may cast some doubt on the reliability of the data base. A solution to the mystery may also lie less in the patriarchal habits of immigrant communities and more in the (real or expected) sexist attitudes of Australian bank managers. The difficulties experienced by women in obtaining business loans have been often documented as has the tendency for even native solo female entrepreneurs to send or seek the company of a man on such a mission. In family partnerships, which are more common among the overseas than the native-born, there is normally no need for the woman, even if she were the prime mover in the business, to visit the bank herself (and, thus, to be available to fill in an exit questionnaire).[19] The impressive size of the Williams data base is unfortunately no guarantee against substantial inbuilt selection bias.

One reason for the ready acceptance of the Strahan and Williams' picture is that it accords with stereotypes derived in part from the working class attributes of earlier generations of migrant women and, in part, from patriarchal images of the Asian cultures of recent arrivals. Yet, it is clear that the new Asian migrants are in many ways quite different from their earlier South European counterparts and that the societies from which they come have been experiencing very rapid changes in recent years. Immigration to Australia since the mid-1980s has seen a sizeable increase of independent and business migrants from Asian countries, some from long established trading and manufacturing diasporas, with considerably greater class resources in funds, business experience and education than the earlier South Europeans with their peasant or working class backgrounds. Unlike the latter, they have come in a period of manufacturing decline, encouraged by immigration policies that give credit points for education, skills and capital. The motives of many are not primarily economic but focus rather on fears of political changes or racial discrimination in their countries of origin or on a desire to get away from pollution and overcrowding, and above all on the search for greater and less intensely competitive educational opportunities for their children. Both men and women have substantial class resources, and while many experience significant problems of non-recognition of their credentials, others have recognized qualifications from earlier periods as overseas students in Australia or from British affiliated institutions recognized here.

The Hong Kong migrants are a case in point. Since 1986, this has become one of Australia's principal source countries. In 1977, the number of Australian immigrant visas issued to Hong Kong residents was only 1,633.[20] By 1990, the annual total had reached 17,486 accounting for 9.5 percent of Australia's total immigrant intake.[21] By the Hong Kong government's own unhappy admission, among the emigrants departing for Canada, Australia and the United States between 1987 and 1989, about 15 percent held degree level educational qualifications, although only four percent of Hong Kong's overall population is tertiary educated. Of the emigrants who had been employed in Hong Kong, 23 percent had been in professional, technical, administrative and managerial positions although only six percent of the colony's overall work force is in these categories. The fear of the take-over by China in 1997 was clearly the primary motive.

To focus on the groups that are the subject of our case study, the ethnic Chinese and Indians of Brisbane and Sydney (a large majority of whom have arrived since 1975), Tables 4.1 to 4.3 provide some data obtained from special runs of the 1986 census. Table 4.1 shows that few of the working women in these groups fit the stereotype of unqualified workers who cannot speak English. The difference between men and women in this respect is small.

Table 4.1   Qualifications and English of employed men and women of Chinese
and Indian ancestry in Brisbane and Sydney (%)

	Brisbane		Sydney	
	Men	*Women*	*Men*	*Women*
Chinese Ancestry				
Good English and Qualifications	41	35	41	41
Good English no Qualifications	42	46	37	38
Poor English and Qualifications	3	2	2	1
Poor English no Qualifications	14	17	20	20
Total Employed	100	100	100	100
Number	1,183	1,002	9,775	7,333
Indian Ancestry				
Good English and Qualifications	55	47	65	59
Good English no Qualifications	44	52	34	40
Poor English and Qualifications	0	0	0	0
Poor English no Qualifications	1	1	1	1
Total Employed	100	100	100	100
Number	519	341	2,047	1,629

Source: 1986 Census (Special Run).

Tables 4.2 and 4.3 provide more detailed data on the proportions of
independents (employers and self-employed) in these groups. Not only are
these figures high (especially for Chinese in Brisbane, in particular those
born in China, Hong Kong and Taiwan), but the gap between men and
women is generally no greater than for the population as a whole and
noticeably lower for some groups. (These figures do not conceal large
numbers of outworkers as no more than two percent of each of these
ancestry groups are classified as 'working from home'.)

The profile makes clear the central importance of ethnic small businesses in the working lives especially of Chinese in Brisbane, where, in
1986, nearly 24 percent of the male and 22 percent of the female labor
force were employers, self-employed or unpaid helpers. If their employees
could be counted as well, it seems likely that a majority of this community
would be found to be working within their own ethnic business sector. The
OMA survey was based on a snowball of personal introductions, comprising 73 Chinese in Brisbane and 31 in Sydney and with 27 Indians in
Brisbane and 13 in Sydney. There were no sharp distinctions between the
four groups as far as the subject matter of this chapter was concerned. We
believe we have a good and varied coverage of Brisbane Chinese from

Table 4.2 Labor force status of non-employee men and women in Brisbane and Sydney

		Self-employed %	Employer %	Family helper %	Sub-total %	%	Total labor force no.
Brisbane							
Chinese	Men	10.0	12.7	1.0	23.7	100	2,631
	Women	10.5	8.7	2.5	21.7	100	2,063
Indian	Men	5.6	4.9	0.4	10.9	100	1,413
	Women	3.4	3.6	1.6	8.6	100	880
Sydney							
Chinese	Men	6.6	8.3	0.5	15.3	100	21,756
	Women	4.8	4.4	1.3	10.4	100	16,510
Indian	Men	4.8	5.3	0.2	10.3	100	6,973
	Women	3.5	2.4	0.5	6.4	100	5,039
All Ancestries	Men	8.2	5.9	0.2	14.3	100	946,632
	Women	4.8	3.3	0.9	9.0	100	646,851

Table 4.3 Independents (self-employed and employers) as proportion
of the labor force, Brisbane and Sydney. Men and women of Chinese and
Indian ancestry, by birthplace (%)

	Brisbane		Sydney	
	Men	Women	Men	Women
Chinese Born in:				
Australia	19	14	16	9
China and Taiwan	40	38	23	17
Hong Kong and Macao	28	25	13	9
Malaysia and Singapore	19	16	17	6
Vietnam	14	15	5	5
Other	19	17	13	9
Indians Born in:				
Australia	9	x	9	8
Fiji	11	8	7	4
Malaysia and Singapore	11	x	21	5
India	9	8	11	8
Sri Lanka	7	5	6	3
Other	18	12	13	7

NB – Often the distinction between China and Hong Kong as place of birth merely
represents a difference of age, as most of the former have Hong Kong as last place
of residence.
x – A number of 5 or less is not reliable because of ABS scrambling for reasons of
confidentiality.
Source: 1986 Census (Special Run).

a variety of birthplaces, class backgrounds and types of business (their
profile is not very different from what the census would lead us to expect),
although the findings for the other three groups may be more tentative.

The study was not initially designed with an emphasis on the place of
women and personal introductions almost invariably led to men, clearly
seen as the appropriate face to present to a university interviewer. In fact,
only 20 interviews (16 Chinese and 4 Indian) took place with women.[22]
Yet, it soon became clear that this male public face was misleading. In a
few cases, the nominated contact explained that he only worked part-time
in what was 'my wife's business'. In several cases where we had been
given an introduction to a woman, she claimed to be too busy, and referred
us to a male partner instead. In one case, the reference to a member of
a business association led us to the retired father of the very assertive

woman who was, in fact, the initiator and owner of the business.[23] Once we started asking about ownership, management and decision making in the business, it soon became clear that in very many cases the respondent saw a female partner (usually a wife, sometimes a mother, daughter or daughter-in-law, sister or sister-in-law) as being on a par with themselves. While we have in the following account relied quite heavily of course on the 20 interviews with women, we have also drawn the quantitative data and many particular accounts, from the information supplied by male respondents about the female partners in their businesses.

3.

The contribution of family members to the businesses surveyed was substantial in terms of labor, management and ownership. In 17 cases in Brisbane, there were two adult generations working together in the same business. In 32 of the 96 Brisbane firms, both husband and wife were working full-time. In a further 23 cases, one of the couples was full-time and the others (four men and 19 women) were part-time. In addition, there were 20 brothers, five sisters, seven brothers-in-law and five sisters-in-law involved and also three cousins and an uncle. Only 24 percent of the Chinese businesses in Brisbane and 14 percent of the Indians made no use of family labor.[24]

The common notion of 'cheap' or 'unpaid' family labor requires substantial qualification, however. In the first place, most of them *were* paid (this made tax sense), and if those who lived in the same household then put some or all of it back into the family budget, this need not distinguish these earnings from what they would have done with wages from a job elsewhere. Indeed, the use of household labor involves the opportunity cost of the foregone contribution of the possible outside earnings. The smallest and most struggling businesses belonged to precisely the families most dependent on such outside earnings and, therefore, least likely to maximize the use of family labor in the business.

The second qualification is that, in general, the importance of the family was seen by respondents not in its cheapness but in its contribution to management resources. Only a handful of the businesses in our survey employed non-family managers, and many had cautionary tales warning of the dangers of doing so.[25] There was a clear positive correlation between the number of family members involved, especially full-time, and the number of non-family employees, branches and the range of activities. In one case, a newsagency and gift shop with a gold lotto agency was in the charge of the wife, while the husband ran an estate agency (both under joint ownership). In another, the man, with several employees, operated a bakery while the wife, also with employees, ran the shop which sold the products. One husband dealt with export/import activities while the wife was responsible for travel agency operations. A husband and wife, both with unrecognized medical qualifications from China, opened a joint practice where he provided acupuncture and she prescribed and sold herbal treatments. The part-owner of a chain of three successful restaurants, employing 15 workers, run in partnership with his wife and brother, remarked that no more branches were contemplated because the three of them could not manage any more. References to family members (irrespective of gender) as 'the management', to the possibility of leaving any of them (but only them) in charge of the till or the premises or in a supervisory capacity were common. In a few cases, women had clearly sought deliberately to take advantage of the loose knit flexibility of the family firm to maximize their own autonomy by initiating new activities for which they were largely responsible.

The third qualification is that in most cases where family members worked full-time in the business, they were also partners or directors of a family trust. Fifty-two percent of the firms in Brisbane and 41 percent in Sydney involved family partners. Only five out of 44 wives who worked full-time in the business were not also owners, and most of these were receptionists in a professional practice, where partnership was legally precluded. Altogether there were at least 16 businesses which had been started essentially by a woman alone (occasionally in conjunction with other family or non-family partners), the husband's wage generally providing the safety net for the family (two had been started by single or divorced women). Eleven of these were still primarily in the hands of women, while the other five had now drawn in a wider range of family members, in two cases having seen the founding woman withdrawing because of ill health. In most cases, however, a woman's full-time involvement was in conjunction with a similar input by her husband.

A closer focus on the relation of husbands and wives in the business can, therefore, help provide a quantitatively clearer picture. All but one of the 16 Brisbane women respondents, and all but four of the 84 men, were married (or in one case in a *de facto* relationship). Allowing for the three cases where both spouses were interviewed, this gives us a total of 92 couples. For Sydney the equivalent number was 37. Table 4.4 shows the relative involvement of these 129 women in these couples' businesses.

Looking first at those wives with little or no involvement in the business it should even here be noted that this can vary over the family's life cycle.

Table 4.4   Business involvement by married women, Brisbane and Sydney

	Brisbane	*Sydney*
Business is:		
Owned and run by wife alone (sometimes with part-time help from husband)	2	2
Run by wife alone, husband is inactive partner	1	–
Run by wife with other partners, husband is inactive partner or uninvolved	1	1
Run primarily by wife, co-owner husband helps part-time	4	–
Started mainly by wife, both co-owners now full-time	3	–
Started by co-owning couple, wife now runs it	–	1
Owned and run by both full-time	22	10
Primary or equal role of wife	33	14
As percent of all couples	36%	38%
Staffed by wife as full-time employee, husband full-time owner	5	–
Run by husband full-time with wife as part-time (owner or employee)	22	4
Run by husband, wife as inactive partner	12	2
Secondary involvement by wife	39	6
As percent of all couples	42%	16%
Wife uninvolved	20	17
As percent of all couples	22%	46%
Total women in couples	92	37
Percent	100%	100%

In one case, a woman who had been only marginally involved, for 5 to 10 hours a week at the time of the interview, was found to be running a petrol station, a new family venture, full-time a few months later. In another case, a doctor's wife was employed as a nurse part-time, with the intention of bringing her into partnership if she could obtain recognition of her own medical qualifications. Several currently uninvolved women had played an equal or primary role at an earlier stage but had now withdrawn, usually because of ill health,[26] and six of the 28 part-time women were said to be fully involved in decision making. Some of these partially involved or uninvolved women had jobs, including some that were clearly careers of their own, and one had her own completely separate business.

In the case of the 35 wives who were partners with their husbands in the business, and working in it with him full-time, the crucial outstanding question is of their involvement in decision making, and we probed this subject with some care. In two cases, the man asserted that he had the final say, and in two cases the woman claimed to get her own way. Three other cases were ambiguous ('joint decisions although most of the time she lets me decide', 'I decide, then I discuss it with her'). In the remaining 28 cases, there was an insistence either that all decisions were jointly made or that individuals decided within their own sphere of activity, with major issues resolved by discussion. When we probed further on 'what happens if you disagree?' we were told either that there were never serious disagreements or that the one with the best arguments would carry the day or that 'We fight it out', 'We talk until we agree'.

In the nine cases where women carry the main or sole work load of the business (irrespective of the formal ownership structure), the majority view was that although she might seek advice or engage in discussions, in the end, 'it's up to her', 'it's really her business', 'I discuss problems with my husband, use him as a sounding board, but I decide'. Two of these women, however, said that they generally chose to follow their husband's advice because they found it good and in a third case, where a previously full-time husband had largely retired, he said that 'she more or less runs it, but I decide'.

We were unable to observe the decision-making process in practice and were only occasionally able to cross-check the perspectives of both husband and wife on this. But the general stated norm is clearly that the extent of involvement in decision making is closely related to knowledge and experience in the business and to the input of time and effort.

4.

The levels of commitment, responsibility and initiative suggested above clearly depend on, but also foster, strong, energetic women with an independent and innovative spirit. They can lead to great personal pride and satisfaction, but can also impose enormous work loads and substantial stress and sacrifice.

One of the more striking stories is of F.H., a young Chinese woman from Indonesia. She stopped work as a shop assistant when she became pregnant and moved interstate to stay with her parents. She learned that a run down printshop, in the basement next door, was for sale very cheaply. She bought it (borrowing money from her parents), taught herself to operate the equipment, starting slowly from the three or four existing clients, and then did canvassing and mail shots and over 18 months had built it up from one or two orders a week to half a dozen a day. She arranged bank loans to acquire better equipment and established a network of contacts with (non co-ethnic) neighboring workshops, for contracting in and out of specialized tasks. She took five days off to have the baby and then returned (this made possible by her mother and a paid child minder). The toddler now plays around the printshop. She had some part-time help from her retired parents, and after six months her husband gave up his job and came up and joined them full-time. Now they also employ two full-time workers and three casuals and are looking for more. When asked how important decisions were made she said, 'We fight. I normally win, but it is getting tougher now. It was really good at the start. I knew more because I started it. Now he knows as much or more'. She was hoping to get around the resulting tensions in part by reorganizing functions, to make their spheres autonomous and to take her out a lot to see clients, and by setting up another related company, in publishing, with a different partner. She remarked that it would have been good to have had more help at the start, 'I really needed a man's brain', but concluded about running a business that 'The freedom is good. The pride is good. But you often have to pay a high price for every experience. If you make a mistake as a worker it does not cost you so much'.

Another case is that of D.C., a woman of 40 with two small children and a third on the way. In Taiwan, she had run her own businesses, in retail and printing, before marriage and after. She has been in Australia for two years now, but her husband, an architect and developer, was still in Taipei completing projects that were likely to take some time. Although he kept asking her to come back for the time, she preferred to stay and wait in Australia. She was taking things 'fairly easy, until the baby is born'. She had been buying land on which she was devising a scheme for him to construct houses in a style to meet the tastes of recent arrivals from Taiwan, and she was also making plans to start herself an import business for tinned food, which could not be found here and would meet an unfilled demand. 'This will be my own business, no partner, and I'll make my own decisions'.

V.A. saw her business as a challenge. She had been working as a social worker for the Chinese community and had observed that 'There was not any provision to help full fee-paying students from overseas to adjust'. She decided to quit her job and establish her own agency for recruiting overseas students. She sought to infuse her concept with a social work philosophy to create something new, free she hoped from the money-grubbing 'stigma' she believes has come to attach to such agencies. She sees herself as 'shaping a new profession which accepts responsibility also for helping overseas students and for protecting their interests. We have to prove we are different. After 18 months old contacts are now coming to regard us as professionals in the field'. For her 'Being your own boss is great. I'm only responsible to myself. It's good that you can try things you think will work, without first having to convince a superior'.

On the other hand, many spoke of the worry and stress, often keeping them awake at night, and of the long hours and exhaustion and the lack of time for their family. 'I would not mind going back to work in a factory,' remarked one Chinese woman who had described herself as 'the boss.' 'At least then I might get some rest.' One Indian woman ran a combined corner shop and take-away, with a small restaurant attached. She opened the shop at six in the morning, every day, and rarely finished clearing up before midnight. Her husband helped in the evenings, but in the day worked full-time as a trade instructor. Her only child, a 12-year-old girl helped as well, but had little time to spare from her school work and from the grueling routine of private dancing and drama classes with which she was being prepared for the best private high school in Brisbane the following year. The school fees were the main reason for setting up the business. 'We are working hard for her future. We put her name down for the school the day after she was born'.

E.J. had been a beautician and then a housewife in Hong Kong. On her arrival, she found her licence was not recognized and 'There was not much else I could do. I'm not well educated. The factories wanted teenagers or people with experience'. Until her husband found a job, she kept the family afloat by selling cosmetics, sent from Hong Kong, from a market stall and then she found part-time work in a take-away. Her children were having difficulty in the public school, however, and their wages would not cover the fees in a Church school where they believed they would get more attention, so she took over the take-away lease. Above all, she dreads being ill. 'No sick leave. No holidays. I hurt my back last Friday. My doctor told me to lie down for three days. I can't do it'. The previous year she had kept the shop open while dizzy with a high fever, because her son's exams were approaching, and he could not be called on to take over even for a few hours. She would continue until he had completed university, in about five years when she intended to give it up. 'I want to have a long holiday, to travel round the world. I have not even been back for a visit to Hong Kong since I left. I work hard now and aim for leisure later'.

Often, these efforts are only made possible by the contributions of other family members to childcare and domestic tasks. One respondent had run a shop and import–export business jointly with his wife who 'Knows 101 percent of what there is to know about the business. I do about 80 hours a week. She does about 70 hours a week in the shop, plus ten hours housework'. Since she had the baby, she had been bringing it with her to the shop each day, while he tried to obtain an entry visa for his sister to come and help with the child. Because the visa had been refused, they were thinking of closing the shop, as the strain was affecting his wife's health.

What surfaces again and again in these accounts, in the triumphs and the sacrifices, in the solo enterprises as well as the collectively operated family firms, is the extent to which they are inscribed within a family strategy, aiming at a generally prosperous outcome for the family unit as a whole, and mobilizing internally the skills, interests and resources of the family members to overcome the crucial initial hardship during the settlement period. The education of the children to tertiary or professional level is often the primary goal.

As such, these women's efforts and achievements are legitimated and supported by other family members in a way that contrasts with other accounts of female entrepreneurs. While women continue to carry most of the burden of childcare and domestic work (which surely takes more than ten hours a week), help here, not only from female relatives but also from men, is not unknown.

> My husband [a university lecturer] helps a lot in the house, without him I could not do it. He picks the children up from school and looks after them. Even makes their sandwiches in the morning, because I work long hours and I need eight or nine hours sleep, he can make do with six. He does the shopping. He helped with housework and cleaning until we employed the girl. If I have a problem I discuss it with him first. When I am on a trip or overseas, he looks in the office around 5:00, signs cheques and keeps an eye on the bookkeeping. He knows about the computer and helps if we are having trouble with it. (V.A., the overseas student agent)

A dentist's wife who had for years been a housewife, while devoting just a few hours a week to her husband's accounts, decided to go into a non-family partnership to run a take-away. 'I discussed with my husband and the children whether I should go in in the first place, as I had to cut back on time spent at home and they now need to help in the house. They all said they would support me'.

5.

The notion of family strategies and goals, of course, challenges arguments which assert that what is really involved is the input of effort by female family members to further the goals and consumption of the males. We believe this is an important and generally unexamined question, which requires the kind of analysis of what goes on within the family that is rarely undertaken. We believe also that it is an empirical question, to which the answer is likely to be different for different groups in different circumstances and that it may change over time. Our study made no attempt to analyze family expenditure patterns, or to systematically examine any differing interests and perspectives of men and women, and it cannot provide definitive answers as far as our groups are concerned. On balance, however, our findings do not point to any general and substantial exploitation of women by men within Indian and Chinese business families in Australia today. Both husbands and wives worked most of their waking hours (although it seems likely that women's double load added up to more hours), both lived in the same generally comfortable houses, ate the same food, and one respondent remarked that, although they drew no individual wages, 'We both get the same pocket money'. Of significance is the extent to which family efforts and expenses are geared to the children's education. This was a goal which seemed equally dear to men and women, and when we asked about what future they would hope for their children, there was only one case where any distinction was made between sons and daughters in this respect. Almost all children of the appropriate age were preparing for or pursuing tertiary studies.

It would seem that this situation may represent the outcome of a process of historical change which has preceded the migration to Australia and which may itself be a consequence of the significant and visible contributions made by women to the family economy, including family businesses, over the last decades. This is particularly clearly so in the case of the Chinese.

The traditional, pre-communist ascribed kinship structures of rural Guangdong (from which many of our respondents originated, often several generations ago), was strictly patrilineal and exogamous, including all the male kin and their wives, with a hierarchy based on gender, generation and birth order, and excluding married sisters and daughters and their husbands and husbands' families. Salaff, in her 1972 study (published in 1982), *Working Daughters of Hong Kong*, argued that the outcome was the exploitation of unmarried working-class daughters, whose earnings were largely handed over for 'family projects' which mainly consisted of the education of their brothers. Since girls would eventually marry out of the family, investment in their education was seen as having a lower priority.

Already for 1972, this conclusion appears overstated in relation to the evidence presented in the book itself. While clearly the labor of older children furthered the education of younger ones, the gender bias was only partial. Some older boys also contributed, and some younger girls benefitted. There were also cases where marriage did not break the economic or residential ties with the girl's family of procreation. Since then, the data show significant change. Ng found women's economic significance in Hong Kong had continued to increase with their workforce participation (in the formal sector) rising from 44 percent in 1976 to 51 percent in 1986.[27] In this study, Ng also found parents denying any explicit favoring of sons over daughters. Mak traced the upward trend of female enrollment in Hong Kong universities from 24 percent of students in 1958 to 40 percent in 1986.[28] Associated with this has been the erosion of the patrilineal family over decades of urban living and diaspora.

Given the great value of family resources and that relatives have become more scarce and scattered, it makes no sense any longer to exclude half of them a priori or to write off one's daughters. Among our Chinese respondents, parents' hopes for a child to join the business were more focused on their willingness and aptitude than on their gender or birth order, and several were advising daughters to follow commerce and law courses in the hope they would be useful for the business. The prevalence in these businesses of kin in the female line, relatives of a wife or married sisters and daughters, their husbands or these husbands' relatives, towards whom there are few strong, traditional, ascribed obligations, is a clear indication of these changes. Among the 69 Chinese businesses in Brisbane were 17 which involved partnerships with extended family members. Eight of these involved non-patrilineal relatives (men and women), linked through females. In another nine businesses such kin had given or received important economic help at some time, in the form of finance or employment. Women and their kinship networks have become as influential as men and as valued as an actual or potential resource in the functioning of these Chinese family businesses. It would also seem to be the case, as Omohundro has shown, in his study of Chinese in the Philippines, that as wives and daughters (and their relatives) became more important in the business, they also gained stature in the family and in its distribution of resources and power.[29]

In recent decades, Australia, like other countries on the Pacific Rim, has again become an important destination for Asian migrants as it was in the 19th century. The volume and composition of the new migrants have increasingly challenged the old stereotypical picture of the existing migrant communities, particularly in portraying women migrants as typically passive, unskilled, unresourceful and submissive underdogs. There is emerging a new element of women entrepreneurs in some Asian communities, because of the changing attributes of recent immigrants from these countries and the changing position of women within these communities. From our survey of small businesses in the Chinese and Indian communities in Brisbane and Sydney, despite the small number of women entrepreneurs interviewed, important new impressions have surfaced. As their personal and class resources have increased, these migrant women have tended to start businesses either as an equal partner or on their own, as part of a strategy to optimize their family's opportunities and advantages. Migrant women as business partners are not necessarily acting in a submissive manner subject to patriarchal supervision and exploitation, as some previous research has suggested. In fact, the determination of these women has, in a number of cases, been the trailblazer, establishing businesses which their husbands have later chosen to join, leaving their prior employment. With more work experience and self-confidence, professional migrant women are tending to seek more personal independence, challenge, achievement and fulfillment by becoming their own bosses. Rather than an undifferentiated experience of exploitation and oppression, for migrant women, running their own business can become a liberating experience.

Many of these women spoke of the pride they had gained out of the new responsibility. Yet the effort the long hours and the worry can grind them down and the toll on leisure and family life can be heavy. For those who had been blocked from using their education and training or who had lost status and self respect in the migration process, this can be seen as an entirely new start, an opportunity to prove themselves afresh. Others commented on the deprivation felt by their children who too rarely had their parents' company. For a few, the negatives weigh most. For some there are no negatives. For a large majority, however, their feelings about their business might well be called a love-hate relationship. 'Having your own business gives you a sense of achievement. I enjoy being my own boss. But what a price you have to pay for that … all the worries, conflicts with partners and long hours. Your social life is screwed up'. 'To run a business you need imagination and you can do your own thing. But the responsibility can also be suffocating at times, and there is little freedom'.

Migration to Australia continues to be an issue of intense debate, particularly in times of economic hardship. Often engulfed in such debates, the dynamic elements of immigration can be ignored. Our impressions of the women immigrant entrepreneurs suggest that there are many as yet untold experiences and stories especially about their contribution as achievers and innovators.

NOTES

1. For example Robin Cohen, *The New Helots, Migrants and the International Division of Labour* (Aldershot: Avebury, 1987); Jock Collins, *Migrant Hands in a Distant Land* (Sydney: Pluto Press, 1988); Saskia Sassen, *The Mobility of Capital and Labour* (Cambridge: Cambridge University Press, 1988).
2. Stephen Castles and Godula Kosack, 'Immigrant Workers and Trade Unions in the German Federal Republic', *Race and Class* 8: 6 (1974); Constance Lever-Tracy and Michael Quinlan, *A Divided Working Class. Ethnic Segmentation and Industrial Conflict in Australia* (London: Routledge and Kegan Paul, 1988); Alejandro Portes, (1978); 'Migration and Underdevelopment', *Politics and Society* 8: 1 (1978); Martin Slater, *Migration and Workers' Conflicts in Western Europe* (Ph.D. dissertation, Massachusetts Institute of Technology, 1976).
3. CURA (Centre for Urban Research and Action), *But I Wouldn't Like my Wife to Work Here. A Study of Migrant Women in Melbourne Industry* (Melbourne: CURA, 1976); S. Westwood and Bhachu, eds., *Enterprising Women. Ethnicity, Economy and Gender Relations* (London: Routledge, 1988).
4. Ian Campbell, Ruth Fincher and Michael Webber, 'Job Mobility in Segmented Labor Markets: The Experience of Immigrant Workers in Melbourne,' paper presented to *The Australian Sociological Association Conference*, Melbourne (December, 1989); Christine Inglis, S. Gunasekaran, Gerard Sullivan and Chung-Tong Wu, eds., *Asians in Australia: The Dynamics of Migration and Settlement* (St. Leonards: Allen and Unwin, 1992).
5. Howard Aldrych, Trevor Jones and David McEvoy (1984) 'Ethnic Advantage and Minority Business Development' in Robin Ward and R. Jenkins, eds., *Ethnic Communities in Business: Strategies for Economic Survival* (London: Cambridge University Press, 1984); Edna Bonacich, 'Middlemen Minorities and Advanced Capitalism', *Ethnic Groups*, 2 (1980); CWW (Centre for Working Women), *Outworkers* (Melbourne: CWW, 1986); Al Rainnie, 'Small Firms, Big Problems: The Political Economy of Small Business', *Capital and Class*, 25 (Spring, 1985).
6. Thomas R. Bailey, *Immigrant and Native Workers* (Boulder: Westview Press, 1987); Susan Nowikowski (1984) 'Snakes and Ladders: Asian Business in Britain' in Robin Ward and R. Jenkins, eds., *Ethnic Communities in Business: Strategies for Economic Survival* (London: Cambridge University Press, 1984); Roger Waldinger, *Through the Eye of a Needle: Immigrants and Enterprise in New York's Garment Trades*, (New York: New York University Press, 1984); Roger Wadinger, 'Immigrant Enterprise: a Critique and Reformulation,' *Theory and Society*, 15 (1986); Kenneth Wilson and Alejandro Portes, 'Immigrant Enclaves: an Analysis of the Labour Market Experiences of Cubans in Miami,' *Americal Journal of Sociology* (1980).
7. Noel Tracy and David Ip (1990) 'The Asian Family Business in Australia: A New Export Base?' *Current Affairs Bulletin* (July, 1990).
8. Phizacklea (1987), 'Minority Women and Economic Restructuring: The Case of Britain and the Federal Republic of Germany,' *Work, Employment and Society*, 1: 3 (1987) Westwood and Bhachu, eds. (1998); J. Sanders and

Victor Nee, 'Limits of Ethnic Solidarity in the Ethnic Enclave,' *American Sociological Review*, 52 (1987).

9.   Richard Scase and Robert Goffee, 'Home Life in a Small Business,' in Mary Evans, ed., *The Woman Question* (London: Fontana, 1982), p. 206.

10. Robert Goffee and Richard Scase, 'Business Ownership and Women's Subordination: a Preliminary Study of Female Business Proprietors', *Sociological Review*, 31: 4 (1983).

11. Leone Still, *Enterprising Women, Australian Women Managers and Entrepreneurs* (Sydney: Allen and Unwin, 1990); Leone Still and D. Guerin, 'Self Employed Women: The New Social Change', paper presented to the Australian Sociological Conference, Melbourne (1989: 8, 15).

12. Goffee and Scase, 'Business Ownership' (1983: 632–5); Still, *Enterprising Women* (1990); D. Watkins and J. Watkins, 'The Female Entrepreneur in Britain: Some Results of a Pilot Survey with Special Emphasis on Educational Needs', in M. Scott, ed., *Small Firms Growth and Development* (Gower, 1986: 193); Still, *Enterprising Women* (1990: 76); Goffee and Scase, 'Business Ownership' (1983: 639).

13. R. Berk and S. Berk, 'Supply-Side Sociology of the Family', *Annual Review of Sociology*, 9 (1983: 381).

14. A.M. Scott, 'Why Rethink Petty Commodity Production?', *Social Analysis*, 20 (Dec. 1986).

15. Much of the material for this paper is derived from the full report, Constance Lever-Tracy, David Ip, Jim Kitay, Irene Philipps and Noel Tracy, *Asian Entrepreneurs in Australia. Ethnic Small Business in the Chinese and Indian Communities of Brisbane and Sydney* (Canberra: Office of Multicultural Affairs, AGPS 1991).

16. For example R. Lampugnani and Robert Holton, *Ethnic Business in South Australia. A Sociological Profile of the Italian Business Community* (Adelaide: Centre for Multicultural Studies, Flinders University of South Australia, 1989: 43).

17. Kenneth Strahan and Alan J. Williams, *Immigrant Entrepreneurs in Australia* (Canberra: Office of Multicultural Affairs, 1988: 33).

18. Figures for females among the self-employed may be suspected of being inflated by outworkers, but this can hardly be the case for employers.

19. Goffee and Scase, 'Business Ownership' (1983: 636); Still and Guerin 'Self Employed Women' (1989: 10); Watkins and Watkins, 'The Female Entrepreneur' (1986: 195).

20. *Metropolitan*, Aug. 23 (1982: 20); R. Skeldon, 'Emigration in Hong Kong' (Hong Kong: Workshop on *Emigration from Hong Kong, Trends and Prospects*, University of Hong Kong, 10 Dec. 1990).

21. Australian Consulate General, Hong Kong, 1990.

22. Given the census data above, it is not surprising, among these 20, to find seven degree holders and collectively many years of prior work experience including as physician, physiotherapist, public servant, social worker, secretary and owner of a supermarket, as well as in factories, shops and restaurants.

23. A number of writers have noted the shyness of women in business or farming, in many diverse communities, of participating in the male atmosphere of business and other public or community organizations, which are often attended by male partners or relatives even if the latter are marginal to the

business (J.T. Omohundro, *Chinese Merchant Families in Iloilo. Commerce and Kin in a Central Philippine City*, Quezon City: Ateneo de Manila Univerity Press, 1981: 98; James, 'Women on Australian Farms', 1982: 312; M. Stratigaki, 'Agricultural Modernisation and Gender Division of Labor. The Case of Heraklion, Greece', *Sociologia Ruralis*, XXVIII: 4, 1988: 254; A. Barbic, 'Farm Women, Work and Decision-Making: The Yugoslav Experience', *Sociologia Ruralis* XXVIII: 4, 1988: 297). Lampugnani and Holton (*Ethnic Business*, 1989) used the membership list of the Italian Chamber of Commerce in Adelaide, and concluded that women had almost no place among Italian business owners.

24.   The Sydney interviews were concentrated to an unrepresentative degree in Chinatown which may have involved too much traveling time from residential areas for part-time workers. The full-time participation by spouses was quite comparable to that in Brisbane but that in other categories was noticeably less. Forty percent in Sydney made no use of family labor, tending more than in Brisbane to non family partnerships, often with old university friends, which we found almost invariably to be incompatible with involvement by family members.

25.   Scase and Goffee (*The Real World*, 1980) argue that small businesses in Britain also find the transition to paid management to be a barrier to growth which few are willing or able to cross.

26.   We did not, however, like Goffee and Scase, find any general tendency to withdrawal by women and their replacement by employees once the business was established. The continuing growth dynamic of these businesses, and the role of women in making this possible, precluded this pattern.

27.   C. Ng, 'Familial Change and Women's Employment in Hong Kong', in F.M. Cheung *et al.*, eds., *Selected Papers of a Conference on Gender Studies in Chinese Societies* (Hong Kong: Hong Kong Institute of Asia-Pacific Studies, The Chinese University of Hong Kong, 1991: 50).

28.   G.C.L. Mak, 'Development of Women's Higher Education: a Comparative Study of China and Hong Kong' in Cheung *et al.*, *Selected Papers* (1991: 221). At Griffith university, in Queensland, Australia, in the last few years, the enrollment (at substantial expense) of full fee paying female Chinese students (mainly from Hong Kong and Taiwan) in commerce courses has, if anything, exceeded that of males.

29.   Omohundro, *Chinese Merchant Families* (1981: 142, 162, 165).

REFERENCES

ABS (Australian Bureau of Statistics) (1988) *The Overseas Born in Australia*, Cat. 4112.0, Canberra: AGPS.

Aldrych, H., T.P. Jones and D. McEvoy. (1984) 'Ethnic Advantage and Minority Business Development' in Ward and Jenkins.

Bailey, T. (1987) *Immigrant and Native Workers*, Boulder: Westview Press.

Barbic, A. (1988) 'Farm Women, Work and Decision-Making: The Yugoslav Experience', *Sociologia Ruralis* XXVIII/4.

Berk, R. and S. Berk. (1983) 'Supply-Side Sociology of the Family', *Annual Review of Sociology*, 9.

Bonacich, E. (1980) 'Middlemen Minorities and Advanced Capitalism', *Ethnic Groups*, 2.

Castles, S. and G. Kosack. (1974) 'Immigrant Workers and Trade Unions in the German Federal Republic', *Race and Class* 8/6.

Campbell, I., R. Fincher and M. Webber. (1989) 'Job Mobility in Segmented Labor Markets: The Experience of Immigrant Workers in Melbourne, December', Paper presented to The Australian Sociological Association Conference, Melbourne, Dec.

Cohen, R. (1987) *The New Helots, Migrants and the International Division of Labor*, Aldershot: Avebury.

Cheung, F.M. *et al.*, eds. (1991) *Selected Papers of a Conference on Gender Studies in Chinese Societies*. Hong Kong: Hong Kong Institute of Asia-Pacific Studies, The Chinese University of Hong Kong.

Collins, J. (1988) *Migrant Hands in a Distant Land*, Sydney: Pluto Press.

CURA (Centre for Urban Research and Action) (1976) *But I Wouldn't Like my Wife to Work Here. A Study of Migrant Women in Melbourne Industry*, Melbourne: CURA.

CWW (Centre for Working Women) (1986) *Outworkers*, Melbourne, CWW.

Goffee, R. and R. Scase. (1983) 'Business Ownership and Women's Subordination: a Preliminary Study of Female Business Proprietors', *Sociological Review*, 31/4.

Hong Kong Government, Office of Members of the Executive and Legislative Councils (1989) *The Brain Drain*, Hong Kong: Hong Kong Government.

Inglis, C. and C.T. Wu. (1990) 'The New Migration of Asian Skill and Capital to Australia. Implications for Theory and Research', Unpublished Paper.

James, K. (1982) 'Women On Australian Farms: A Conceptual Scheme', *Australian and New Zealand Journal of Sociology*, 18/3, Nov.

Lampugnani, R. and R. Holton. (1989) *Ethnic Business in South Australia. A Sociological Profile of the Italian Business Community*, Centre for Multicultural Studies, Flinders University of South Australia.

Lever-Tracy, C. and M. Quinlan. (1988) *A Divided Working Class. Ethnic Segmentation and Industrial Conflict in Australia*, London: Routledge and Kegan Paul.

Mak, G.C.L. (1991) 'Development of Women's Higher Education: a Comparative Study of China and Hong Kong', in Cheung *et al.*, eds.

Ng, C. (1991) 'Familial Change and Women's Employment in Hong Kong', in Cheung *et al.*, eds.

Nowikowski, S. (1984) 'Snakes and Ladders: Asian Business in Britain', in Ward and Jenkins, eds.

Phizacklea (1987) 'Minority Women and Economic Restructuring: The Case of Britain and the Federal Republic of Germany', *Work, Employment and Society*, 1/3.

Omohundro, J.T. (1981) *Chinese Merchant Families in Iloilo. Commerce and Kin in a Central Philippine City*, Quezon City: Ateneo de Manila University Press.

Portes, A. (1978) 'Migration and Underdevelopment', *Politics and Society*, 8/1.

Rainnie, A. (1985) 'Small Firms, Big Problems: The Political Economy of Small Business', *Capital and Class*, 25, Spring.

Sallaf, J. (1982) *Working Daughters of Hong Kong*, Cambridge: Cambridge University press.

Sanders, J. and V. Nee. (1987) 'Limits of Ethnic Solidarity in the Ethnic Enclave', *American Sociological Review*, 52.

Sassen, S. (1988) *The Mobility of Capital and Labor*, Cambridge: Cambridge University Press.

Scase, R. and R. Goffee. (1980) *The Real World of the Small Business Owner*, London: Croom Helm.

——. (1982) 'Home Life in a Small Business', in Evans, M., ed., *The Woman Question*, Fontana.

Scott, A.M. (1986) 'Why Rethink Petty Commodity Production?', *Social Analysis*, 20, Dec.

Skeldon, R. (1990) 'Emigration in Hong Kong', Workshop on Emigration from Hong Kong, Trends and Prospects, University of Hong Kong, 10 Dec.

Slater, M. (1976) *Migration and Workers' Conflicts in Western Europe*, Ph.D. dissertation, Massachusetts Institute of Technology.

Still, L. (1990) *Enterprising Women, Australian Women Managers and Entrepreneurs*, Sydney: Allen and Unwin.

Still, L. and D. Guerin. (1989) 'Self Employed Women: The New Social Change', Paper Presented to the Australian Sociological Conference, Melbourne.

Strahan, K.W. and A.J. Williams. (1988) *Immigrant Entrepreneurs in Australia*, Canberra: Office of Multicultural Affairs.

Stratigaki, M. (1988) 'Agricultural Modernisation and Gender Division of Labor. The Case of Heraklion, Greece', *Sociologia Ruralis*, XXVIII/4.

Tracy, N. and D. Ip. (1990) 'The Asian Family Business in Australia: A New Export Base?' *Current Affairs Bulletin*, July.

Waldinger, R. (1984) *Through the Eye of a Needle: Immigrants and Enterprise in New York's Garment Trades*, New York: New York University Press.

——. (1986) 'Immigrant Enterprise: a Critique and Reformulation', *Theory and Society*, 15.

Ward, R. and R. Jenkins, eds. (1984) *Ethnic Communities in Business: Strategies for Economic Survival*, London: Cambridge University Press.

Watkins, D. and J. Watkins. (1986) 'The Female Entrepreneur in Britain: Some Results of a Pilot Survey with Special Emphasis on Educational Needs', in Scott, M. *et al.*, eds., *Small Firms Growth and Development*, London: Gower.

Westwood, S. and P. Bhachu, eds. (1988) *Enterprising Women. Ethnicity, Economy and Gender Relations*, London: Routledge.

Williams, A.J. (1987) *The Characteristics and Performance of Small Business in Australia, 1973–1985*, Newcastle: University of Newcastle.

Wilson, K. and A. Portes. (1980) 'Immigrant Enclaves: an Analysis of the Labor Market Experiences of Cubans in Miami', *American Journal of Sociology*, 86(2).

Wong, E.Y.T. (1991) 'An Investigation into the Employment of Women in Hong Kong', in Cheung *et al.*, eds.

5 Immigration Policy, Cultural Norms, and Gender Relations Among Indian-American Motel Owners
Nandini Narain Assar

INTRODUCTION

Indians now make up a significant proportion of immigrants to the US. The number of Indians in the US doubled between 1980 and 1990, and currently stands at one million (Ghasarian, 1995). Mexicans account for 15 percent of all documented immigrants to the US, and are the most numerous; Indians account for 5.3 percent and rank fifth (Isbister, 1996). Immigrant Indians have achieved considerable economic success, particularly in the motel business.

For Indians, affiliation with a linguistic or regional sub-group is more relevant and stronger than identification with the national group (Sheth, 1995). About 33 percent of Indian immigrants are from the state of Gujarat in western India[1] (Weiner, 1990). An estimated five to eight percent of these Gujarati immigrants are Patidars[2] (Mehra, 1993). Although Patidars are a small proportion of Indian immigrants to the US, they predominate and have achieved outstanding economic success in the motel business in the US. They were introduced to the motel business during WWII and now control 12,500 motels and hotels, with a market value of over $26 billion. Industry estimates are that in five years, they will control 50 percent of all hotel and motel assets in the US (Woodyard, 1995). Patidars already control 65 percent of budget motels nationwide (Lister, 1996). The motel business is commonly referred to as the 'Patel-Shah industry'. (Shah and Patel are the two most common last names among Gujarati motel-owners.)

My contention is that cultural characteristics of Patidars as a group are a perfect fit with the needs of the US labor market. This match is a major contributor to their economic success in the motel business. I will examine the nature of the link between economic contribution and decision-making power. To get at this, I examine whether the family reunification policy (which is the centerpiece of US immigration law) operates to resist or reinforce gender hierarchy among Gujaratis. I claim that 'traditional' gender hierarchy is contested when there is a direct relation between economic contributions and decision-making power and maintained when they are disconnected.

The pattern of family reunification is closely connected with the rate of business start-ups in labor-intensive industries. In countries where family reunification and self-employment have not been encouraged, there is no evidence of immigrants' involvement in entrepreneurship (Phizacklea, 1988). The connection between immigration policy and family enterprises is pertinent to Gujaratis in the US: motel owners live together on the premises, reducing labor costs, and saving substantially on rent, utilities, childcare, and transport costs. In the pilot study, I found that about 85 percent of Gujaratis who came in under family reunification rules enter family businesses, mainly motels (Assar, 1990). A motel provides at once real estate, living quarters, a business, and employment for the entire family (Jain, 1989).

The work consists mainly of cleaning and laundry, skills in which women are already trained and socialized, and which are easily incorporated as an extension of the domestic domain. We can observe gender hierarchy in how motel work is allocated, and it is also highlighted by experiences of tension or contradiction. The first contradiction is that even though Gujaratis prosper in this line of work, they object to the nature of the work. Cleaning rooms and making beds is devalued work. Like domestic workers,

> They must confront, acknowledge, and convey the undesirable nature of the work they do to their children, as an object lesson and an admonition, and at the same time maintain their children's respect and their own sense of personal worth and dignity. (Dill, 1980)

This devaluing of the work influenced my experience in doing the study. One potential participant angrily declined when I approached him to be a part of the project when he learned that I wanted to observe him at work. He was offended, I believe, because he thought it was demeaning for him if I watched him clean toilets and make beds. Despite this dissatisfaction, there is no move to change occupations. There are not many attractive alternatives, and motels are economically profitable.

Family businesses are easily seen as being in line with the ideology of joint resources and inputs, with the family as the unit of analysis.

Recent research on various immigrant groups suggests a direct relationship between economic contributions and decision-making power, indicating a change to more egalitarian patterns after migration when women's labor substantially contributes to economic success (Kibria, 1993; Lamphere, 1987; Pessar, 1986). Hondagneu-Sotelo's (1994) findings regarding Mexican immigrants are in line with this logic. However, this direct relationship is mediated by immigration status and cultural patterns.

Salient cultural patterns of Patidars are hypergamy, dowry, hierarchy in social status among sub-groups, economic emigration (which began in colonial times to East and South Africa, the Caribbean, UK, Singapore, Thailand, Malaysia, and Hong Kong), emphasis on patrilateral kin, obligation to extended family, and pooling of family resources (Pocock, 1972; Breman, 1985; Hardiman, 1987, 1992). Marriage relations are highly significant: 'The Patidar achieves his social self through marriage' (Pocock, 1972).

Shared understandings among the dominant members of a group define cultural norms for the whole group. Ideological constraints are embedded in material relations of production and reproduction that reinforce perceptions of what is 'natural' and therefore justified. Relationships based on kinship/community ties define the division of labor and rewards, not economic calculations. Power relations operate in families and households in ways that defy economic logic. These relations are based on culturally ascribed roles that are not reducible to contributions to the family (Nash, 1988). Is there an interaction between family reunification policy and cultural patterns? Is the impact of US immigration policy gender-specific *and* culturally-specific? The attention in this chapter is on immigrant women who contribute labor to economic success while being secluded from the labor market.

An understanding of what is actually happening in the lives of particular immigrants under current policies will be significant for the future. The extent and direction of US immigration reform will set the stage for the economy in the next century. Immigration reform is a contested arena today. Ranging from calling for a halt to future immigration (Brimelow, 1994) to advocating easier access (Simon, 1989), public discussion centers on whether immigrants contribute to the living standards and productivity of the US economy, or drain national resources. That is, the focus is on the impact that immigrants have on structural features of the US economy. The debate is ideologically based and politically charged because the stakes are enormous. It calls for nuanced analyses of immigration rules that are ostensibly neutral, but have a differential impact based on gender and ethnicity.

THEORETICAL FRAMEWORK LOCATING THE STUDY

Despite the fact that the volume of global men and women immigrants is nearly equal, there is a tendency among scholars and legislators to automatically classify women as dependents. As spouses or daughters, women have primarily non-economic roles. The assumption is that women migrate simply to be with their husbands and families (Isbister, 1996). Thus, women's labor is visible only when they enter the labor market (Toro-Morn, 1992).

Currently, slightly less than half of global immigrants are women. However, in contrast to global trends, women constitute the majority of immigrants to the US in recent years (Tyree and Donato, 1986). This can be attributed to the greater propensity of men in the US to marry brides from abroad. Since the immigration reform of 1965, the number of brides admitted to the US has trebled. The majority of immigrant women are married, and more than 39 percent gain acceptance to the US as spouses. One explanation could rest on the centerpiece of US immigration law – the family reunification policy – which encourages immigration in a family context. Marriage provides a way to achieve immigration when it would otherwise be difficult (Jasso and Rosenzweig, 1990).

Further, anyone who applies for immigrant status under the family reunification rules is exempt from labor certification. This is centrally important since more than 94 percent of documented immigrants between 1965 and 1990 entered the US under the family reunification rules, and as such, were exempt from labor certification. After the 1990 reform, the proportion entering under family reunification dropped but still accounts for approximately 70 percent of documented immigrants (Heer, 1996; Isbister, 1996). That means that the US state does not recognize the vast majority of documented immigrants to be labor, or consider their impact on the labor market.

Similarly, women are also assumed not to be economically productive unless they are part of the labor force. It seems appropriate, according to this approach, that women and families not be considered labor unless they enter the labor market. By focusing on individuals, this analysis, based on neoclassical economics, draws attention away from dominating structures like capitalism and patriarchy.

The second framework connects the process of immigration to economic and political forces on a global scale. From this perspective, industrial growth in the West was based on the incorporation of regions from which surplus was extracted. This approach highlights the conditions that link a country/region to the global economy. Women are considered, by attending to their employment generated by export processing zones. Even here, women are visible only when they enter the labor force. The focus on social structures draws attention away from strategies and responses of people as they negotiate these constraints, resist or subvert intended outcomes, or transform the structures themselves. For example, Gujaratis have successfully devised a migration strategy that allows them relatively smooth access to the US.

Neither framework on its own is sufficient to understand immigration; attention to both is necessary. To understand men's and women's migration, analyses must span micro and macro levels, *and* attend to gender (Blumberg, 1991). Gender is a location in the social hierarchy, which changes when people immigrate. Although there is now research available on the topic of women and immigration (Pedraza, 1991; Tienda and Booth, 1991), gender is usually considered only when women are the focus. Part of our lack of knowledge stems from a lack of clarity regarding the role of gender in the process of migration. Gender is not merely a demographic variable; it is a category of analysis, a set of social relations that influences and organizes migration (Hondagneu-Sotelo, 1994; Repak, 1995; Seller, 1994; Friedman-Kasaba, 1996). From this perspective, gender is equally relevant to understanding men's migration as well as women's.

One example of the nexus between the macro (international division of labor) and the micro (gender division of labor) can be seen in relation to US immigration policy. Who is allowed entry and on what terms organizes social relations in immigrant groups. Thus, the process of migration is influenced both by the capitalist world economy and by various systems of patriarchy. This study explores the gendered impact of immigration policies: aspects which strengthen women's status, and those that facilitate/ exacerbate women's domination. The analysis, while focused on the structural features that shape migration of Gujarati men and women to the US, is also concerned with their responses to the limits and facilities these features seek to impose on them, a combination of both dominant approaches. Immigrant women's work is delinked from the labor market and performed in a family context; at the same time, it is an economic contribution.

The general consensus among scholars, international lawmakers, US government officials, and a majority of the US population, is that current US immigration policy is both gender-neutral and generous (Simpson, 1984). The rules are couched in human rights terms, are ostensibly based on non-economic criteria, and define the family in social, not economic terms. However, family relationships are also implicitly viewed in economic terms. For example, marriage is viewed as an economic relationship so that married sons and daughters of US citizens are considered a lower priority than the 'First Preference' assigned to unmarried sons and daughters.[3]

Gender issues, when they have emerged in migration studies, usually also depict women as either remaining home to support households during men's absences, or accompanying men as dependants. However, policies that view families as 'dependant' seem grossly misnamed in the context of increasing contributions of family labor. This nexus of family/tradition, economic activities, and migration plays out in differential ways for men and women immigrants. For example, families may make economic gains after immigration, without improving the status of wives (Cackley, 1993).

In a recent study of Mexican immigrants, Hondagneu-Sotelo (1994) found that public policy affects family relationships. Of special significance for my work, she found that after immigration, the level of gender hierarchy in immigrant Mexican families is rooted in the conditions of migration. That is, in cases where women migrated with full immigrant status, they were able to negotiate relatively egalitarian family relations. In cases where women migrants had undocumented or conditional status, they experienced an exacerbation of 'traditional' patriarchal relations.

How does the link between conditions of migration and family relations work in a group that combines economic success and documented status? What is the impact on gender hierarchy of immigration policy and cultural norms? Family reunification immigration policy in the US is instrumental in selecting specific kinds of immigrants whose costs of migration are met by social networks and family relationships rather than by the state. The key qualification for acceptance is the minimal demands they make on the state. Family reunification policies multiply opportunities for immigrants on the condition that they accept the definition and constitution of family in particular, prescribed ways, and contribute their labor in family enterprises.

In mainstream analyses using the household model, migration is an adaptive or reactive response: members of the household pool income and resources, and have shared interests and goals. The assumption is that migration is one of several micro-level choices available to migrants. However, using the household as the unit of analysis is inadequate for examining the relative position of men and women within families. Although family relationships (in the case of immigrants) often span several locations, some joint resources are pooled, and some interests and goals are shared among members; there are contradictory interests among members as well. How these contradictory interests typically play out indicates the level of gender hierarchy in the immigrant group.

If immigrant small business is a form of cheap labor, as Bonacich (1984) asserts, the state does not recognize that fact. Immigrants entering under first, second, fourth and fifth preference categories are exempt from labor certification. Women accounted for 55 percent of all persons admitted as relatives of US citizens, or permanent residents during 1972–9 (UN Secretariat, 1995). Thus, immigrant women who work in family businesses are not seen as workers because their labor is subsumed in 'traditional' family ideology. Contrary to stereotypes, most Indian immigrants do not enter the US under the third preference category as professionals. In 1992, 86 percent of Indian immigrants were admitted on the basis of family reunification (Sheth, 1995).

At this juncture three theoretical points are important:

(1) Analyses typically conceptualize labor in terms of productive/reproductive, or as being in either the public or private domain. However, my focus here – the work in motels – spans both spheres. Relationships among men and women span both domains: they work together and live together. Even the location does not submit to categorization as being in either one or the other category. The literature on household labor does not relate to work and home being the same place. What is the relationship between the domestic domain and capitalism? Non-wage relationships based on kinship and community ties define the division of labor and rewards in motel work in ways that defy economic calculations.

The bulk of the work can easily be viewed as an extension of the domestic domain – it involves cleaning and laundry. It requires no additional skills or training for women, but most men do need training since they are not usually well-versed in domestic skills. However, since the enterprise always has a woman present, the training for men and children is provided easily within the family relationship. (I saw nor heard of no instance in which a man ran the motel and took care of the family entirely on his own, without employees, for an extended period. I did meet, interview, and hear about several women who were completely responsible for both their family and the motel, either long-term when the husbands were disabled or deceased, or short-term when the husbands were away on a visit). Women's central role in the motels was highlighted by several participants:

> *… all the women, majority you can say 90–95 percent women are in this business. They can do anything in the motel. The men cannot do everything without them.*
> How is that?
> *I don't know … but they cannot do all the work, they cannot do all the work!*

Another participant puts it directly:

*Main thing, [the] wife is running [the] business ... Patel men stand
up and talk on stage ... they say – 'Let me thank my wife, she is my back-
bone. That's why I am standing and giving a speech because she is running the motel there and I am here'. That's the first thing they say, every
meeting we go now.*

The work requires minimal English language skills. Even though immigrant women typically have fewer language skills than immigrant men,
the differential is less significant in this line of work than in most others.
While many Gujarati men and women do become fairly fluent in English,
some do not. Although they raised families in the US, lived here for 17 +
years, and worked in the motel all this time, I came across several women
who could not converse well in English and had not learned to drive. Their
interviews were in a mixture of Hindi and Gujarati. I interviewed all the
men mainly in English. Lack of conversational English is an indication of
women's isolation from the wider society. So, when the men have valuable
skills, they are not always shared with the women.

(2) In immigration law, family is defined precisely in ways which often
do not fit the norms of immigrant groups. In this way, the policy directly
interacts with immigrant family structure. For example, the conjugal tie is
given priority in the family reunification policy, when it may be the
mother-son tie that is central. Or, as in the case of Gujaratis, there is not a
qualitative distinction between immigrant kin and community networks.
Gujaratis, for example, typically continue to function in ways where the
distinction between family and community is difficult to make.

(3) The mutual structuring of family and enterprise is based on family
forms and ideology of immigrants as well as the filter of immigration
rules. The fit of immigrant families with the needs of the US labor market
hinges on the difference of 'traditional' immigrant families from the mod-
ern/nuclear family. A clear polarity exists between these two notions of
family (Nandi, 1980). Families may sometimes not live together, but the
traditional extended family is a psychological and economic reality in
immigrant communities.

DESCRIPTION OF THE STUDY

What is the relation between the family reunification policy, and the cultural norms of Gujartis and the gender hierarchy in family relationships?

Since a majority of Gujarati immigrants are involved in small family businesses (Assar, 1990), and they dominate the motel industry in the US (Lister, 1996), I interviewed Gujarati motel-owners and their families. The focus on Gujarati motel owners is theoretically driven: access to family labor is a key competitive advantage for immigrant businesses. Motels are also a clear example of the blurring of public and private domains. The work is performed by unpaid family labor, and the gender division of labor is based on cultural norms. Even the physical separation of work and home is challenged because most owners reside on the premises of the motels. Family businesses are easily seen as being in line with the ideology of joint resources and inputs, if the family is the unit of analysis. However, examining whether there is a link between contributions and rewards within the family will allow us to see what is going on inside this unit and to chart the impact of social structures on family relationships.

The labor of women in motel-owning families consists mainly of laundry and cleaning, work easily seen as an extension of the domestic domain, facilitated by the fact that everyone lives on the motel premises. The women require no additional training or language skills, because there is no direct relationship to the labor market and minimal contact with clients. However, lack of proficiency in English means that Gujarati women must survive entirely within the Gujarati community and its 'traditions'.

Both spouses work together in motels. Only where the wife is unable to 'help', labor is hired. Women are relatively removed from decision-making. One Gujarati motel-owner said he could not tell his wife about his proposed business deals before they were finalized, because 'women cannot keep secrets' (Jain, 1989). One participant said that business decisions are 100 percent the father's, because there is a wide difference in the levels of education between his parents. However, the parents have both worked full-time to support the family for 27 years. It becomes imperative, then, to unpack the black box of 'family' to examine the links between contributions to joint resources and sharing of decision-making power.

In addition to women, children of motel-owners typically 'pitch in' after school and during weekends, holidays, and vacations. They start young. Sons typically continue to help out at the family motel after they leave home. Daughters typically work in the motel until marriage. One participant put it clearly:

> *Sons are more likely than daughters to take an interest in the business. Many young men who have professional qualifications are quitting their jobs now to work with their families again. Daughters ... well, maybe if the son-in-law shows an interest, then it may work out.*

METHODS

This project demands that the researcher gain access to family decision-making processes which could potentially highlight differential access to joint resources. As a result, this information was difficult to elicit. My location as an Indian immigrant woman is a decided asset. I am familiar with the general cultural codes, but I am not Gujarati. In other words, although as an Indian immigrant woman, I am an insider in relation to the wider society, I am not part of the Gujarati community, so I am an outsider as well. I had both statuses simultaneously. Since I am Indian, I shared Indian culture – food, language, clothing, and general ethos – with participants. Since I am not Gujarati, I did not have preconceptions about particular cultural norms, and could hear them without the filter of 'Gujarati-ness'.

Participants were explicit about seeing me this way – they said they would not feel as free to discuss intimate family and community dynamics with another Gujarati, as they would be worried about repercussions from within the community. They did not see a possibility that I could use the information they offered for personal gain or against them. They knew it was not relevant in my life because I do not live within the traditions of their community.

I used observation, conversation and semi-structured, taped interviews to get at the data. I approached prominent local Gujaratis, explained the project and requested referrals to Gujarati motel-owners in the area. Armed with these referrals, I contacted motel-owners. At first, I visited them to get acquainted with their businesses and families. My access to the family and home is facilitated by the fact that they live on the premises of the motels. After the initial contact, I returned as needed to conduct tape recorded semi-structured interviews with each person. Each interview was done in privacy. I stayed overnight, if possible, to observe the daily routine. Then I asked each family for a referral to another motel-owner. I left it open in each case that I may need to return for follow-ups.

I was after a snowball sample. The sample is relatively homogenous in several dimensions: immigrants who are successful, documented, and from one cultural milieu. My goal is to analyze the mutual impact of immigration policy, cultural norms, and gender hierarchy. The interaction of public policy and 'tradition' in family relationships can be seen more clearly than in samples where internal variation clouds the issues.

ABOUT THE PARTICIPANTS

I interviewed Gujaratis in the motel business and their families and employees. The interviews were semi-structured and tape recorded ranging in

length from 30 minutes to 3 hours, depending on the participant's engagement and response.

I selected the participants based on three criteria: the most important
one was that I would be referred by someone they knew; then, I looked
for small motels without many employees, where family labor was the
mainstay of the operation; and finally, I looked for Patidar families, so that
my sample would be relatively homogenous. In all cases, I went with a
referral from someone the participants knew. Some participants were involved in both small and large franchised motels. Finally, most participants
are Patidars, although I did interview some non-Gujarati women married
to Patidars.

Most of the interviews were within a 250-mile radius of where I live.
Most of the participants are located in three southeastern states. The location of motels is not significant in the context of this study, as Gujaratis
running motels are a nationwide phenomenon. Gujaratis in the motel business are not confined to any region. The project could be done in anywhere
in the US, with similar findings.

FINDINGS

Four themes emerge from the focus of the interviews that illuminate the
links between capitalism and various patriarchies. The common thread that
runs through all the four themes is that systems of hierarchy hinge on the
status attached to different kinds of work – indeed whether it is considered
work or not-work is determined by the context and not by the labor.

1. Conditions of Work

Among Gujaratis, the green card had become a currency in marriage negotiations after the immigration reform of 1965. In the early seventies and
eighties, when women came to the US as brides, or as part of a family
unit, they did not know what it meant to be a small-motel owner. Most
Gujarati women did not anticipate the nature of the work that would be
necessary for them to engage in as the owners of budget motels.

> *… I had impression [about] this motel, you can just do the office work
> and just get out of it, you know. But it involves each and every thing.
> Sometimes you have to do some labor work too. So, it was a big change
> for me. Like when I came here, I had to do some laundry too … I never
> expected that I would do that kind of work when I was in India. Because
> we feel it's a labor job – you can hire any one to do it. … [I]n this*

business, you have to be ready any time, because of the employment problem – employees can walk out any time!
Even in a big place like this?
Yes. It happened last July or August here. At 10:30, we got the call that the night janitor is not coming to do the job and we had no substitute. So me and my husband came here, and we worked whole night. In India, you have all kinds of help – money can buy anything there. But here, it's difficult, very difficult. ...

Some women said that their families abroad were unaware of their life conditions because there was no chance to visit for 17 years or more. Even when there were visits and information flowed, there were still barriers, as the following excerpt highlights:

Do people in India have a good idea of what your life is like?
No. Absolutely not. Absolutely not. If you tell your friends, life is like that, they won't understand. Till they come over here and see all the facts over here, they won't be knowing anything, even though you were writing everything, still they won't understand anything. They think you have all the machines 'over there' to do the work. You know, but who has to put in machines? We have to. They don't understand till they come over here and look with their own eyes. Then their eyes will open. Their eyes won't be open if you tell. If you tell your sister, then she will think 'You don't want me to come down there'. See, on opposite side, the grass is greener. ... They don't understand ... no, not at all. ... Who has good job satisfaction? ... They think that money grows on trees. You know what I mean. ... It's not easy at all, I am telling the truth ... telling my life, you know. You think when you are over there that a job is waiting for you – No! It's not waiting for you. You have to work for the job, you have to get a good degree to get a certain kind of job. ... No.

It is now better-known among Gujaratis abroad that family motels are a labor job. As a result of this information, there is resistance from women in Gujarat. That is, the green card has lost value in the marriage market, as compared to the seventies and eighties. Several participants addressed this point directly, for instance, one said:

People in India like to come here. ... Because of the [dollar], the attraction was too much up till now. But see, the trend is changing too, that is my experience. One of my nephews has gone to get married over there, and he interviewed so many girls. ... So many girls gave the requirement that they don't want to come to America to do labor work like that ... they refused. So, trend is changing.

2. Economic Domestic Work

Gujaratis typically think about their motels in terms of an extension of the domestic domain. The following excerpts highlights this point directly:

> *You have to give them towels, whatever they need, and if they are not in the room, you make the bed and everything for them and clean up... bathroom and everything. See, Indian mentality is there: that I am educated, why should I do cleaning job? ... No, you have to do it. The time comes, you have to do it because you want things, you have to do like 30 rooms house. ... You have to ... afterwards you thinking about that – this is a 30 room house, we are cleaning every day. ... Ya, I am not going to clean people's stuff. No. You have to ... time comes, you have to do everything. This is a part of business.*

Thinking about motels as an extension of the domestic domain has several crucial implications for family relationships:

(a) it supports the rhetoric that women are not 'working' outside the home. It keeps women segregated from the labor market, their experience does not translate into the wider society. The conditions of work are determined by family and kin relationships. This is an important 'tradition' that can be sustained, even as women contribute full-time to the economic support of the family. Women do not accumulate their own individual resources because they are unpaid workers, regardless of significant contribution to family income (In-Sook Lim, 1997).

(b) it takes advantage of women's domestic skills which are rooted in 'traditional values': cooking, cleaning, laundry, serving food, and so on, while simultaneously devaluing the same skills as 'women's work' which men do not engage in. Here one can see the direct link between capitalism and patriarchy – the structure of the US labor market supports unwaged family labor – such work is also low-wage, low status when performed outside the domestic domain.

3. Resource Utilization

Gujaratis are economically successful because (a) they are good at cutting fixed costs and (b) they have access to financial resources at terms that are much more favorable than what is commercially available. Cutting fixed costs typically means a shortage of living space. Immigrant families cannot attain the middle-class ideal of a single family home while running a budget motel. Young people who grew up in motels voiced a consensus that this was the most important condition that affected their lives. Since immigration rules favor family relationships, Gujaratis who come to the US are able to share living space intimately, sometimes for extended periods, with subsequent newcomers and kin. Having access to another motel room when needed is a huge advantage. Sharing living space and expenses with extended family is exactly in line with the ideal of the Hindu joint family, another perfect cultural fit. Here again, we can see the interlocking nature of patriarchal tradition and the demands of a capitalist economy.

Access to non-commercial terms usually involves pooling of family and community resources, in such ways that when particular members intensify their contributions, they do not gain comparable status in the family or community and they also do not expect to make a profit. It is interesting to contrast the strategies and situation of Gujaratis with the common perceptions of immigrants draining state resources.

4. Gender Hierarchies

Gender hierarchy is reproduced in the kind of work men and women do. That is, some jobs are out-of-bounds men and others for women, although the rhetoric is distinct for each. There is, however, a growing and explicit understanding of the centrality of women's contributions to the economic success of motels. For example, one motel owner shows a clear understanding of what is going on:

> *For Indian ladies, life in United States is harder than what it is in India. In India, at that time (I don't know what's going on right now) but, only job they had was to take care of the family – I mean, prepare nice dinner and take care of all the family chores. Here, their job is still there: they have to take care of cooking, cleaning and all the family – on top of that then, they have to work. She works whole day with me, taking care of motel, plus she has to take care of the family: cooking, cleaning and all that. I can help and I do help her, you know, that's just help. But she is the one, who does most of the work.*

Participants stated directly that men were unable to do all the work necessary to run a budget motel. Every family interviewed reported that men would not clean bathrooms either in the motels or in homes. When it became inevitable, men would clean for motels. Participants unanimously agreed that men did not clean in their homes, and most men were also exempt from other domestic work. However, several women who are raising sons specifically pointed out that they are training their sons to do all the work that the mothers do and including jobs that fathers did not do. I observed evidence of their claim.

Women and adult sons reported male domination in decision-making processes, explained by differentials in education among spouses. In 'traditional' family relationships, men are raised to 'call the shots'. It translates well into the family business in that although spouses work together, the decision-making is definitely in the men's domain. Here is yet another point at which capitalism and patriarchy work in tandem. This excerpt from a second generation motel-owner puts it succinctly:

> *Say my mother wants a divorce from my Dad. What is she going to do? She has no education. She has never been on her own. She probably doesn't even know how to use the credit card. So she stakes a lot. She stakes a lot for her kids too.*

CULTURALLY SPECIFIC IMPACT OF FAMILY REUNIFICATION POLICY

Whether families are beginning a chain of migration, are an intermediate link, or at the end of a chain is linked to degree of hierarchy in gender relations within the family. Four rationales for gaining entry into the US were evident for families who began a chain: for education, as investors, as professionals, and finally, without immigrant status.

Men came to the US for higher education and were then able to find jobs and recruit spouses from abroad. Families who had economic resources to bring with them could get in as investors, provided they created jobs in the US economy. Families immigrated first to Canada, where immigration laws are less stringent. Then they simply crossed the border as Canadian citizens to do business in the US with no restrictions. Professionals whose qualifications translated into the US labor market were able to recruit spouses and bring their siblings and parents. These instances were relatively rare; the more general experience is that education, experience, and skills from abroad were not well-received in the US However, even when immigrants' qualifications were accepted, they typically experienced the glass ceiling and eventually decided that a family business provided more security than the vagaries of the labor market.

Families who began the chain migration as investors, for education, or without immigrant status were subject to high levels of financial and cultural stress. I found exacerbated levels of gender hierarchy in these cases. When both partners had immigrated with professional qualifications independently of each other, I found highly equitable relations.

In the next category, among families who were the first link in the chain, having immigrated with the help of a sibling or parent, levels of gender hierarchy are related to whether or not they took on a subsequent link in the chain. When they sponsored more family members to join them, they needed higher levels of economic returns to provide for them. Supporting two or more people for an extended period involves a considerable expense, even when the new immigrants have access to community financing. It includes training them to succeed in the business – and this is accomplished by having them work together with the established family members. All this is possible and works seamlessly because the residence and workplace are located in the same premises. Participants expressed consciousness of the necessity for increased input to meet family responsibilities. I found higher levels of gender hierarchy among families who made subsequent links than in families where there were no subsequent links. When the next link in the chain is forged, it serves to reinforce 'tradition' in two ways: (i) the new immigrants are immersed in it when they arrive; and (ii) it requires increased contributions from more established members, which are met by further cutting costs and sharing living expenses.

The interlocking processes of patriarchy and capitalism are evident in the process of chain migration. 'Tradition' is evoked when particular families sponsor subsequent links in the chain-migration – they are assuming family responsibilities; they want to do something that will help family members to improve their situation.

Family is also evoked in the immigration policy – the importance of maintaining the family as a social unit is well accepted (Simpson, 1984). However, there is a theoretical contradiction in this consensus. In international law, the family is a 'natural' unit: 'The family is the natural and fundamental group unit of society and is entitled to protection by the law and state' (International Covenant on Civil and Political Rights). A similar statement is found in the Universal Declaration of Human Rights (Perruchoud, 1989). However, in US immigration law, the family is conceptualized in social terms:

> Reuniting of families, which is very important for the well-being of migrant workers, should be actively encouraged in accordance with UN standards concerning the protection of the family. (Pekin, 1989)

Clearly, the family is a different category from migrant workers. As noted earlier, policies which view families as dependent, seem grossly misplaced in the context of increased family labor. Assumptions about gender and work are apparent in this framework. And as noted earlier, families are seen in economic terms in immigration policy.

I am wary of a wide consensus in which the family is simultaneously a natural and a social group. Natural and social are contradictory definitions and cannot logically be applied to the same phenomenon. Family ideology is evoked in the business as well – women work in the motels because their labor is necessary for economical survival. When women increase their contributions of labor, gender hierarchy is destabilized. It is maintained and perpetuated when more members of the family immigrate. Economic crises and employer sanctions have displaced immigrants in the labor market towards family enterprises. Family reunification multiplies opportunities for immigrants on the condition that they accept definition of the family in particular prescribed ways.

Finally, among the second generation of immigrants (in which I include those who were born abroad and substantially raised in the US, as well as those who were born here), gender hierarchy is related to whether or not they were involved in the family business. This generation has moved to the next level in the motel business, often in partnership with other Gujaratis, where community financing is very important. They operate large franchised motels and hotels usually with many employees. Where both spouses worked in the business, gender hierarchy was reproduced again in the kind of work they did. Where one spouse was employed outside the family business, gender relations were more equitable. If they recruited a bride from abroad, 'tradition' was reinforced, and gender hierarchy was evidently exacerbated.

Among the unmarried second generation, the women professed egalitarian expectations in marriage, which they saw as precluding recruiting a groom from abroad. All the second generation women I interviewed were college-educated. Second generation men's responses were ambiguous, reflecting the position that they were open to recruiting a spouse from abroad.

The findings support the contention that the impacts of immigration policy are culturally specific. Gujaratis who applied for immigration based on family reunification rules report a smooth immigration process for the entire period from the early 1970s onwards. It would appear that the widespread claim that the policy is based on the family as a social and not economic unit is valid. However, when we ask why Gujaratis have been a huge economic success as compared to other groups from India and elsewhere who also migrate under family-reunification rules, then the culturally specific aspects of immigration policy are brought into sharp relief.

CONCLUSIONS

Two reasons for Gujaratis' economic success are (a) community financing for family businesses on terms that are far more favorable than what is commercially available and (b) increased levels of women's economic contributions.

Community financing is important because it forms a buffer for Gujaratis from the US labor market, in which they experience biases against dark-skinned 'foreigners'. It is a method of sharing and redistribution of community resources that resists the central motif of capitalism – profit. When Gujaratis provide financial resources to each other, they do not expect to make a profit. This aspect of 'tradition' reinforces the isolation of the group as a whole from the wider society. Gujaratis make their profits from their business interactions with customers and non-Gujaratis.

Similarly, increased levels of women's contributions also operate as a buffer from the labor market. It frees Gujarati women (and men) from competing for employees, or for employment in the wider labor market, in which they are disadvantaged. The conditions of women's labor are delinked from the labor market, and performed within the constraints of family and kin relationships. Family relationships are governed by 'tradition'. In this way, two forms of patriarchy (US and Gujarati) operate in tandem: women increase their labor but retain their 'traditional' status in the family. This facilitates further migration, which in turn fuels retention of 'tradition'.

US immigration rules privilege those family relationships which are conducive to retention of 'traditional' family structure. This structure is a perfect fit with the labor market in the US as it allows for increased labor from women immigrants whose conditions of work separated from the labor market. That is, Gujarati women have integrated into the US economy structurally, facilitated by cultural and labor market segregation. Therefore, the US state can (and does) refuse to recognize immigrant families as labor, while at the same time the economy benefits from immigrants' inputs.

NOTES

I want to thank the participants for their generosity, kindness, and candour, which helped me to highlight the depth, complexity, and nuanced analysis of the issues. I would like to acknowledge my colleagues in the work group for their support, encouragement, and close reading of this work while it was in progress: Sharon McGuire, Meeta Mehrotra, Nancy Gard McGehee, and Marjukka Ollilainen.

1. There are 25 States in India.
2. Patidar is a caste. The word means 'landowner'. Before migration, they are mainly farmers. Although they make up about 18 percent of the population in Gujarat, they are the dominant caste in terms of wealth and status.

3.   Recent changes in the rules specify that the family member who sponsors
     another for immigration also needs to provide the financial support. Prior to
     January 1997, the financial support could come from someone other than
     the sponsoring family member.

REFERENCES

Assar, N., *The Mutual Impact of Family Structure and Business Practices Among
    Indian Immigrants: An Exploratory Field Study*, conducted under the guidance
    of Prof. E.N. Glenn at SUNY-Binghamton, manuscript, 1990.
Blumberg, R.L., *Gender, Family, and Economy: The Triple Overlap*, Newbury
    Park, CA: Sage Publications, 1991.
Breman, J., *Of Peasants, Migrants and Paupers*, Delhi: Oxford University Press,
    1985.
Brimelow, P., *Alien Nation: Common Sense about America's Immigration
    Disaster*, New York: Random House, 1995.
Burawoy, M., 'The Functions and Reproduction of Migrant Labor: Comparative
    material from Southern Africa and the United States', *American Journal of
    Sociology*, 81, no. 5 (1976): 1050–87.
Cackley, A.P., 'The Role of Wage Differentials in Determining Migration
    Selectivity by Sex: the Case of Brazil'. In *Internal Migration of Women in
    Developing Countries*, New York: United Nations, 1993.
Cheng, L. and E. Bonacich, eds., *Labor Immigration Under Advanced Capitalism:
    Asian Immigrant Workers in the US before W.W.II*, Berkeley: University of
    California Press, 1984.
Dill, B.T., 'The Means to Put my Children Through: Childrearing Goals and
    Strategies Among Black Female Domestic Servants'. In *The Black Woman*, ed.
    La Frances Rodgers-Rose, Beverly Hills and London: Sage, 1980.
Friedman-Kasaba, K., *Memories of Migration: Gender, Ethnicity and Work in the
    Lives of Jewish and Italian Women in New York, 1870–1924*, Albany: SUNY
    Press, 1996.
Ghasarian, C., 'The Asian Indian Community in Northern California: Cultural
    Continuities and Reformulations in New Contexts', *Multicultural Review*, 4,
    no. 4 (1995): 20–2.
Hardiman, D., *The Coming of the Devi*, Delhi and New York: Oxford University
    Press, 1987.
——, *Peasant Resistance in India*, Delhi and New York: Oxford University Press,
    1992.
Hondagneu-Sotelo, P., *Gendered Transitions*, Berkeley: University of California
    Press, 1994.
Isbister, J., *The Immigration Debate: Remaking America*, West Hartford, Conn.:
    Kumarian Press, 1996.
Jain, U., *The Gujaratis of San Francisco*, New York: AMS Press, 1989.
Jasso, G. and M.R. Rosenzweig, *The New Chosen People: Immigrants in the
    United States*, Imprint: New York: Russell Sage Foundation for the National
    Committee for Research on the 1980 Census, 1990.

Kibria, N., *The Family Tightrope: The Changing Lives of Vietnamese Americans*, Princeton, NJ: Princeton University Press, 1993.

Lamphere, L., *From Working Daughters to Working Mothers*, Ithaca, NY, and London: Cornell University Press, 1987.

Lister, H., 'Accidental No More', *Lodging*, the management magazine of the American Hotel and Motel Association, Dec. 1996, p. 54.

Lim, In-Sook, 'Korean Immigrant Women's Challenge to Gender Inequality at Home: the Interplay of Economic Resources, Gender, and Family', *Gender and Society*, 11, no. 1 (1997): 31–51.

Mandel, M., 'It's Really Two Immigrant Economies', *Business Week*, 20 June 1994, p. 74.

Mehra, Achal, 'Keeping Up with the Patels', *Little India*, 31 Dec. 1993.

Mogelonsky, M., 'Asian-Indian Americans', *American Demographics*, 1, no. 17 (1995): 32–9.

Nandi, P.K., *The Quality of life of Asian Americans: An Exploratory Study in a Middle-Size Community*, no. 2, Monograph Series, Chicago: Pacific/Asian American Mental Health Research Center, 1980.

Nash, J., 'Cultural Parameters of Sexism and Racism in the International Division of Labor'. In *Racism, Sexism, and the World System*, eds. Joan Smith, Jane Collins, T.K. Hopkins, and Akbar Muhammad, New York: Greenwood Press, 1988.

Pais, A.J., 'Motels go Modern', *India Today*, 31 Dec. 1995.

Passel, J. and M. Fix, 'Setting the Record Straight: What are the Costs to the Public', Public Welfare 52, Sp. (1994): 6–15.

Pedraza, S., 'Women and Migration: The Social Consequences of Gender', *Annual Review of Sociology*, 17 (1991): 303–25.

Pekin, H., 'Effects of Migration on Family Structure', *International Migration Review*, 27, no. 2 (1989): 281–93.

Perruchoud, R., 'Family Reunification', *International Migration*, 27, no. 4 (1989): 504–24.

Pessar, P., 'The Role of Gender in Dominican Settlement in the United States'. In *Women and Change in Latin America*, eds. June Nash and Helen Safa, South Hadley, Mass.: Bergin and Garvey, 1986.

Phizacklea, A., 'Entrepreneurship, Ethnicity, and Gender'. In *Enterprising Women: Ethnicity, Economy, and Gender Relations*, eds. Sallie Westwood and Parminder Bhachu, London: Routledge, 1988.

Pocock, D., *Kanbi and Patidar*, Oxford: Clarendon Press, 1972.

Repak, T.A., *Waiting on Washington: Central American Workers in the Nation's Capital*, Philadelphia: Temple University Press, 1995.

Seller, M.S., *Immigrant Women*, revised 2nd ed., Albany: SUNY-Press, 1994.

Sheth, M., 'Asian Indian Americans'. In *Asian Americans: Contemporary Trends and Issues*, ed. Pyong Gap Min, Thousand Oaks, CA: Sage Publications, 1995.

Simon, J., *The Economic Consequences of Migration*, Cambridge, MA: Blackwell, 1989.

Simpson, A.K., 'The Politics of Immigration Reform', *International Migration Review*, IX, no. 3 (1984): 486–504.

Tienda, M. and K. Booth, 'Gender, Migration, and Social Change', *International Sociology*, 6 (1991): 51–72.

Toro-Morn, M.I., 'When Wives Follow Husbands: Is it Labor Migration?' Paper presented at the annual meeting of the Society for the Advancement of Socio-Economics, New School for Social Research, New York, 1993.

Tyree, A. and K. Donato, 'A Demographic Overview of the International Migration of Women'. In *International Migration: The Female Experience*, eds. Rita James Simon and Caroline Brettell, Totowa, NJ: Rowman and Allanheld, 1986.

Weiner, M., 'The Indian Presence in America: What Difference Will It Make?' In *Conflicting Images*, eds. S.R. Glazer and N. Glazer, Glenn Dale, Maryland: The Riverdale Company, 1990.

Woodyard, C., 'Roadside Revival by the Patels', *Los Angeles Times*, Friday, July 14, 1995, Part A, p. 1, col. 1.

6 Third World Immigrant Women in American Higher Education

Cecilia G. Manrique and
Gabriel G. Manrique

THE NEW IMMIGRANTS IN ACADEME

The immigrant in academe is not a new phenomenon. Indeed, immigrant professors in the USA have had a long and distinguished record. Albert Einstein just happens to be the most prominent among the many immigrants who have contributed to the vitality of American colleges and universities. What is relatively new is the increased number of non-European immigrants who have joined US faculties. Prior to the enactment of the 1965 Immigration and Nationality Act, there were already non-European immigrants on US faculties including the 1957 winners of the Nobel prize in physics, Chen Ning Yang and Tsung-Dao Lee. However, it was not until after 1965 that their number increased significantly. The National Science Foundation (NSF) estimates that as of 1992, there were 49,000 foreign-born Asians and 3,100 foreign-born black Africans among the engineering and science Ph.D.s in the USA. In contrast, the combined number of foreign-born Asian and black Africans among the ranks of Ph.D.s in 1962 was less than 1,600.[1] Between 1979 and 1988, the number of Asian faculty in the USA increased by 85 percent with most of the increase coming from foreign-born faculty.[2] And in 1993 alone, there were approximately 6,620 college professors among the legal immigrants admitted to the USA.[3]

By non-European immigrant faculty, we are referring primarily to those who come from Asia, the Indian Subcontinent, Africa, the Middle East, Mexico, Central America and South America. For the purposes of this chapter, we will refer to these last three areas as 'Latin America'. With a few exceptions such as Japanese immigrants, the faculty we are referring to come from the so-called 'third world' countries.[4] Their increased presence in the USA reflects the overall patterns of post-1965 migration to the USA, a pattern of 'South-North migration' which has meant that 85 percent of immigrants to the USA since 1980 have been from the third world.[5]

While their contributions to human capital in the USA have been significant, immigrant faculty also provide American higher education, and by extension, American society, with opportunities for managing the diversity of cultures that has been the direct result of the latest and current wave of immigration to the United States. As the debate about immigration, diversity, assimilation and multiculturalism intensifies in the United States, it is imperative that we look to all the possible opportunities for managing such diversity.

CHINESE (AND OTHERS) NEED NOT APPLY: A BRIEF HISTORICAL BACKGROUND

Prior to 1965, the immigration laws of the United States were expressly discriminatory against persons from non-European countries. The Chinese Exclusion Act of 1882, the Gentlemen's Agreement of 1907 between the USA and Japan, and the 'Asiatic Barred Zone' contained in the 1917 Immigration Act were openly and directly aimed at severely restricting immigration from Asian countries. And between the 1920s and 1965, in an effort to preserve the ethnic status quo in the USA, a system of national origins was adopted to establish limits on the number of immigrants coming from various countries. First, the law required that a ceiling on the total number of immigrants to be accepted into the USA be established (for example, 154,277 in 1929). Then, a foreign country was allocated a quota of immigrants based on the proportion of the USA's population claiming that country as their national origin. Not surprisingly, European countries which were the main source of early immigration to the United States like Great Britain received large quotas (65,000) while Asian and African countries received very small quotas. China's quota of 100 immigrants per year was the minimum number set by the National Origins Act. It is not surprising that with these discriminatory policies towards non-European immigrants, there would be very few non-European immigrants on US faculties prior to 1965.

Changes to immigration and refugee laws of the USA beginning in 1965, quite unintendedly and unexpectedly, led to a shift in the major source of immigrants to the USA – away from European and towards non-European, predominantly third world countries. The Immigration and Nationality Act of 1965 abolished the discriminatory system of national origins for accepting immigrants to the USA, which opened the door for more non-European immigrants. The national origins system was replaced by one that favored family reunification which, through what demographers call 'chain migration',[6] opened the door for even more non-Europeans to immigrate to the USA. There were subsequent amendments to immigration laws that included: the treatment of refugees as a separate category with its separate numerical limit; the granting of amnesty to illegal immigrants who were in the USA in 1987 and who had resided in the USA continuously since 1982; an increase in the annual level of legal immigrants admitted to the USA; and the strengthening of provisions for employment-related immigration. These amendments, and in particular the amendments favoring employment-related immigration, made it possible for more non-European Ph.D.s to join college faculties in the USA after 1965.

Of course, changes in immigration laws are not sufficient to explain the increased presence of non-European immigrant faculty members. The demand and supply conditions also had to be favorable for the hiring of such faculty. On the demand side, the changes in immigration law coincided with the growth in college enrollment on many campuses in the 1960s and 1970s. And even when the overall growth of campus enrollment slowed on many campuses in the 1980s, some disciplines continued to gain in popularity. As enrollments grew, it became apparent that there was a shortage of qualified native-born faculty to meet the demand. In areas such as engineering, computer science, and business, particularly in finance and management information systems, there were simply not enough native-born Americans pursuing the Ph.D. and of those earning their Ph.D., many were choosing non-academic careers.[7] Thus, the demand conditions were favorable to hiring foreign-born Ph.D.s.

On the other hand, there were important factors that led to an increase in the supply of foreign-born Ph.D.s. The USA's widespread global involvement after the Second World War increased other people's awareness of the opportunities in American higher education. This was particularly true among the educated elite of the third world countries allied with the USA during the Cold War. Their knowledge of, and exposure to, American colleges and universities no doubt increased their interest in continuing studies and professional development in the USA. Furthermore, political and economic upheavals led to more immigration from the third world. The fundamentalist revolution in Iran, successive coup de etat and civil wars in various African countries, wars in the Middle East, the debt crises in countries such as Mexico and the Philippines, the wild price swings of commodities sold by countries like Venezuela and Chile, and the population explosion in the Indian subcontinent all created incentives for third world Ph.D.s to leave their country and stay in the United States. Thus, as US immigration laws were changing to make it possible for large numbers of non-Europeans to migrate, there were ample numbers of educated non-Europeans who were eager to come to the United States to further their study and who were eventually willing to stay to fill the faculty slots that were opening up in campuses across the United States.

THE ORIGINS OF THIS PROJECT[8]

Our project began in 1993 when we prepared to survey immigrant faculty of non-European origin. We first compiled a partial list of immigrant faculty across the USA. Then, we developed and pre-tested a survey instrument designed to gather information on the immigrant's background and various characteristics as well as information on his school. The survey was also designed to elicit responses to a variety of questions pertaining to their reasons for coming to the United States, their path to the United States, their experiences with discrimination, if any, and their views on topics such as immigration and cultural diversity. The survey, to which more than 2,400 faculty members responded, revealed interesting information about the immigrant experience. We were also encouraged to pursue this project by respondents who expressed the need to tell the immigrant's story.

To further understand the immigrant experience, we conducted extended personal interviews with some of our respondents. Material collected from lengthy interviews can complement survey data by providing depth and explanations for decisions made at different points in time and under different circumstances.[9] Hundreds of our survey respondents indicated their willingness to talk to us at length. They were all eager to be part of the telling of the immigrant story. Unfortunately, because of our time and resource constraints, we were able to interview only 62 of them. Nevertheless, those that we talked to provided us with a wealth of personal stories and insights to complement our survey data.

What we found in our study is a very diverse group that is eager to blend with, and contribute to, their adopted country. In that respect, they are no different from other immigrant groups. We also found a group that is struggling with its identity. We found a group keenly aware of its past and of being different from the majority of the population, but a group that is also keenly aware that it has been offered a 'golden door' not only to immigration but assimilation. After all, immigrant faculty recognize that in spite of the problems they have encountered, they are a privileged class of immigrants. We found a group of individuals who, though highly educated and quite successful, has not been spared from the problems of prejudice and discrimination. We found that each one has a compelling story – a story of the difficult decision to migrate and the consequences of staying. And we also found that each story enriches the varied tapestry that is the American experience.

IMMIGRANT WOMEN IN ACADEMIA

Women in general receive very confusing signals in the workplace. For non-European immigrant women, the signals can be even more confusing. On the one hand, they are told that because of their gender, race, and national origin, they should be employable because they can add to the diversity of faculties. Thus, their gender, race and national origin is a 'triple crown' that is supposed to help in the market place. One Indian professor was even advised by another Indian professor who had been quite successful in getting employed to go to job interviews dressed in traditional garb so that she could play her 'alienness' to the hilt. But on the other hand, when these same three characteristics become sources of discrimination, then they turn from a triple crown to a 'triple whammy' which can hit hard at women immigrants.

The issue of sex discrimination in higher education is a long-standing one which has been crying out for remedies. Manifestations of sex discrimination include, but are certainly not limited to, the refusal to hire, tenure, and promote women. Concerns about campuses that are unfriendly towards women have been heard and continue to be heard among academics.[10] And even when there have been attempts to incorporate women into the ranks of academe, the effort is said to still fall short.[11] But as difficult as the road has been for women in academe in general, the plight of minority women in academe is made even harder by other people's attitudes towards skin color or ethnic background. Minority women must cope with the added burden of being a marginalized person who is viewed differently by the majority.[12]

For the women in our study, there is a third strike that can be hurled against them. As women of non-European origin and most often of non-Caucasian descent (and therefore an example of a 'person of color'), they face many of the same barriers and prejudices that other minority women face in academe. But their all too obvious 'alienness' as recent immigrants to the USA creates other obstacles for them. At the very least, they are viewed as different from the vast majority of the professoriate – a notion that is reinforced by the stereotypes that Americans may have of women from Asia, Latin America, Africa and the Middle East. Such stereotypes can range from that of the docile Asian to that of the Middle Eastern woman who is not to be heard and barely seen. Even in historically black colleges and universities, as we surmised from our interviews, African immigrants are likely to be viewed as aliens for whom the terms 'black' or 'African-American' does not apply. What is worse for all immigrant women to the USA is that they can be cast as intruders in academe – intruders with a different set of customs, beliefs, and accents.

While affirmative action programs have been well-intentioned in seeking to redress imbalances in the work place and in higher education stemming from past prejudices, affirmative action programs have had negative consequences as well. Nowhere is this clearer than in the statement made by Professor Shahnaz's colleague which typifies a prevailing attitude about women – that if they are hired, it is largely because they are a woman, that they are even more likely to be hired if they are a minority woman and that furthermore a female immigrant (or anyone quite different from the rest of the faculty) is likely to be hired because she has the added bonus of contributing to campus diversity. Such 'affirmative action-induced' attitudes create a paradox for the immigrant female faculty. The three attributes that create barriers to her hiring and advancement on many campuses – gender, race, and national origin – are also the very same attributes that other people assume led to her preferential hiring and advancement. Thus, before she is hired and after she is hired, the non-European immigrant woman is faced with the triple whammy. In any case, as another respondent put it to us, 'You diminish me when you say that I should not have a problem getting hired because of what I represent and then you turn around once I am hired to deny me many things because of what I represent'.

The derogatory '3 for 1' label can be destructive in a number of ways. The accusation that one is hired to fill in more than one slot immediately implies that one is not hired on the basis of one's qualifications. In turn, one can be led to question her own worth in academe. As one of our respondents put it, 'it – the 3 for 1 label – sets you back in your attempts at self-affirmation'. In the case of Professor Shahnaz, the protestations of her dean notwithstanding, she was still left with self-doubt as well as uncertainty about what her colleagues really thought of her. The label is also harmful in another way. It justifies the attempts by others to discount the contributions of immigrants and to confirm negative stereotypes they may have of immigrants. Another respondent was more direct in her assessment of her position and her colleagues.

Of course I've heard via a number of sources in other departments that there are faculty here who say I am an affirmative action hire. They see me as this Hispanic schmuck who was willing to come to their college even though I know they are disappointed that I don't look like their stereotype of a Hispanic. And so I have to pay the price of having to show them how good I really am. It is not enough for me to do my job. You have to be very good so it overcomes the fact that you are not from here. And you can't afford to make a mistake because the mistake you make will not be judged as an honest mistake but because of what you are – a foreign Hispanic woman.

Thus, immigrant women are caught in the trap of doing more, in fact many times more than other faculty, and still not measure up to the incredible flexible yardstick.

In the rest of this chapter, we will compare the responses of women immigrants to that of the men. Having already looked at the experiences of non-European immigrant faculty in general, we attempt to differentiate between male and female immigrant faculty. This may allow us to see if indeed gender, as it does in many areas, also affects the immigrant experience.

DISCRIMINATION AND PREJUDICE

Our study in general found that 38 percent of all respondents reported having experienced workplace discrimination either from fellow faculty or administrators. When we compared the responses of men to women, we found a difference – 36 percent of men and 42 percent of women reported having experienced discrimination. Table 6.1 breaks down the sources of campus discrimination, and it confirms that women experience more discrimination than men. This is particularly true of discrimination suffered at the hands of one's colleagues within the department.[13] The proportion of women who said they had been discriminated against by colleagues in their department (30 percent) was one and a half times the proportion of men who reported experiencing discrimination within their department (20 percent). That the differences between men and women are not as large when asked about discrimination by colleagues outside the department and by administrators suggests that for immigrants at least, gender is more of a problem among those one is in closest contact with and where the opportunities to discriminate are greatest. We also find that female faculty are less inclined than males to agree that their institution has policies and procedures in place to effectively handle cases of discrimination. This too may reflect some differences in the experiences of male and female faculty.

Gender differences are also evident in response to questions about experiences with acts of prejudice. Thirty-seven percent of women as opposed to 31 percent of men reported having experienced acts of prejudice from at least one source. Table 6.2 shows the differences between the responses of men and women with responses to experiencing acts of prejudice by specific groups. The differences in the responses between men and women, although not particularly large, is consistent across the various parts of the

Table 6.1   Immigrant experiences with discrimination

Statement	Percent of respondents who agreed with the statement	
	Females	*Males*
1. I have been discriminated against by colleagues in my department.	20	30
2. I have been discriminated against by colleagues outside my department.	26	28
3. I have been discriminated against by administrators in my institution.	25	30
4. I know of other foreign-born faculty who have been discriminated against.	47	51
5. My institution has policies and procedures in place to effectively handle cases of discrimination.	54	48

Table 6.2   Immigrant experiences with prejudice

Statement	Percent of respondents who agreed with the statement	
	Males	*Females*
1. Colleagues in my department have directed acts of racial prejudice towards me.	12	17
2. Colleagues in other departments have directed acts of racial prejudice towards me.	15	18
3. Administrators have directed acts of racial prejudice towards me.	12	17
4. Students have directed acts of racial prejudice towards me.	23	27
5. People in the community where I live have directed acts of racial prejudice towards me.	32	35

campus – faculty, administrators, and students – and also outside the community. It thus appears that in addition to any discrimination and prejudice faced by a non-European immigrant, women immigrants must also cope with the gender factor – an indication of the presence of the triple whammy. Although there are clear differences in the distribution of responses between men and women, the numbers only tell part of the story. After all, when acts of discrimination in the workplace occur, the perpetrators are unlikely to admit to discriminating, much less say if they are discriminating based on gender, national origin, or race. However, by looking at the some of the comments of our respondents, one may be able to conclude that some of the discrimination and prejudice are brought about by gender as well.

A COLOR, A GENDER, AN ACCENT?

'Do they see me as a color, a gender, or an accent?' Some experiences of female immigrant faculty may help explain why questions such as these are ones they occasionally ask themselves. Such questioning starts soon after she arrives in the USA because the unwelcome mat can be pulled out from under a young female immigrant early in her stay in the USA. One of our respondents vividly recalls her rude introduction to academe in the USA. As a newcomer from India who was still a graduate teaching assistant in one professor's class, she was told by a college student, 'Speak up you Indian b____ or don't you have a voice?' Another immigrant professor related a frightening experience at a public meeting on a controversial aspect of American foreign policy that she attended. She usually wears clothes that are commonly worn in her country of origin, and that day was no exception. To her surprise, she was pushed against a wall by an American male student who yelled in her face, 'You'd better watch out you stinking foreigner. I am sick of you damned foreigners. We can bomb you to hell.' It is possible that an immigrant male could also be subjected to this kind of treatment. But in societies like the United States where women have been treated as less than equal to men, immigrant females are perhaps more vulnerable to such open harassment.

One respondent reflected on how she was socialized into the academic world in the USA.

I was socialized early on into thinking that here in the USA, as a woman, I was not equal to men. In my own country, there would not have been a problem regarding my gender in many professional fields but particularly in the university. I would have been the equal of men. I personally would not have let my gender hold me back from doing more in my college had I been in my own country. Here, I tended to hold back because of the way women are viewed as being less than equal. Remember, I started here in the 1970s. Over the years, I have experienced many instances in our department, when my proposals do not get accepted as often or as quickly because I am a woman.

And when women think over their experiences with university committees, it is not unusual for them to observe like professor Wang did that,

I have experienced this patronizing attitude when you say something. It is almost as if they were patting you on the head and saying, yes, yes, we understand what you mean. But the hidden message is, keep quiet and stay in your place. In addition, I have observed that committees tend to be assigned by gender. Women tend to sit more on the 'house keeping' committees of the university. But substantive committees such as budget, tenure and promotion are still limited to the men.

Hints, subtle and otherwise, about a woman's place can also be dropped very early on and are, thus, part of the socialization process of the immigrant faculty. A respondent recalled that during one of her first job interviews, the male professor interviewing her derided her for wearing pants and proceeded to tell her that even if this was common practice in her country of origin, she would be expected to wear something else if she were teaching at his institution. While this question of attire may seem so trivial, the incident contains two whammies – putting a woman in her place by telling her what to wear and denigrating the customs of one's country of origin. A similar undercurrent can be found in the experience of another articulate and outspoken female professor during one of her job interviews. She was told that perhaps in her country of origin female professors were common and that is why she was used to speaking up too much. She was left with the distinct impression that she would have to know 'her place' at the university.

It also appeared that female immigrants, more so than male immigrants, were questioned about their right to teach 'American' subjects. Typical of this is the experience of one professor was told by a student, 'how dare she teach Greek civilization which is the root of western civilization when she was not even a white person, let alone an American'. That this happens more often to female immigrants may be partially explained by the greater presence of females in the humanities and social sciences where 'American' subjects are common. Male immigrants who are more likely to be found in engineering and the sciences encounter this problem less often. However, it is also possible that such instances occur because students are more likely to question the authority of female immigrants rather than that of males. Immigrant female professors wonder if the intimidation attempted by the students are caused by what students may see as a vulnerable mix of gender and national origin. The following incident illustrates this point.

The respondent who related the incident described below wonders if the following incident would have occurred had she been male faculty. One of her students, unhappy with the grade he got for his paper, came to her office and tried to intimidate her into giving him a higher grade.

> It was intimidation at this point, male to female, white to non-white. It was so transparent that I did not have to guess. Sometimes you just know where it is coming from and you cannot quantify it. I am not obsessed by my color or my gender but when something like this is done, the body language, the stance, the looking over, and the physical intimidation are simply unmistakable. I just could not abide by what was being done to me. So I shut my office door and asked him to sit down. With all the control I could gather, I told him that I had just one thing to say to him, 'Don't mess with me or I will slay you.'[14] Then I immediately opened my office door before he could recover from the shock and in a voice loud enough for my department chair to hear across the hall I said, 'And if you would like the chairman to check over your paper, feel free to do so.' I am still sorry that I used that language with a student but I was so very angry then.

Of course, incidents where immigrant women encounter prejudice are not limited to campuses. Some of the incidents related by female respondents were quite amusing particularly when they involved mathematics. In one incident, a respondent caught a mistake in a salesman's calculation of a 20 percent discount, a mistake she pointed out. In a condescending tone, the salesman replied, 'Lady, let me show you how to get 20 percent'. Unfortunately for the salesman, he saw in front of him only a Hispanic woman with an accent and he was rightfully embarrassed when she said, 'I may not speak English very well but I am a mathematics professor and I teach this for a living'. In another case, a respondent was advising a group about the proposed buyout of their company. The man negotiating for the buyers presented numbers which were patently misleading and which our respondent challenged. The man's response was to try to explain to the 'dear lady' that these were intricate financial matters which she would find hard to understand. Unfortunately for him, the 'dear lady' was a business professor who understood intricate financial matters. He was ultimately replaced by another negotiator. In yet another case, a respondent was negotiating the purchase of a Japanese-brand car. The salesman tried to justify selling the car to a seemingly unsophisticated foreigner at a much higher price because of what he described as major changes in the foreign exchange rate. The salesman had to change his pitch when the faculty member politely informed him that she was a professor of international trade and it seemed to her that because of the appreciation of the dollar against the yen the car should be sold for much less than the sticker price.

While seemingly trivial or just plain amusing, these incidents that immigrants have faced, particularly women immigrants, help to explain the frustration reflected in one respondent's lament: 'Like anyone else, I want to be taken seriously. It bothers me that to be treated fairly, you have to tell people, "See, I have this position, I have this degree." I just want to be treated like any other human being. I do not want to have to explain myself'.

SEPARATION OF RACE AND GENDER

It may be difficult for women immigrants to distinguish among the factors that cause the discrimination and prejudice that they experience. Is it from their race (i.e., a non-Caucasian, or a person of color), from their gender, or from their national origin (i.e., non-European)? Our survey did not ask respondents directly if they could attribute their experiences to their gender. However, because we did ask them certain questions about the role of their race, we may make certain inferences about the role of gender as well. Questions one and two in Table 6.3 indicate that non-European female faculty actually view their race as less of a barrier than non-European males.

Table 6.3 Effect of race on professional advancement

Statement	Percent of respondents who agreed with the statement	
	Males	*Females*
1. My race is a barrier to my effectiveness as a teacher.	16	14
2. My race is a barrier to my professional advancement and/or promotion.	29	26
3. My speech accent is a barrier to my effectiveness as a teacher.	23	19
4. Because of my race, I have to try harder to prove myself professionally.	66	66

Females also viewed their speech accent as less of a barrier. And question four indicates that male and female immigrants feel equally strongly that because of their race, they have to try harder to prove themselves professionally. One can thus infer, albeit tentatively, that if non-European male and female faculty do not differ in their view of how race affects their professional career, then differences in their experiences with respect to discrimination and prejudice may be attributable to gender. This is perhaps the signal that immigrant women have been receiving on US campuses.

The awareness that they must labor under the cloud of the triple whammy confuses women immigrants. As one of our respondents reflected,

> sometimes I cannot sort out why my colleagues are not comfortable with me or why they don't like me. Is it because I am a foreigner or because I am a woman? And if I am not sure, then it is hard for me to do the things that will help me get tenure. They say I have to adapt, but adapt to what – the gender issue, the race issue, or the alien issue?

It does not help that they are often alone in their department or even in their college – alone either as a woman or as a non-European immigrant. The gatekeepers of academe tend to be even less inclined to hire non-European women. And even when there are other women in the department or college, the experiences of immigrant women may not necessarily be better. Our survey revealed that there was no difference in the relative frequency of discrimination by departmental colleagues experienced by an immigrant woman whether or not there were other women in her department. In fact, some of our respondents have found that the open hostility of female colleagues have been worse than those of males. This experience of an immigrant professor of English is not at all unique: Her female colleague who was to go up for tenure one year after her, sought to undermine her chances for tenure by encouraging students to complain about her accent – an issue that never came up with students until this female colleague tried to use it to improve her own chances for tenure. In another instance, an immigrant woman was constantly denied laboratory resources by a female colleague who claimed to know more than 'these foreign faculty'. And of course, in some of the strange twists of affirmative action in academe, white women end up being pitted against minority or immigrant women.

FOR WOMEN IMMIGRANTS – A REVERSAL OF FORTUNE

Gender discrimination is not unique to the USA and may even be more prevalent in other countries. Thus, despite the experiences with discrimination and prejudice that our respondents have experienced, immigration to the United States remains an attractive option for female faculty. For female faculty, gender can be another factor in calculating the relative costs and benefits of immigrating. For example, a female faculty considering immigration to the USA is easily made aware that gender discrimination exists in the USA. This would be one of the costs of migrating that may deter her from coming to the USA permanently. However, if she is also aware that gender discrimination is relatively worse in her country of origin, she may still be inclined to migrate to the USA.

It is also commonly understood that immigrants to the United States come for economic reasons. There are of course other powerful reasons why people migrate such as the fear of persecution in their country of origin. However, the high probability that one can raise one's standard of living by coming to the United States is a compelling reason for migrating that is shared by many immigrants regardless of educational level. For the women in our study however, there is an added twist to the reasons given for migrating which differentiates male and female immigrants. Although economics may play a significant part in the decision to migrate, both our survey and our interviews reveal that non-European immigrant women often migrate to carve out a role and a life that is significantly different from what would be traditionally expected of them in their home country.

The new wave of immigrants come from countries where the views of women's roles and, therefore, the options for women are still 'traditional' – centered on marriage and the raising of the family. When these women come to the United States, oftentimes to study, new avenues open up for them. Immigrant women find that these avenues, once taken, are very difficult to leave. We found this to be a recurring theme among the women in our study – that economics is not necessarily the main reason for the decision to migrate. The results of our survey showed that male faculty overwhelmingly stated that compared to what they currently have in the USA the standard of living they would be able to afford in their country of origin would be lower. On the other hand, relatively more females stated that their standard of living in their country of origin would be higher than what they currently have. As one of our informants put it, 'I used to think that I immigrated for economic reasons but I am realizing now that that was not the reason. I left to do something different from what was expected of women such as myself'.

In Table 6.4, we compare male and female responses to questions that ask respondents to rate their prospects in their country of origin relative to their current situation in the USA. The table shows that both males and females are optimistic about job opportunities in their country of origin.

Table 6.4 Comparison of job opportunities in the USA and immigrant's country of origin

Statement	Percent of respondents who replied			
	High		Low	
	Males	Females	Males	Females
1. The probability of finding employment in my country of origin commensurate with my training and education.	68	62	14	18
2. The probability that I would be offered a permanent college faculty position in my country of origin.	73	58	12	18

However, men are clearly more optimistic than women about their job prospects in both college teaching and non-teaching fields. In response to question two which asks them to rate the probability of being offered a faculty position, 73 percent of men but only 58 percent of women thought it was high. A comparison of the proportion who rated such probability as low also shows that women were more pessimistic than men about finding a job in their country of origin.

It is interesting to note however, that although women were less optimistic than men about employment opportunities in their country of origin, they were more optimistic about what their standard of living in their country of origin would be compared to what they currently have in the USA. Table 6.5 shows that proportionately more women than men think that their standard of living in their country of origin would be higher than what they currently have in the USA. Twenty percent of females but only 14 percent of males thought that their standard of living would be better in their country of origin. The difference is higher among those who responded that their standard of living would be worse in their country of origin. Only 37 percent of females but 48 percent of males said that it would be worse in their country of origin.

One explanation for the difference between men and women is the lack of support that immigrant women felt they have in the USA. This is particularly true of immigrant faculty on campuses far removed from urban centers and where there are few, if any, immigrants or minorities. One respondent went so far as to say that she felt like an exile in her campus and her community in the Midwest. 'This place is the absence of anything that is related to me. The complete void of anything that is culturally

Table 6.5   Comparisons of resources in the USA and immigrant's
country of origin

Statement	Percent of respondents who replied			
	Better		Worse	
	Males	*Females*	*Males*	*Females*
1. Compared to my standard of living in the USA, my standard of living in my country of origin would be	14	20	48	37
2. Compared to my standard of living in the USA, my standard of living as a faculty member in my country of origin would be	12	19	61	55
3. Compared to the USA, my access to research and library facilities in my country of origin would be	4	6	77	77
4. Compared to the USA, my academic freedom in my country of origin would be	7	6	43	47

familiar to me is striking. At times, I still feel like I am lost in space and that makes it very hard to cope'. Our female respondents repeatedly alluded to the support from an extended family, a wide network of friends, and the availability of hired help in their country of origin which contributes to their ability to attain a higher standard of living. In contrast, faced with the multiple tasks of raising a family, managing the home, advancing a career, and adapting to a new culture, immigrant women find little such support in the US.

There is another possible explanation for why relatively fewer immigrant women think that their standard of living in the USA is not much better than what they would have in their country of origin. Male immigrants may experience less salary discrimination in the United States than female immigrants. This would mean that male immigrants would perceive a much larger difference between their income in the USA and what they think their income would be in their country of origin. On the other hand, if there is salary discrimination against women in the United States, then women immigrants would not perceive as large of a difference between the salary they obtain here and what they could get in their country of origin. Finally, and perhaps not surprisingly, we found no difference between genders with regard to perceptions about access to research and library facilities and there is a small difference in their perceptions about academic freedom.

The differences between men and women are not limited to perceptions about economic opportunities in the USA. There are significant differences between them in their perception of their social status and opportunities for professional advancement, as shown in Table 6.6. While 67 percent of males thought their social status would be better in their country of origin, only 54 percent of women thought so. This may be an indication of the lower status of women in other countries. In addition, proportionately fewer women thought that their opportunities for professional advancement would be better in their country of origin. One-fourth of the female respondents thought that opportunities for advancement were worse in their country but less than one-fifth of men thought so. Taken together, these indicate that one of the attractions of the USA for immigrant women, in spite of the discrimination they encounter in the USA, is the relatively higher social status and professional advancement they can achieve by staying in the USA.

For immigrant women, therefore, the breaking of one's moorings and starting alone as an immigrant can impose significant costs. However, the same break from one's moorings can be desirable in that it eliminates some of the restraints imposed upon them as women in their country of origin. The following statement by a young professor expresses the sentiment of many other respondents, 'I definitely feel better off here as a woman. I can dish out a lot more here and not be reprimanded for it. At home, I would not be as free to speak. And by this time, if I had gone back, I would have been married off and arranging seven forks and seven knives for fancy dinners we would host'. Another statement addresses an even more basic sentiment, 'Here [in the USA], I don't experience the same kind of treatment from men that I get when I go back home, particularly if I am alone. I refer to it as the "look." You know, the looking over as if you were a piece of meat'.

Table 6.6 Comparisons of opportunities in the USA and immigrant's country of origin

Statement	Percent of respondents who replied			
	Better		*Worse*	
	Males	*Females*	*Males*	*Females*
1. Compared to my social status in the USA, my status in my country of origin would be	67	54	6	9
2. Compared to the USA, my opportunities for professional advancement in my country of origin would be	43	34	18	25

Table 6.7   Views of campus diversity – by gender

Statement	Percent of respondents who agreed with the statement	
	Males	*Females*
1. My institution's efforts to recruit faculty from diverse racial backgrounds are effective.	41	43
2. My institution's efforts to retain faculty from diverse racial backgrounds are effective.	40	39
3. My institution should recruit more faculty from diverse racial backgrounds.	52	66
4. My institution should devote more resources to cultural diversity.	56	69

Perhaps the experiences of non-European immigrant women can help to explain why women, compared to men, are more inclined to favor programs to expand the cultural diversity of their campuses. As victims of the triple whammy, they may be more sympathetic to, and more understanding of the needs to improve the campus atmosphere – to make it less chilly for women, for minorities, and for immigrants. Table 6.7 shows that the ratings male and female respondents gave their respective institution's efforts to recruit and retain faculty from diverse racial backgrounds were approximately equal. Less than half of both groups rated such efforts as effective suggesting that universities and colleges still have a long way to go towards achieving diversity. But the major difference between men and women was in their responses to questions about what their institutions should be doing. A much larger percentage of women faculty said that their institutions should recruit a more diverse faculty and should devote more resources to cultural diversity. As one female respondent told her college president who was apparently pleased with himself for being able to attract her – a female, a non-white, and a recent immigrant – to his college which he himself described as 'pure lily white', 'Don't be happy that I am here. Work on bringing more of us here. Think of what several more of us can do for the students and for the whole campus'.

FROM "THREE-FERS" TO ACHIEVERS

Highly educated and motivated individuals, regardless of gender, ethnicity, or national origin, have the potential to make significant contributions to their adopted country. But in addition to the expertise that all faculty are expected to have, non-European immigrant women can enrich universities in other ways. Their perspectives provide balance to the dominant perspectives in traditionally male-dominated institutions. Their ethnicity provides diverse cultural perspectives, perspectives that are important as students learn to function in an increasingly multicultural, multiethnic and multinational work place. And their different national origins reinforce the learning of cultures beyond this country's borders. In addition, the very presence of immigrant women on campus can provide role models for the increasing number of students from minority or immigrant backgrounds. For these important reasons, as well as for mandated reasons such as affirmative action hiring, women immigrants may be sought out by colleges and universities.

What we have attempted to point out in this chapter are some of the forces that are at work against non-European immigrant women particularly once they are allowed inside by the gatekeepers. The very factors that may make them desirable to colleges and universities may also be used against them. The misuse of gender to hold back women in academe, as well as the misuse of ethnicity and race to the extent that they reflect being part of a minority group, are factors that have been examined in other works. When 'alienness' colors all of these other factors, then academe can become even more forbidding to women immigrants. We have also attempted to show that women immigrants have reasons, other than economics, to migrate. These reasons, in particular the chance to break from constrictive stereotypes and roles in their own country, are powerful motivators for making substantial contributions to research and teaching in the United States. Such contributions can be even more substantial if the campus climate is receptive to immigrant women. In that case, rather than being 'three-fers', they can become achievers of their full potential which many of them believe can be realized in the USA.

NOTES

1. From the National Science Foundation data on foreign-born engineers and scientists.
2. Harold Orlan, 'Affirmative Action in Higher Education', *Annals of the American Academy of Political and Social Sciences*, September, 1992, pp. 144–58.

3. Linda Chavez, 'Guest Workers Might Ease Immigration Flow', *USA Today*, August 2, 1995.
4. The term 'third world' is both a convention and a convenience that is used widely in the economic development literature. The authors also recognize that the classification of countries changes over time as in the case of the economically successful 'tigers' of Asia like Singapore, Korea, and Taiwan which, it can be argued, have 'graduated' from 'third world' status by 1995.
5. Reginald T. Appleyard, 'South–North Migration, Conference Report of the Ninth International Organization for Migration Seminar on Migration', *International Migration Review*, XXV, no. 3, pp. 610–19.
6. In its simplest form, chain migration takes place when an immigrant sponsors his or her parents for immigration to the USA. In turn the parents can sponsor their other children for immigration to the USA. If the original immigrant were married, the spouse could also sponsor his or her parents who could also sponsor their children.
7. According to an NSF survey of engineers and scientists, the number of native-born persons earning a Ph.D. in engineering declined through much of the 1970s and even though their numbers increased in the 1980s, it is still has not returned to the previous levels. During the same period, the number of foreign-born Ph.D.s in engineering has continuously increased.
8. Funding for the project came from the University of Wisconsin System Institute on Race and Ethnicity, and several faculty development grants from the University of Wisconsin-La Crosse and Winona State University.
9. The same point is made by A.W. Helweg in 'Why Leave India for America? A Case Study Approach to Understanding Migrant Behavior', *International Migration*, 25, no. 2, pp. 165–78.
10. Examples of works on sex discrimination in higher education include Joan Abramson, *The Invisible Women: Discrimination in the Academic Profession* (San Francisco: Jossey-Bass, 1975); Jennie Farley, *Academic Women and Employment Discrimination: A Critical Annotated Bibliography*. The atmosphere for women is examined in Bernice Sandler, 'The Campus Climate Revisited: Chilly For Women Faculty, Administrators and Graduate Students' (Washington, DC: Project on the Status and Education of Women, Association of American Colleges, 1986) and in Lynne Welch (ed.), *Women in Higher Education: Changes and Challenges* (New York: Praeger Publishers, 1990).
11. For example, as of 1995, women still constitute only 11 percent of the tenured faculty at Harvard University (as opposed to the 23 percent average nationwide), 'Harvard Held Up', by Lynell Hancock and Claudia Kalb, *Newsweek*, December 11, 1995, p. 81. In this, they talk of the difficulty for women in Harvard and why women alum are trying to block the capital fund drive until Harvard does more. Harvard has hired one woman per 250 positions that have opened up.
12. Several of these issues are discussed by minority women in Lynne B. Welch (ed.), *Perspectives on Minority Women in Higher Education* (New York: Praeger Publishers, 1992).

13. The percentages of females who agreed with the statements about discrimination are all higher than the percentages for men. But the difference between men and women is greatest in reporting on discrimination within departments. The difference between men and women is also large when asked if they know of others who have been discriminated against.
14. The actual words used by this professor, as she told the story to us, were much more graphic and much less polite. We have simply chosen to paraphrase her remarks.

Part II
The Social Status of International Female Migrants

7 Mail Order Brides: The Legal Framework and Possibilities for Change
Lisa Simons

'Island ladies seek loving husbands from overseas. Cebuanas (ladies from Cubu, Philippines) are joyful and fun, mellow, soft, sincere, vulnerable, zestful, compassionate, loyal. ...' A man interested in meeting one of these 'ladies' can begin a search on the Internet in catalogs where he can scroll through pages of photos, clicking on a picture to get more information, and read a short biography which states her interests and hobbies. Spokespersons for these agencies claim that many happily married couples have met this way. But news like the following draws less favorable attention to the practice: 'A gunman killed his pregnant mail-order bride and one of her friends and critically wounded a third woman as they waited to testify against him in a marriage annulment hearing' (*Washington Times*, 1995). This case, although extreme, is representative of abuses that can result from the unequal status of men and their immigrant wives (Leung, 1990).

This chapter examines the mail order bride industry, using the case of women's migration from the Philippines to the US as an example. The migration of Filipino women to the US for marriage to American men can be studied as a microcosm of the larger international sex industry (Barry, 1979; Barry *et al.*, 1984). Several dimensions of the topic are introduced including the historical, legal, political, economic, and cultural factors involved in the migration of women for the purpose of marriage.

This research is necessary because knowledge of the causes and consequences of female migration will contribute to advancing the status of women. Gender differentiated migration has been insufficiently documented and studied because migration has traditionally been viewed as gender-neutral. Marriage migration, in particular, has been almost entirely ignored in scholarly research. Migration has throughout history been a route to improving people's status and opportunities. We do not, however, have adequate answers to questions about female migration. The purpose of this chapter is to contribute to the emerging body of research on women and migration.

Part I describes the mail order bride business. Part II examines the legal response to the mail order bride industry, describing various attempts to reveal the elements of this sector of the sex industry as a violation of civil, constitutional, and international law. Drawing primarily on scholarship in recent law review literature, I evaluate the various legal attempts to construct arguments that will reform and/or transform the practice of mail order marriages. The conclusion illustrates reasons for guarded optimism regarding women who migrate to marry (or marry to migrate). The current degrading status of women as international commodities on the marriage market may change as litigation joins forces with social and political currents to produce potentially liberating results for women.

I. MAIL ORDER BRIDES

American men marrying foreign women is not a new occurrence: foreign women have long captivated the male imagination in popular culture, and the traffic of women for marriage and/or prostitution in the eighteenth and nineteenth century was widespread (Barry, 1979). There has, however, been a notable rise since the early 1980s in the numbers of women entering the US as mail order brides. 'In 1970, only 23 Asians were issued fiancee-petitioned visas; while in 1983, the figure jumped dramatically to 3,428' (Joseph, 1984). There are also reasons for heightened awareness of this increase. By the 1970s, the mail order bride industry was flourishing as decolonization created new patterns of global migration while militarization fueled relations between US servicemen and Asian women. Third world countries began to find avenues of power and influence in the UN, catching the attention of more people in the industrialized countries and giving international feminism an audience for women's interests. Women's liberation has become a popular focus for the media, providing an easy way to explain tension between men and women. During the 1970s, feminist scholars published some pioneering research documenting the international sex industry and the role of mail order brides in that context (Barry, 1979; Rubin, 1975; Boserup, 1970). Although the mail order bride industry is an old one, there is increasing public consciousness of its existence, growing scholarship on its history and implications, and emerging national and international legal efforts at renewing previous efforts to control and/or mitigate its harmful effects.

A common starting point for people seeking information about the mail order bride industry is to request catalogs from companies that advertise in national magazines such as Rolling Stone, the National Review, Esquire, and Playboy. There are also 'how-to' books written by men who are self-proclaimed experts on the subject. Another increasingly popular option for those with Internet access is to go to any number of the many web sites with on-line catalogs of available women or other introduction services with information for men to meet foreign women. Web sites offering help for American men seeking foreign wives provide an introduction to the process, tips for avoiding scams, and testimony from the men who are using the services.[1] The sites also offer explanations for the growth of the mail order bride industry in the past twenty years. Free information on the Internet gives advice 'for the purposes of helping men'. Newsgroup postings alert readers to the fact that more men want mail order brides today because of men's unhappiness with American women. The tone and level of discourse aptly captures the sensibility driving the mail order bride business:

> Because of the attitudes held by so many of today's American women, a huge number of American men are becoming increasingly unhappy with them. ... The reason [the men] are not married is because, among the women they find available, they can't find the kind of wife they want. *The feminist movement is to blame.* The feminist movement has caused immense social damage in this country. It has harmed not only men, who can't find the kind of wives they want, but women as well ... many American women can't find husbands ... because they have chosen for themselves a career path other than that of wife.

The testimony from men who are using or planning to use the international dating services represents a wide cross-section of backgrounds, education and economic status. What they have in common is the above-stated attitude towards American women.

The web site explains that while the typical man looking for a foreign wife used to be a middle-aged divorcee, in the 1990s, many younger men are not even bothering with American women first. One of the self-proclaimed experts, Gary Clark, notes that American men need not be rich for foreign women to find them attractive. The cost of procuring a foreign wife should be affordable to a middle-class man. He surveys some of the most reputable mail order bride companies and offers tips on how much one can be expected to spend as well as advice on how to avoid scams.

Cherry Blossoms is the catalogue of one of the oldest and, according to Clark, most reliable mail order firms – Rainbow Ridge. It contains photos of 500 women in each bimonthly publication. Each photo and brief biography has a code number, and men can, as it says in the instructions, 'order your girl by number. Send $10 per girl'. The best deal, according to Clark, is to pay $269 for all the addresses listed in a six month period. The man's address will be sent to the next 500 women who join the new listings. Rainbow Ridge lists women from all over the world, whereas some companies specialize in certain areas (http://www.filipina.com).

The agencies do not charge the women to be listed in their catalogues. They find interested women by placing 'brides wanted' ads overseas. Prospective brides answer questionnaires and send photos. Although this can be done at no cost to the women, some use modeling agencies to take their photos; some pay for 'coaching' services for help in filling out the questionnaires and answering letters to the men who respond to their ads.

Estimates from investigative reporting show extensive growth in activity. In 1986, there were approximately 100 mail order marriage companies in the US. By 1996, the estimate had doubled to 200 (Federal News Service, 1996). One company, American Asian Worldwide Services in Orcutt, California, grossed $250,000 in 1985 (Ferraro, 1986b). Their catalog goes out to over 3,000 men whose average age is 40. Tessie Florence, a native of the Philippines, runs the organization out of her home. She met her own American husband through an ad he placed there in 1979. Like many people who operate these agencies, she claims that her happy marriage through an international personal service provides motivation to help others achieve gratification in the same way (Ferraro, 1986a).

Precise statistics on the industry are not available as this is an unregulated, unmonitored, and largely unstudied phenomenon. The Immigration and Naturalization Service (INS) does not keep records on the industry, but it is estimated that each year anywhere from 2,000 to 4,000 American men find wives through mail order bride agencies (Federal News Service, 1996). There has been recent congressional interest in the mail order bride phenomenon: part of the current immigration reform proposal is a response to claims that the industry ought to be held accountable for extensive fraud and abuse.[2] Senator Herbert Kohl is sponsoring a provision of the immigration bill to study the mail order bride industry to see how many immigrant brides are abused and how many are prostitutes.

Congressional interest in this aspect of the international traffic in women is not necessarily motivated by a concern for women. Rather, it follows a pattern of alarmism about unregulated business conducted on the Internet. The exploitative potential of any exchange is often used as justification for restrictive legislation. The mail order bride trade becomes conceptually linked with other 'evils' in what some see as a 'disturbing new development in the still unregulated information superhighway – already used to distribute pornography globally' (Rose, 1995). An odd alliance has developed out of the interest in regulating sex on the Internet: the government supports investigations into the mail order bride industry, as do feminist groups who fear that the toleration of this trade on the Internet will further condone abusive treatment of women and entrench stereotypical attitudes about sex roles.

The mail order bride promotional material provides a deceptively simple answer to the question: What drives the industry? According to much of the media, it is the eternal human desire for love and marriage. It is only natural, the story goes, that as global economic and political interdependence grows, so do social and personal relations. Personal ads have long been a feature of local newspapers. Therefore, as international travel became accessible to the masses, personal ads became transnational. From this perspective, it is difficult to find fault with the mail order bride agencies. According to agency organizers, testimonials from 99 percent of their clients demonstrate happy, successful marriages (Klass, 1995).

Marriage, however, is a multidimensional issue. Marriage to foreigners is even more so. The courts' recognition of the contentious political nature of marriage dates back to the Blackstone tradition (Blackstone, 1993). One man's decision to order a catalogue, choose a woman, write her letters, and perhaps eventually marry her, can sound uncomplicated. If we look at the intricate layering of forces that takes place prior to this free market exchange, before the 'individual' makes his choices, we see a more complete picture of the mail order bride industry.

Immigration is a result of combined push/pull factors. In the marriage industry, the pull factors include the consumer demand for women (driven partly by the previously noted reaction to the women's movement) and the promise of providing a better life for immigrant women. The push factors include the desire of women from low income countries to move to higher income countries: the benefits (including greater economic as well as social opportunities in a country with less traditional gender roles) are expected not only for the immigrant spouse but also for her additional family members for whom she may petition for future entry into the US.

The politics driving the Philippine exportation of women is linked to the colonial past. US military bases in the Philippines (as elsewhere) promoted the local prostitution industry. Some of the women working as prostitutes who developed relationships with US officers eventually came to the US as war brides (Anderson, 1993). When the US scaled down its military operations overseas, many of the women who had been making a living as prostitutes found themselves out of a job. They were looking for a way to come to the US to continue the only work they could find to earn the money needed to support their families.

The economics and politics of the mail order bride industry are linked by foreign policy. When developing countries have large debts owed to the International Monetary Fund and the World Bank, a lucrative enterprise is to export women into the international labor market (Enloe, 1990). Filipina workers provide their country with remittances that add up to as much as $6 billion annually, which is enough for the Philippine government to pay the interest on its loans. Women leave the Philippines to become domestic workers worldwide, leading President Fidel Ramos, in 1991, to call these women 'heroines of the Philippine economy' (Enloe, 1990; Rosca, 1995). However, the women who emigrate as domestics or as brides often end up in the sex industry (Bunch, 1984). Some organizations seeming to be bridal or domestic agencies are actually fronts, procuring women for the sex industry (Barry *et al.*, 1994).

Traditional beliefs about women as national symbols as well as guardians of culture play a part in the psychological aspect of political domination. There is a history of evidence supporting belief in the saying that to experience a country one must experience its women. International relations scholar Cynthia Enloe (1990) has documented the connections among colonialism, sexism, militarism. She discusses how nationalism can take pride in itself by relying upon stereotyped roles of foreign women. Myths celebrating oriental subservient femininity are used in tourist brochures and in advertisements for mail order brides, airlines and hotels.

Advertisements boast that Asian women are 'faithful, docile, exotic'; the ads note that the women are petite (often under 100 pounds), exceptionally feminine, and mostly virgins. One ad, in language that typifies the catalog marketing reads:

> Congratulations, you have taken the first step toward discovery of an eternal treasure that will happen when you find your number one Asian lady whose main objective in life is to please her husband. The enthusiasm shown and the pleasure they derive in accomplishing this goal is almost embarrassing.... We wouldn't be at all surprised if you entertained thoughts of polygamy. (Hanson, 1987)

Other companies have similar claims: '[w]here else will you find a girl who will clean your toenails with a toothbrush?', 'passionate lovemaking guaranteed', 'Two Million Submissive Doll-Like Women For Sale' (Meng, 1994).

II. THE PRESENT LEGAL RESPONSE TO THE MAIL ORDER BRIDE INDUSTRY

Inadequacies and Proposals for Change

Immigration law is presently the only source of national control over the mail order bride industry. This control, however, is partial, inconsistent, and ultimately ineffective. It neither prevents fraud nor protects vulnerable immigrants.

The INS grants an immigrant bride conditional status for two years during which at any time she may be deported if she leaves the marriage. After this waiting period, she may change her status to permanent resident alien. The INS has always been justifiably concerned about marriage fraud. US immigration law has long allowed immigrants married to US citizens or permanent residents to bypass waiting periods and numerical limits. Thus, the INS created and applied the 'Marriage Viability Requirement' to ensure that the citizen spouse and immigrant had a 'bona fide' marriage (Richins, 1980).

Questions arose regarding the due process requirements, and the viability standards were declared unconstitutional.[3] However, by 1985 there was enough alarmism in the popular media about marriage fraud in the mail order bride business for the INS to request that Congress grant statutory authority for a liability standard. In 1986, Congress passed the Immigration and Marriage Fraud Amendments (IMFA) providing the INS with permission to create rules and regulations designed to combat marriage fraud. The centerpiece of the IMFA is the conditional permanent resident (CPR) status.[4]

Restrictive immigration tends to be caused by fears that immigrants place a drain on a nation's cohesion, identity, or strength (political, economic, social). Targeting the immigrant women in the mail order bride business is in keeping with this historical pattern of responses to cultural threat: the most vulnerable members of society are the easiest to blame.

The story, as told by the popular press, fits a script repeated throughout history. Different immigrant groups are singled out according to various politically motivating factors ranging from foreign policy concerns to national immigrant advocacy lobbies. The fear is that an incoming group threatens the US by draining resources and/or constituting a threat to citizens jobs, health or morality (Reimers, 1992).

In this case, the IMFA was passed by vilifying the aliens believed to be exploiting generous US immigration law by deceitfully marrying unsuspecting US citizens. Aliens marry, in this view, as a quick way to get into the country only to drain public assistance resources. Those trying to circumvent the law by marriage fraud might include 'undesirables' such as criminals, terrorists, drug dealers and prostitutes. According to INS discourse, mail order brides are part of this trend of potential system abusers (Meng, 1994). The rhetoric of the INS is echoed in warnings contained in mail order bride information on the Internet and elsewhere about the less reputable companies or individuals who seek only the chance to manipulate upstanding men into marriage.

The law, taken literally, is gender-neutral in that it applies simply to a foreigner who marries a US citizen. One can argue, however, that this creates a disparate impact, affecting women more negatively than men. Foreign women, particularly mail order brides, marrying American men are more vulnerable than foreign men marrying American women. The Marriage Fraud Amendments were written to fight any fraudulent marriage, but the publicity fueling the passage of these amendments was focused on the mail order bride traffic. Thus, it is arguable that the disparate impact was deliberate in the original intent of this law.[5]

Following the INS logic, the burden of proof must be on the immigrant spouse: the threat of deportation during the conditional status period is designed to ward off potential fraud. From the point of view of the husband as the consumer, this scheme makes good sense.

The INS sets up a series of hurdles for immigrant women who want to change their legal status. The immigrant woman must undergo a confusing process to get her CPR status changed to that of permanent resident (Meng, 1994). The Immigration Act of 1990 contained legislation aimed at providing immigrant waivers of conditional status in the case of battery or extreme cruelty.[6] Critics of the change charged the INS with unduly complicating the procedure with evidentiary requirements which in effect undermined the intent of the legislation.[7] The required level of proof was impossibly high; it also burdened women by focusing on their mental state rather than on that of the abuser (MacKinnon, 1987; Schneider, 1991).

Responding in part to the criticism that the petition procedures give husbands free rein to abuse their immigrant wives, the 1994 amendment to the IMFA includes the Violent Crime Control and Law Enforcement Act.[8] This allows immigrant women in some cases to self-petition for a change in status. But this act too has unreasonable conditions. Reminiscent of nineteenth century standards for women applying for government welfare, the 1994 act requires that the CPR still be married and demonstrate (1) that she is of 'good moral character'; (2) the marriage was entered into 'in good faith'; (3) that she or her child was 'battered by or has been the subject of extreme cruelty perpetrated by [her] spouse'; and (4) that she or her child will face 'extreme hardship' if deported. Divorced immigrant women face a different standard for changing their CPR status: they may apply for joint-petition waver by showing battery *or* good faith *or* extreme hardship.[9]

The complicated evidentiary standards are not the only hurdle an immigrant CPR must face while petitioning to legalize her status. The IMFA process includes an INS interview with the couple, or with only the women if she files a self-petition. The INS is infamous for its harrowing interviews (Anker, 1992). The INS officer has wide discretion in the interrogation procedure, and the often intrusive personal nature of the inquiry can present a challenge to privacy rights.

Shifting perspectives to that of the mail order bride, the CPR scheme looks quite different. It is from the immigrant point of view that we can begin to see how the feminist legal scholars have likened the mail order bride position to sexual slavery (Barry, 1979). The conditional status has been called a 'license to abuse' (Anderson, 1993). Legal scholar Michelle Anderson's (1990) study of the impact of conditional status on female immigrants is an investigation of two sub-populations of female immigrants: mail order brides and military brides. The findings include evidence that a large number of female immigrants are abused and that the abuse is heightened by the current statutory and regulatory framework that exists to combat fraud. Risk of battery is not limited to conditional residents, but the power disparity and circumstances surrounding conditional residency amplify vulnerability.

The immigrant spouse is unlikely and often unable to avail herself of the limited opportunities to adjust her legal status regardless of how much proof she may have to support a case for self-petition. The strict 'capricious and arbitrary' evidentiary requirements can be prohibitive, and immigrants are susceptible to the ever-present threat of deportation. Many mail order brides, like some immigrants and most refugees, are unfamiliar with the language and political structure in the US, are without close friends or family, and are financially dependent on their husbands. Thus, the women face incentives to stay with abusive husbands, despite the existence of formal channels for potential escape.

The CPR scheme forces immigrant brides to stay in marriages and legitimizes exploitation by requiring the women to meet the 'viability' standards for their two year conditional period. Legal scholar Eddy Meng characterizes the CPR rules as consumer protection for the men:

the standards actually prescribe what immigrant women must do to fulfill their two-year warranty: offer sexual services (that is, consummation of marriage, having children, using birth control), offer domestic labor (that is, housework, chores), or void the warranty by being abused (that is the domestic violence exception)... the viability standard... not only creates obstacles for mail-order brides to leave... but also tells them that they may be deported unless they give their consumer-husbands their money's worth. (Meng, 1994)

If the exchange of women is part of the smooth operation of society, those who do not willingly cooperate are a problem. Thus, it is easy to understand why women's autonomy must be controlled. If a mail order bride violates assumptions about women as passive commodities, it disrupts society's system of promises and debts.[10]

Reform

This chapter has illustrated some of the legal complexity arising from the mail-order bride business. I now turn to a review and evaluation of various attempts at reform. The dynamics of this industry resist simple categorization and render any one strategy for change insufficient. The power behind systems of oppression is not easily isolated and eradicated (Barry *et al.*, 1984). Thus, this section will look at multiple strategies for addressing both macro and micro level issues: the root causes fueling the industry as well as the subordination of women within the context of immigration law. The strategies most commonly discussed in the law review literature fall generally under two large categories, dismantling CPR status and targeting the demand side of the business.

CPR Status

The CPR status is open to charges of violating three broad constitutional rights: privacy, due process, and equal protection. The INS inquiry to determine the bona fide nature of the marriage is a procedure, in theory and practice, that infringes upon the 'zones of privacy' established in *Griswold* v. *Connecticut.*[11] The very idea of suspecting that marriages are fraudulent is an affront to the Court's own construction of the marriage contract as 'sacred'. But given the reality that the noble ideal of marriage is subject to exploitation, some questioning may appear acceptable. In *Paul* v. *Davis,*[12] following *Griswold*, protected zones include 'matters relating to marriage, procreation, contraception, family relationship, and child rearing and education'.

A critique of investigating marriages points to assumptions behind the inquiry. The INS interrogations presume sex role stereotypes of male and female behavior and obligation. Such sex typing has elsewhere been deconstructed by the court as vestiges of time worn misperception and mistake.[13]

Traditional deep rooted assumptions about what marriage is for – male access to women – support otherwise constitutionally suspect practices. The CPR scheme assumes a strictly prescribed view of marriage. Take, for example, a couple who decide not to raise children, or choose to abstain from sex, or want to have separate bank accounts. Quite apart from the issue of wife battering, this is a further instance where CPR legalizing status is in danger of being withheld because the couple does not meet traditional notions of marriage.

Due Process

The standards for proving marriage viability and good faith are arguably so vague and arbitrary that they contravene the legal norm that law must be 'sufficiently explicit' so that people subject to it can understand what behavior makes them liable (*Connally* v. *General Construction Co.*, 1926).

In addition, in light of the 1994 Violent Crime Act – which purports to help battered women – the INS is arguably exceeding its constitutional authority by breaching congressional intent. If the intent of the 1994 amendment is to make less stringent the evidentiary standards for proof of battering, then the INS's different standards for married and unmarried women makes the standard even more strict for the former.

Equal Protection

The above point illuminates the INS's possible violation of congressional intent. The same charge can be made with respect to equal protection. The different standards applied to married, divorced, or separated women fail to acknowledge that the women are similarly situated regarding the issue at hand – abuse. Marital status ought to be irrelevant if the congressional intent is indeed the equal protection of women from violent men.

Limitations of a Constitutional Approach on Immigration

There is a certain futility in attempts to take on constitutional issues in areas where the court traditionally gives broad deference to Congress. Immigration is one facet of national security, foreign policy, and state sovereignty which tends to be highly resistant to change except as deemed necessary in response to a direct threat. The plight of CPRs is not an issue

with enough weight for the court to overstep its tacitly observed boundaries in the balance of power of American politics. Additionally, although
the state department and the INS acknowledge that GIs are involved in
marriage fraud, allegations of large scale military involvement in prostitution rings and marriage agencies are dismissed as hearsay. There is general
agreement that it is considered improper to investigate a GI's motive for
marriage (Cao, 1987). Furthermore, the constitutional challenge outlined
here only applies to the CPR scheme: it does nothing to challenge the mail
order bride traffic or the legitimacy of the industry itself.

Legislative Approach

One could argue that rather than challenge the CPR program as unconstitutional, the INS ought to do away with it on the basis of inefficiency.
The CPR scheme is poorly designed: it is unclear, unfair, and it does not
accomplish its stated goal of combating marriage fraud. The Select
Commission on Immigration routinely reports to the government on the
current state of immigration, providing suggestions for reform. The Select
Commission has focused extensively on fraud in the context of illegal
immigrants and employer sanctions; they have not, however, put any
emphasis on problems with the IMFA. This appears to be an area of contention only among immigrant support agencies and a few legal scholars
who have investigated the mail order bride industry.

Eddy Meng suggests that the INS should return to the pre-IMFA process
whereby alien spouses of US citizens were screened at consulate offices at
the time they filed their visa applications (Meng, 1994). There were anti-
fraud officers at all major cites for issuing visas. The interview procedure
was no different than it is under IMFA. The distinction is that if the spouse
was granted a visa, immigrant status was that of lawful permanent resident
upon arrival. The process was as effective, in terms of a fraud screen, as
the process is now under IMFA. The important point for the immigrant
women is that the previous scheme did not contain the coercive threat of
deportation. Despite the sound logic of Meng's proposal, a return to pre-
IMFA regulation is politically unlikely. The IMFA fits an agenda that benefits from publicly targeting immigrants as potential system abusers.
Immigrant women are an insufficiently mobilized political force to attract
any legislative activity on their behalf.

The International Context and Legal Response

The elaborate networks of power and ideology maintaining the mail order
bride industry work together to frustrate change: any single attempt at

stemming the traffic or criminalizing individual husbands may appear insignificant in the face of such an enormous industry (Hauge, 1995). The mail order bride industry can be seen as one window from which to observe links among race, gender, and subordination in international relations. The enormity of the issue and the fact that it is so deeply enmeshed across lines of race and sex can make efforts at change appear futile. But at the same time, these multiple points of control offer multiple points to challenge the industry. Scholars, researching the international perspective on human rights, racial and sexual justice, and North/South relations, see the mail order bride industry as one place from which to challenge existing global arrangements that encourage and maintain a business that demonstrably does harm (Bahar, 1996; Bunch, 1990; Charlesworth, Chinkin, and Wright, 1991).

International efforts at stopping the traffic in women (Barry, 1979) entail transnational coalition-building across racial, sexual and cultural lines. The problem in its entirety demands social and cultural change as well as legal attempts at reform and ultimately transformation. Economic and political development that entails education and opportunity for women could potentially change conditions enough so that women would face smaller incentives to use marriage as a way to leave their home countries (Boserup, 1970).

CONCLUSION

Widespread criticism of the forces behind the mail order trade could potentially attenuate the power of long held myths underlying the need for the 'services' of Asian women. Admittedly, the reconstruction of American men may appear to be a quixotic fantasy. There is some evidence however, that this change is underway (Brooks, 1995; Stoltenberg, 1989 and 1994). One piece of evidence of this change is the growth that the mail order bride industry has experienced in accordance with the rise of the feminist movement. As some men begin to adapt to emerging norms of shifting sexual ethics in an age when egalitarian relationships are becoming more common, other men fight back to regain 'lost' control (Minkowitz, 1995).

The angry anti-feminist rhetoric in the mail order bride promotional material evinces the success of feminism: the very fact that the men who write the advice columns feel the need to quote and rebut Robin Morgan on sexual slavery can be heralded as a triumph. Early on in the mail order bride industry, there was no perceived threat; at the same time, there was not so great a need for the service, as 40 years ago, many American men were quite happy with their American wives. As of yet, the feminist movement has changed more women than it has changed men.

The rule of law has long been integral to social change yet at the same time presents feminists with a paradox. Using the law with its inscribed male biases, in an attempt to deconstruct those very biases, does not always result in the intended effects of advancing the position of women. The goal of feminist jurisprudence is to show how the male bias allows dominance to be wielded and maintained and from this bias dismantle it. International law is concerned with interstate commerce, use of force, human rights, refugees, and delimiting the extent of state sovereignty. The mail order bride trade operates at the intersection of national and international politics and is one link in a chain of structurally embedded sexism and racism.

An analysis of domination and subordination as an explanatory paradigm of male/female relations, as well as interstate relations, is a solid platform for legal attempts to reform and transform the mail order bride trade (MacKinnon, 1987). A feminist perspective investigates the traditional ideals of freedom, equality and consent because the abstract legal concepts can leave intact the power structure which precludes women and men from being similarly situated in light of these ideals. The equality that feminism seeks to secure is not freedom to be treated without regard to sex, but freedom from systematic subordination because of sex.

NOTES

The author would like to thank Deborah Stone of the Heller School of Social Work at Brandeis University for the encouragement to pursue this project and for help on an earlier copy of the manuscript.

1. Internet searches reveal extensive information on this industry. Examples of web sites offering services or information on meeting foreign women include:

    < http://www.vix.com:80/pub/men/romance/pen.intro.htm >,
    < http://www.loveme.com >, < http://pacificcentury.com >.

2. The fraud that the help-information for men material warns of is of two sorts. First, there is the deceptive woman (who just wants a visa) and second, there is the deceptive agency (which just wants your money and won't deliver the 'goods').

3. There was a series of cases in the 1970s questioning the procedural due process requirements when aliens were being denied adjustment and/or deported. See, for example, *Bark* v. *INS*, 511 F.2d 1200 (9th Cir. 1975) and *Whetstone* v. *INS*, 561 F.2d 1303 (9th Cir. 1977). In *Chan* v. *Bell*, 464 F.Supp. 125 (D.D.C. 1978), the court held that the INS did not have the statutory authority to use the marriage viability standard in deciding status adjustment cases.

4. 8 U.S.C. §§ 1184(d), 1186a (1994).

5. I am not suggesting that those debating the law consciously formulated a way to punish vulnerable immigrants. It is possible however, that the cultural stereotypes of women as devious and manipulative are the assumptions operating behind the legislation. A close reading of the Congressional Record would provide more information: my impression from the media excerpts from the Congressional Record do support this disparate impact result as deliberate.

6. 8 U.S.C. § 1186a(c) (4) (1994).

7. Waiver applications had to be substantiated by testimony from police, judges, medical personnel, school officials, social service agency personnel; and supported by professional evaluations: the INS only recognized licensed clinical social workers, psychologists, and psychiatrists. 8 C.F.R. § 216.5(e) (3) (vii) (1997).

8. Violent Crime Control and Law Enforcement Act of 1994, Pub. L. No. 103–322, 108 Stat. 1796 (portions codified at 8 U.S.C. § 1154).

9. 8 C.F.R. §§ 216.4(a), 216.5(a)(1994).

10. For example, witness the customary female genital mutilation that takes place in much of the underdeveloped world.

11. 381 US 479 (1965).

12. 424 US 693 (1976).

13. In *Dothard* v. *Rawlinson*, for example, the Court upheld a narrow interpretation of the BFOQ exception, permitting discrimination against women by allowing maximum security prisons to refuse hiring female guards. Justice Marshall, who issued a dissenting opinion, nicely articulates a feminist sensibility. Although this is a dissent, it is still significant precedent for any Supreme Court justice to fall soundly on the feminist side of a sex discrimination controversy. Marshall disagrees with the court's 'rationale [which] regrettably perpetuates one of the most insidious of the old myths about women that women, wittingly or not, are seductive sexual objects.' *Dothard* v. *Rawlinson*, 433 US 321, 345 (Marshall, J., dissenting).

REFERENCES

Anderson, Michelle J. 'A License to Abuse: The Impact of Conditional Status on Female Immigrants'. *Yale Law Journal*, 102 (1993): 1401–30.

Anker, Deborah E. 'Determining Asylum Claims in the US: A Case Study on the Implementation of Legal Norms in an Unstructured Adjudicatory Environment'. *New York University Review of Law and Social Change*, 19 (1992): 435–528.

Bahar, Saba. 'Human Rights Are Women's Rights: Amnesty International and the Family', No. 1 (Winter 1996).

Barry, Kathleen. *Female Sexual Slavery.* Englewood Cliffs, NJ: Prentice-Hall. 1979.

Barry, Kathleen, Charlotte Bunch, and Shirley Castlely, eds. *International Feminism: Networking Against Female Sexual Slavery.* New York: International Women's Tribune Center, 1984.

Blackstone, William. 'Blackstone on Coverture'. From *Commentaries on the Laws of England 1765–69,* Book I, Ch. 15. Excerpted in Lindgren and Taub (eds.), *The Law of Sex Discrimination,* 1993.

Boserup, Ester. *Women's Role in Economic Development.* New York: St. Martin's Press, 1970.

Brooks, Gary R. *The Centerfold Syndrome: How Men Can Overcome Objectification and Achieve Intimacy with Women.* San Francisco: Jossey-Bass Publishers, 1995.

Bunch, Charlotte. 'Women's Rights as Human Rights: Toward a Re-vision of Human Rights'. *Human Rights Quarterly,* 12 (1990): 486–98.

Cao, Lan. Note, 'Illegal Traffic in Women: A Civil Rico Proposal', *Yale Law Journal,* 96 (1987).

Charlesworth, Hilary, Christine Chinkin, and Shelley Wright. 'Feminist Approaches to International Law'. *American Journal of International Law,* 85 (1991): 613–45.

Enloe, Cynthia. *Bananas, Beaches, and Bases.* Berkeley: University of California Press, 1990.

Federal News Service. 'Hearing of the Senate Judicary Committee', 28 March 1996.

Ferraro, Thomas. 'Immigrant Marriage Fraud; Alien Sham Marriages: Passports to America'. *UPI,* 4 Aug. 1986a.

——. 'Mail-Order Marriage: Marriage Agencies Legal, but There are Concerns'. *UPI,* 10 Aug. 1986b.

Hanson, Christopher. 'Mail-Order Bride Business Booms in Backlash to US Feminism'. *Reuters News European Service,* 27 April 1987.

Hauge, Carol H. 'Prostitution of Women and International Human Rights Law: Transforming Exploitation Into Equality'. *New York International Law Review,* 8 (1995): 23–50.

Joseph, Raymond. 'American Men Find Asian Brides Fill the Unliberated Bill: Mail Order Firms Help Them Look for the Ideal Women They Didn't Find at Home'. *Wall Street Journal,* 25 January 1984.

Klass, Tim. 'Mail Order Bride Business Booming Despite Seattle Courthouse Slayings'. *Los Angles Times,* 10 Sept. 1995, p. B3.

Leung, James. 'Many Mail-Order Brides Find Intimidation, Abuse: Marriages Made in China for US Citizenship'. *San Francisco Chronicle,* 4 Sept. 1990, p. A9.

MacKinnon, Katherine A. *Feminism Unmodified.* Cambridge, Mass.: Harvard University Press, 1987.

'Man Kills Pregnant Wife Before Annulment Case'. *Washington Times,* 3 March 1995, p. A9.

Meng, Eddy. 'Mail-Order Brides: Gilded Prostitution and the Legal Response'. *Michigan Journal of Law Reform,* 28 (1994): 197–248.

Minkowitz, Donna. 'In the Name of the Father', *Ms,* Nov./Dec. 1995.

Reimers, David. *Still the Golden Door: The third world Comes to America.* New York: Columbia University Press, 1992.

Richins, Nancy K. 'The Marriage Viability Requirement: Is It Viable?' *San Diego Law Review*, 18 (1980): 89–106.

Rosca, Ninotchka. 'The Philippines' Shamful Export: Emigrant Women'. *The Nation*, 17 April 1995, p. 15.

Rose, Emily. 'Adverts Selling Women Flood on to the Internet'. *The Guardian*, 13 Nov. 1995, p. 3.

Rubin, Gayle. 'The Traffic in Women: Notes on the "Political Economy" of Sex'. In Rayna R. Reiter (ed.), *Toward An Anthropology of Women*. New York: Monthly Review Press, 1975.

Schneider, Elizabeth M. 'Particularity and Generality: Challenges of Feminist Theory and Practice in Work on Woman Abuse'. *New York University Law Review*, 67 (1991): 520–68.

Stoltenberg John. *Refusing to Be a Man: Essays on Sex and Justice*. Portland: Breitenbush Books, 1989.

———. *The End of Manhood: A Book for Men of Conscience*. New York: Dutton, 1993.

8 Sri Lankan Tamil Immigrants in Toronto: Gender, Marriage Patterns, and Sexuality

Lynn Morrison, Sepali Guruge, and Kymberly A. Snarr

'Our culture is so deep, and so traditional, and so ancient, that I would feel that only another person that shares those values and has been moulded from that culture would be able to understand.'

BACKGROUND TO THE STUDY

Canada is currently home to over a hundred different linguistic and cultural groups (Guruge and Donner, 1996). In Toronto alone, there are over 80,000 Sri Lankan Tamils, and they are considered to be one of the fastest growing immigrant groups in the country (SACEM, 1994). The greatest influx of Tamils to Canada has been in the last 10–13 years during which time they arrived as refugees escaping violent civil war. These Sri Lankan Tamil refugees comprise the first generation bringing their own distinct beliefs, identity, social, and cultural practices to Toronto.

The goal of this study is to assess the changes occurring in the Sri Lankan Tamil community of Toronto since the time of their migration. Using qualitative research methodology, this study assesses changes due to a transition between two cultures and how these may affect marriage patterns, partner choices, sexuality and gender roles. With the exception of a recent and very extensive multi-phase study undertaken by Canadian researchers on HIV/AIDS which included South Asia (Adrien *et al.*, 1996), very little research to date examines specific refugee communities and their changing sexual behavior in Canada. In contrast to other studies which have amalgamated various cultural groups according to broad geographic locations resulting in generalized findings, this study focuses on a specific cultural group rendering the findings highly applicable to that community.

This study examines the transition between two cultures, that of Tamil to Canadian, and how this transition affects marriage patterns, partner choices, sexuality and gender roles. This research also explores whether these issues have changed since coming to Toronto, whether Tamils are in the midst of a cultural transition and becoming more 'Canadianized' and the conflicts these may pose. This is particularly relevant as Tamil women are moving from a highly structured patriarchal society in Sri Lanka to a country where patriarchy is a fading part of the culture.

Immigration is a very difficult and stressful event, the effects of which continue in the new country where the traditions may be in contrast to those of the home country. There was a specific focus on Tamil women in recognition of the fact that social issues encompassing women worldwide include basic inequities in familial, marital, and sexual relationships. During the course of our work in the Tamil community in Toronto, situations involving women's isolation, abuse, and suicide were serendipitously uncovered. The urgency and severity of these matters dictated its inclusion as part of the overall issue of gender and immigration.

Most of the Tamils who have come here are from the Northern or Eastern provinces of Sri Lanka or the capital city of Colombo. Sri Lanka, which was historically under colonial rule and formerly known as Ceylon, is currently home to 18 million people comprised of three major ethnic groups: Sinhalese 74 percent, Tamils 18 percent, and Muslims 7 percent. Approximately 60–70 percent of Tamils are Hindus, with the rest being Christian; whereas the majority of Sinhalese are Buddhists (Wanasundera, 1991).

For the past several centuries, there have been conflicts between the Tamils and Sinhalese. The early 1980s marked a flare-up in this long-standing conflict resulting in a civil war during which hundreds of Tamils were killed and hundreds more lost their homes and businesses. Because of this, the Canadian government made some changes in their immigration policies to accept more Tamils into Canada (Kendall, 1989). They come to Canada with a strong sense of identity which has been nurtured throughout their long history in Sri Lanka; they leave behind a cohesive community which had been further strengthened by the political and cultural strife they experienced.

STUDY DESIGN

This ethnographic study was based on key informant and in-depth interviews. Both Tamil men and women were invited to participate in order to elucidate the changing sexual and social context of their lives including issues of pre- and extra-marital sex, and love versus arranged marriages and how these may differentially affect women and men's autonomy and expectations in choosing their life partner. In consultation with several community leaders, an interview format was developed to contextualize women's lives in the Tamil community.

Sampling Design

Non-probability quota sampling was used to collect the data. This method of sampling 'approximates representative sampling without using random selection ... and ... guarantees that at least all subpopulations of interest (strata) are represented in the final sample' (Bernard, 1988). The 'subpopulations' of the Tamil-speaking Sri Lankan community in Toronto included both genders across the reproductive age groups represented in five-year increments. In addition, respondents were selected from various parts of the city of Toronto to increase representativeness and maximize variance. The data was collected during an 8-month period in 1994 and 1995. Study participants were recruited through community agencies, cooperatives, and key informants. Both Christian and Hindu Tamils participated. There were 32 interviews each approximating one to one and a half hours, and 13 key informant discussions.[1]

The data collection involved personal interviews using a semi-structured questionnaire. Most closed-ended questions were followed by open-ended questions allowing for information not otherwise preconceived by the researchers to be explored allowing for unpredicted information to be gained.

Each interview began with basic demographic information (age, sex, religion, town or city of origin, employment, marital status, and length of residence in Toronto). Respondents were then asked to describe what their life was like in Sri Lanka and how they felt it had changed since coming to Canada. There was a particular emphasis on marriage and courtship since each is guided by strong cultural tradition which may or may not be influenced by Canadian mores.

The interviews were anonymous to increase the comfort level of the respondents due to the sensitive nature of some of the questions. The interviews were conducted at locations and times that were comfortable and convenient for the respondents including: community centres, homes, or other places such as coffee shops. One of the limitations of this study is the fact that only English-speaking Tamils were interviewed. The resources were not available to employ a translator. Upon discussion with key informants regarding this issue of language barrier, they stated that unfortunately many non-English-speaking Tamils tended to be the most isolated and often did not come to the attention of community workers until a crisis had occurred. This is, therefore, an area that would require further attention by community agencies, researchers, and funding organizations.

Analysis

The nature of qualitative analysis is the search for patterns (Bernard, 1988) and a quest to understand the existence and reasons for those patterns. The answers to the open-ended questions and the discussions that evolved from them were analyzed qualitatively by systematically looking for similarities and dissimilarities among the responses (Berg, 1995). The analysis consisted of a broad coding of the data into general themes and sub-themes supported by quotes whenever possible (Berg, 1995). Particular attention was given to possible patterns in responses, primarily between genders and also between the various age groups. The length of stay in Toronto or other countries of habitation was also taken into consideration.

FINDINGS

The following is a presentation of our data which specifically examined dating and pre-marital sex, arranged versus love marriages, partner choices, extra-marital sex, and empowerment issues of women within their personal lives and relationships. It is recognized that as a newly arriving group to this country, the Tamils are exposed to many contrasting traditions, customs, values, and mores. Canada can be broadly categorized as a country in which dating and pre-marital sex are the norm. Most marriages are based on love and although extra-marital sex is not condoned, it does occur fairly often (in comparison to Sri Lankan Tamils). This first generation group was examined with a particular emphasis on whether their behaviour with regard to any of these issues has changed, and whether they are indeed in transitional flux. The overriding thrust of the study involves exploration into the level of 'Canadianization' which is defined as the process of acculturation to Canadian norms and values.

Dating and Pre-marital Sex

According to traditional Tamil Hindu and Christian social norms, a sexual relationship is reserved exclusively for married life. Therefore, pre-marital and extra-marital sex is not tolerated, and common-law relationships are not accepted (Jegatheeswaran, 1997). Dating was virtually non-existent until their exposure to Canadian norms of dating, going out, and having sex. In addition, cross-cultural dating and sexual liaisons were a significant occurrence since coming to Canada. The following quotes illustrate the varying opinions and dilemmas.

Female (mid-20s): 'Dating is frowned upon'.

Female (late 20s): 'Five percent of dating [non-Tamil] leads to marriage ... youngsters here do not have parental guidance'.

Female (mid-30s): 'some of the Tamil men if dating someone here in Canada [non-Tamil] that before marriage he may have sex but not in Sri Lanka'.

Male (mid-20s): 'Tamil people date non-Tamil because they don't have enough Tamil people'.

Male (early 30s): 'I rarely see dating a Tamil woman here [due to availability] and most Tamil women, they are with their parents, so dating is not easy'.

All of the respondents agreed that sex before marriage is not acceptable within the community, particularly for women; although there was a complacency among men having pre-marital sex. Both genders explicitly stated the importance of a woman maintaining her virginity until marriage, but there was a detectable change in attitude if a woman was to have sex while dating her eventual husband. Such changes are particularly detectable among the younger university-aged people although a gender double standard is still evident. Some of these younger-aged male respondents dated and picked up girls at bars and discos while others are using the services of commercial sex workers here in Toronto. Having pre-marital sex seemed to be more the case among those male respondents who did not have their family in Toronto which perhaps alleviated strong cultural constraints against pre-marital sex. Men, once in Canada, have far more opportunity to seek sexual partners in a milieu where there can be anonymity from the rest of the community, which is in sharp contrast to the extensive communication network found in Sri Lanka.

Key Informant (female):[2] '... usually one person from the bride-groom's family, one person from the bride's family, will go and check the sheet on the first. But now most people have changed they don't go through with all that. ... Men are also expected to be [virgins], but they are not that strict strangely with the men as with the women. The women they are very strict about, but the men, they're prepared to accept things or tolerate it. ...'

Male (early 50s): comments that a woman is expected '... to enter into marriage a virgin, families will not accept a son's wife if they know she has had sex'.

Female (mid-20s): 'It is very, very frowned upon ... sex has always been a taboo' but later stated with regards to women that '... the amounts are increasing now'. If women were found to have had pre-marital sex, it became a matter of marital negotiation since the prospective groom's family '... feel they haven't got what they bargained for ... they feel they have been cheated'.

Male (mid-20s): talking about women having sex with their boyfriends, '... I know many people [having sex] like Christian Tamils, they are very flexible, their parents are not strict. ...' He also remarked upon the availability of Tamil women '... the girls are so strict [they are not having sex]. ...' He further states that '... they [the men] go out to street bars ... or prostitutes ... if I want to find girls [non-Tamil] I have numbers. ...' In regard to shifting sexual behaviors, he commented '... some people [Tamils] are changing now, here they are becoming like Canadians, so they don't give a damn. ...'

Male (late 20s): refers to men talking about having sex before marriage, '... many of them brag a lot, mostly talk but no action'. He alludes to generational changes when questioned about sex before marriage '... [it is] not acceptable by old generation [your generation?] More acceptable, yes'.

Male (early 30s): states that '... back in Sri Lanka you were not able to do the things you are able to do here ... I could date somebody Canadian here ... and make sure no one else knows'.

He also states that the number of men having pre-marital sex is increasing as the length of residency in Toronto increases.

Male (early 30s): talks about the availability. 'I don't think people in Jaffna nor in Colombo ... have a chance. People who come to Canada ... they can go like prostitutes ... people [Tamils] are changing'.

Arranged Versus Love Marriages

According to traditional Tamil beliefs, marriage is a spiritual and unbreakable alliance which is not workable without the blessings and guidance of parents and elders (Jegatheeswaran, 1997). Marriages are arranged within the same caste and constitute, in essence, an agreement not just between two individuals but between the two respective families. Each family has certain responsibilities and obligations to ensure that the marriage thrives. Because of the extraordinary support, young people feel a sense of security in making this lifelong commitment. When a suitable candidate is found, the parents and close relatives begin a very discrete screening process through the extensive network of relatives and friends. Being of the same caste, same religion, having matching horoscopes and suitable socio-economic and educational backgrounds are all important factors in selecting a candidate. In addition, any suggestion of the potential suitor's past alliances are also investigated.

Key Informant (female): '... they check the birth time of the girl and the birth time of the boy and they will get round the horoscope. Usually when the baby is born they already draw up the horoscope. So they have matching points on horoscopes, on characteristics'.

Key Informant (female): stated that inquiries are made into the families of the potential bride and groom to investigate '... if they have been going out with somebody, what kind of life they have been leading, and economically they check to see how much they can earn, where they can support their family, live in the same lifestyle they have been used to'.

Dowries, an integral part of the marriage proposal and negotiations, are given to the groom by the girl's family and can include property, money, jewelry, and house. For example, the more educated a young man is, the greater the expected dowry will be.

Key Informant (female): '... if you want somebody with higher education you going to pay more money for it. So they demand more money, so the dowry became higher, so say if somebody wants to marry a doctor, the boy is educated, he's now a doctor, they say, okay he is educated his dowry for him should be higher, you should pay more money if you want to marry that boy'.

Traditionally, if the couple gives their consent to their respective parents, the engagement ceremony and wedding plans are discussed by the two families. It is quite common for two people to wed who have never seen each other before the wedding day. In contrast to the traditional form, a potential couple in Canada may meet before the wedding, or, at times, even before the proposal is finalized, but this usually occurs in the company of an elderly relative. Young Tamils in their twenties and thirties in Canada are now being influenced by the traditional Canadian marriage pattern which is based on love or convenience.[3]

Key Informant (female): '... now they go out... they do meet each other, they may like some-body else [other than the arranged suitor]. If they don't like it [the arranged suitor] then they can say "no, I don't want to get married"'.

Although most respondents believed in traditional arranged marriages, many voiced advantages and disadvantages of both. Our research indicated that younger men were veering away from arranged marriages after having lived away from Sri Lanka for a period of time. In contrast, female respondents felt more strongly about retaining the traditional form but did accept love marriages. Some voiced the concern that love marriages occur between inexperienced or immature individuals. All respondents, nonetheless, felt there could be problems in either type of marriage, but arranged marriages offered a tangible sense of security, family support and approval. Additionally, it alleviated the shortage of prospective Tamil brides in Canada by making arrangements with families still in Sri Lanka.

Male (early 30s): 'we as Sri Lankans are not being taught to take a woman out for a meal and to treat her nice ... and how to date her nice ... parents usually have to arrange something and then again you will be quite accepted into your own family circle and culture.'

While this respondent thought 80 percent of Tamils have arranged marriages he himself is having difficulty in finding a partner because he wants to go beyond the traditional characteristics a man looks for in a Tamil woman, such as submissiveness and acceptance of prescribed gender roles.

Female (mid-20s): '... sometimes very difficult for to find someone by themselves ... most are arranged, most of the people think of marriage relationships as commitments and these relationships last longer'.

Male (early 20s): 'most of them [Sri Lankans] are very shy and I think it would be very hard for them to find somebody right for them ... the parents will step in for them, they have no choice ... but personally I think it shouldn't be like that anyway'.

Female (mid-30s): 'I married arranged marriage because I don't want to take any risks ... but these marriages also have problems, same chance as love marriage' but about love marriages 'I don't know, they are not mature people, so they have a lot of problems after they get married and they don't have understanding [of each other]'.

A love marriage is regarded as an independent decision and contract undertaken by two individuals, not necessarily their families although their approval was sought. Therefore, any problems arising in the marriage did not constitute family involvement but was relegated to the two individuals to sort out. Conversely, some respondents felt there may be fewer problems because the partner choice was decided upon by the individuals. Love marriages implied a lack of family support for the couple and, in turn, perhaps nullified the son's obligation to help his family. Others yet felt an ambivalence regarding the whole issue of arranged versus love marriages.

Female (late 20s): 'only for enjoyment, not for long-time partner'.

Female (early 30s): 'Love marriage I would say if both parties are sensible, then that marriage is ideal, if they know each other truly, then that marriage is ideal. Instead of just infatuation or overnight love or puppy love as we call it. See him the first day, get married on the third day, and falling out on the 31st day, that's not life'.

Key Informant (female): '... even the love marriages become similar to arranged marriages, after marriage, marriage is marriage, the husband starts to control the wife and the wife becomes the regular wife'.

Partner Choice

To date, marriage partners are generally selected within the Tamil community although our research indicates that this is changing. When asked about marriage partners, both genders by and large said it would be unacceptable to marry a non-Tamil although a few males said they would consider it as an option. The female respondents generally said that it was easier to stay within the culture. Several of the men said they would preferably marry women from back home in Sri Lanka rather than ones who have been living in Canada for the last 4 to 6 years. Although none of the respondents explicitly said why they felt this way, their reasons seemed to indicate that it would be 'easier', that Tamil women from Sri Lanka would not have learned the 'western ways' or have become 'Canadianized'. They fear that such women may cause problems after they are married. This is grounded in the reality which all respondents recognized as the inherent lack of availability of young Tamil women in Canada.

Key Informant (female): 'The men feel that when the women come here and they lived here long in Canada they are beginning to get the western influence and the marriages may not last long. Or they might think that they have gone with boyfriends and girlfriends and they might have more freedom. So they like to have the girls from back home who have been brought up the traditional way, traditional outlook so they might stay home to look after the children, not go out to work'.

Male (early 30s): 'most of the people think that the girls here they change to Canadian culture, they get more freedom, these ones, so [men] get scared so [men] go back to Sri Lanka ... they [women now in Canada] know the laws very well ... they have rights and everything'.

Key Informant (female): 'They think that okay they have had their freedom so they might be sleeping with some-body else. So we don't want to get married to her, they don't know'.

When Sri Lankan men were asked about what characteristics they would look for in a potential bride, the men said that the woman had to be pretty, had to have an education that was equal to or less than theirs, and if the potential bride did work, she was not to make more money than him. When a female key informant was asked about men's expectations of their future wives' unequal financial and educational backgrounds, she replied, 'They feel that the women might dominate them if they are more educated, and they might feel inferior'.

Female (mid-20s): 'women who have been here are too strong headed and they [the men] don't like that, they want to be the boss.' 'One is the dowry thing, when they go back they aren't marrying someone for free, they are getting immense amounts and you would be surprised how much people are going to pay back home ... to get their daughters out of the country because of all the problems.' 'I know I definitely would not tolerate a lot of their [the men's] attitudes' but arranged marriages would be easier 'because our culture is so deep, and so traditional, and so ancient, that I would feel that only another person that shares those values and has been moulded from that culture would be able to understand'.

Male (mid-20s): "They don't have enough [women] ... you don't find someone" but even when men go back to Sri Lanka and bring back a woman 'Even when they come, they change, they know that there is 911 ... nobody can beat [them] ... here they have freedom'.

Another woman in her late thirties commented on the issue of marrying outside the culture that:

'... it is difficult to live with them [people from other cultures], the culture, the language, all changed'.

Male (early 30s): 'the culture is quite strong [and if] a Tamil married a Tamil, they would have moral and all the support from their parents ... as well as when you get married you get a dowry ... your house is taken care of or a brand new car' but in regards to arranged marriages 'this is the way the culture functions ... so you just take it you don't want to argue'.

Male (late 20s): 'A lot of my friends are from mixed marriages, they have good values and they are happy'.

Extra-Marital Sex

Respondents were also asked about their views and opinions regarding sex outside of marriage. Both genders stated extra-marital sex was not acceptable within the Tamil community, but numerous respondents did state that it could occur under certain conditions. These included the long-term separation of a husband and wife or dissatisfaction of the sexual relationship within the marriage. Interestingly, the female respondents had more opinions regarding sex outside of marriage. There was the mention of talk and gossip by both genders if an affair did occur thus re-enforcing the power and influence of the community. Families, especially the older generation, stand as bastions of cultural norms.

Female (mid-20s): 'After marriage if men are alone out of country or family back home, this happens mostly with the men if the parents are not in the same place'.

This sentiment was also expressed by a male in his early 50s: 'In transition, when away for long periods of time ... if the separation is long'.

Female (mid-40s): 'Probably they have more chance ... they go out and we don't know what they are doing'.

Female (early 30s): 'There are guys that travel all the way out on the pretense of having some job ... or some urgent matter ... for family purposes but they are having sex ... it even happens back home so anything is possible.

Female (early 30s): 'Depends on the situation ... the wife or the man doesn't get enough of what he wants, then he will probably sleep somewhere else ... in Toronto it's happening in a lot of Sri Lankan families now. The reason being ... the root is probably financial problem and depressions and people and families go apart and then end up in other relationships ... even in Sri Lanka it happens'.

Key Informant (female): '... men coming here alone, leaving their wife and children behind in Sri Lanka, so they go to prostitutes here and when they go back or their wives come here, they have sex with them, in case if they contract any of these STDs obviously they transmit it to their wives'.

Voices in Sexual Decision-Making

Our attempts at assessing whether a woman had any power in sexual issues were fraught with difficulties because of its very sensitive and private nature.[4] Most of the women said they find out about sex the night of their weddings. It was not a topic of discussion between mothers and daughters or with married sisters. When asked if they had a voice or were empowered in their sexual relationships, it was found that both genders had respect and consideration for their partner's needs and desires. Although the majority of male and female respondents stated that they did have the right to refuse sex, they were also very aware of satisfying their partner's sexual pleasures. The following represents the varying opinions on this subject matter:

For example, a female in her mid-twenties stated;

'I feel that I am my own person and I feel that if I don't want to do something I shouldn't be forced.'

In addition, another woman in her mid-twenties stated: 'We have the right to say no as marriage is not built on sex'. A woman in her late 30s felt that the ability to refuse sex is '... not right but understanding ... it's equal, partner'. Male (early 30s): 'in the morning ... it usually drains a lot from me, she may want to do it again, I'm physically tired so I have to satisfy her needs'.

However, this was not the case for all respondents. Female (early 30s): 'Many times I try to say no, I just don't want to have it. I try to sleep with the child, just tired'. Female (late 40s): 'I just kept quiet'.

Women, Isolation, Abuse, and Suicide

Although this topic was not a part of the original interview schedule, discussions of violence and suicide occurred spontaneously by the key informants many of whom were leaders and activists in the Tamil community. The findings, although not fully corroborated, indicate a very serious social issue deemed too important to neglect.

Informants discussed the widespread wife abuse and referred to several Tamil women who had jumped to their deaths from their apartment buildings in the winter of 1994. They felt that the isolation that many women experience when first arriving in Canada has aggravated an already existing situation of powerlessness. This isolation has been particularly acute for those women without family here to intercede on her behalf if she is being abused.

Strong community values and beliefs that were easy to impose in Sri Lanka, where everyone knows what is occurring in each other's households because of the open concept of the housing, was also highlighted by the key informants. Doors were not kept locked and people entered at will. Therefore, if something was taking place in the household that was not appropriate or acceptable that involved abuse within the family, it was not tolerated by the nearby family. In Canada, we do not have a good view into our neighbor's house, and doors and windows are kept locked. Our environment is much more exclusionary and enhances the isolation and loneliness these women feel. This is compounded by the fact that for many Tamil women, the families are still in Sri Lanka and they are initially very dependent on their husband as their only link to survival.

The poignancy of the following quotes illustrates the tragic circumstances some women are in.

Key informant (female): '... women are so completely isolated because they are economically dependent on their husbands. Women don't know their way around the city, just another form of control, virtually isolated ... women have no voice'.

Key Informant (female): 'Sometimes they [the husbands] are ill-treating some of them [the wives], that we have heard. Usually he collects the welfare, marriage, sometimes the wife does not know anything that's going on, especially if she cannot speak English, she's isolated. That's why we heard of all this suicide. Because they are cut off, they have no relatives, no one to go to. They trusted this man and they come here and then he lets them down and they have no way of doing anything. It's very sad'.

Male (early 30s): 'That's the husband. That's the reason. The husband comes and beats them. They jump from apartments, last week I think a girl jumped from the west end. I have heard of about ten cases I think in the last two or three years'.

The method of suicide, which was predominantly by jumping off the balcony, was addressed; to which the key informant stated:

'Yes, because they have no other way, they have no where to go. All they know is they [can jump] off their balcony. And it's very hard to get to them because they don't come out, they don't meet any body and we don't know that these people exist until they commit suicide'.

With regards to the occurrence of suicide in Sri Lanka, she stated:

'Sri Lanka no, it's not very common. Usually if there is any problems it's within the families, the families will get together and try to patch it up. She has support'.

Another key informant (female) stated that women who have been here a long time are beaten because the men feel women here have so much freedom and deserve the beatings. She also stated that the Sri Lankan Tamil women need to be taught to have self-respect, self-confidence, and to be strong.

A key informant (female) in the health-care sector felt very strongly about the issue of violence against women:

'I have seen it happening a lot, too much for me to handle and I do sometimes refer them to some of the centres but mostly to a women called [omitted] ... but it is still a large and unresolved issue and many of them keep coming back to me, and one or two occasions I have called in the police ... even now I have a patient that is practically forced into sex every day, the husband is punishing ... and this is the way of him punishing her until he eventually locks her out of the house, she wait in the road the whole night ...

When asked about violence and sexual abuse, one male (early 30s) respondent stated:

'Yeah, I understand that in sex both must agree, but a lot of men force ... a lot of beating is going on ... it's quite acceptable back home. The men like, mostly everybody is doing it so ... it's not a big issue. But it's going to be the generation is changing in Jaffna, they are having strict rules ...'[5]

Many abused victims suffer in silence for fear of breaking up the marriage or the threat of deportation. A husband who has sponsored his wife from a war-torn country holds untold power over that woman. Additionally, many of these women cannot access the resources available to Canadian women, assuming they are even aware of them, due to language and other personal and cultural barriers. Nevertheless, suicide seems to be one of the tragic outcomes to Tamil women's immigration experience to Canada.

DISCUSSION

The data indicates that there is a degree of change in Sri Lankan Tamils' attitude with regards to sexuality, marriage patterns, and gender role expectations since their immigration to Canada. In traditional Tamil households, any discussion of sexuality and related subjects is considered shameful and taboo (Kendall, 1989). Similarly, the findings of this study suggest that the topic of sex, if discussed at all, is discussed in extremely vague and general terms. This issue is also addressed in Singer *et al.*'s (1996) multicultural study which found that sex was not talked about between generations, contributing to misinformation and miscommunication about sex and sexuality. This emphasizes the dilemma Tamils are confronted with upon arrival in Canada which has a much more open approach to sexuality, dating, and marriages based on love. It is the high school and university-aged people in particular who are exposed and influenced on a daily basis through their new Canadian peers, school curriculum, and media.

The level of acculturation is an individual process based on numerous factors that can include family support and pressure in Canada, existence and cohesion of the community, and length of residency. These factors are not mutually exclusive but woven into a complex web. While Meston, Trapnell, and Gorzalka (1996) found that length of residency in Canada did not affect changes in the sexual behavior of Asian university students, our study does indicate a change in attitude towards the acceptance of dating and pre-marital sex and for some Tamils this is translated into behavioral changes. In fact, Tamil men perceive a change in the sexual behavior of Tamil women corresponding to the length of time they have been in Canada. Other studies have found that immigrant youth are confused by the conflicting messages and values of the new culture in Canada and their traditional heritage, leaving them feeling like they are caught between two cultures (Singer *et al.*, 1996).

Some single males may be changing their views on sexuality, while maintaining particular aspects of the traditional marriage pattern and partner choice. In many cases there is a definite preference for a bride who is still residing in Sri Lanka and has not been exposed to Canadian culture. The preference is reinforced by the fact that the overwhelming majority of single Tamils in Canada are men. Although arranged marriages were recognized as the cultural norm, there is a growing acceptance of love marriages although it has not been acted upon by the majority of Tamils to date.

In addition to changing views on sexuality and marriage, the Tamil community is facing several other challenges due to immigration including changes in gender specific roles. The Sri Lankan Tamil community is a largely male-dominated society in which males and females are socialized into very specific roles and expectations. Women in Sri Lanka are still struggling for equality and universality with regards to controlling their lives, their bodies, and their sexuality. For example, the move to change the penal code to include marital rape and sexual harassment as criminal offences was only made in 1995 (Abeyesekera, 1997).

In general, the distinct roles of 'men as head of the family' and 'women as the care givers' have been prescribed by many of Canada's immigrant groups (Singer *et al.*, 1996). Both male and female Sri Lankan Tamils experience profound role changes upon coming to Canada, including changes in the breadwinner roles and expectations that are crossing traditional gender roles. Similar patterns of change have been experienced by other immigrant groups coming from one culture into another (Gill and Matthews, 1995). Gill and Matthews state that if the changes are too rapid or drastic, it becomes very difficult for families to cope with. The research of Singer *et al.* (1996) notes that role changes create conflicts that are not easily resolved. They state that women fear violence or desertion by their husbands if they step out of their cultural role.

A previous study of Asian immigrant wives in the United States indicated that there was an expectation of a high participatory rate in the labour force by the women whose husbands had difficulties obtaining adequate employment (Stier, 1991). Similarly, it has become essential for many of the Tamil women to work outside the home although these jobs are mainly low-paying, low-status jobs. For many women from various immigrants groups, their first job in Canada may be their first paid employment (Singer *et al.*, 1996). These women are trying to maintain a balance between their traditional role expectations and Canadian life style and expectations.

Many women end up having to juggle their job and household work. Although they may tolerate this situation to maintain family harmony, this affects their health and well being and can lead to depression (Beiser, 1993). Lynam's (1985) work among immigrant women in Canada found that they needed support and felt alienated from other people or resources, particularly if close friends or family members were missing. In fact, the smaller the social network, the greater the likelihood of developing mental health problems (Mueller, 1980). This in turn increased their dependancy on their spouse adding further stress to the family situation.

As has been found among other immigrant groups to Canada, men often had to accept lower status positions with a consequent loss of income. Forfeiting a culturally-valued role may result in a loss of identity and cultural dislocation creating confusion within an individual which would also affect family dynamics and relationships (Gill and Matthews, 1995). Discrimination, loss of professional status for some and fear of being unable to provide for their family result in feelings of frustration and isolation in the immigrant men (Singer *et al.*, 1996).

One of the outcomes to the changes in gender experiences has been an increase in the reports of violence against women within the Tamil community. The exact cause of this increased violence was not investigated as it was beyond the scope of the research mandate although respondents commented on the increased tension in households due to the complex web of factors in the immigrant experience. One of the factors that the respondents eluded to involved the loss of the extended family and their involvement in each others lives. Extended family in many immigrant groups was a source of social support and social control and without it, values and behaviors have been found to change (Singer *et al.*, 1996). Loss of extended family is one among many as yet untangled contributing factors in the abuse of women.

CONCLUSIONS

This chapter is an attempt to raise consciousness and awareness of the Sri Lankan Tamils' struggle with the 'being-versus-becoming' dilemma of migrating into a new culture. The effects of immigration are felt differently by the two genders depending on their age, religion, length of residency, and presence of family in Canada. As a new immigrant group, the majority of Sri Lankan Tamils have resided in Canada for just over one decade. Our data suggests that with regards to marriage patterns and sexuality, they are in the midst of a transition and having to cope with strong external influences since coming to Canada. At this point in time it is unknown whether a full transition will be made or whether the strength of the community in Toronto will maintain traditional norms and values. It is undoubtedly a period marked by flux and anxiety. Some of the changes within this period of flux have lead to increased disempowerment, isolation, and violence against women. These are issues that women face globally.

Researchers and feminists in Canada have been voicing their concerns regarding the lack of proper attention to women's issues in this country, and as a global problem. Tamil women are at double disadvantage because women's issues are in general ignored, under-addressed, or neglected (Meleis, 1991), and secondly, because they are not Canadians. As such, not only are they hindered in accessing services, but when they do they are treated as the 'other'. Canadians, living in a multicultural society, need to increase their awareness of the issues newcomers, such as the Tamils, are confronted with when arriving to our country. It is the responsibility of the immigrants themselves, their new neighbours in Canada, as well as social service agencies, researchers, educators, policy-makers, and health-care professionals to understand and facilitate their transition.

NOTES

Acknowledgements: We would like to express our gratitude to the community workers with whom we worked closely, as well as to all the respondents who gave so freely of their time. We also wish to thank Janette Cole-Wilkin for her assistance in transcribing. Thanks as well to Dr Frances Burton and Dr Jim Flynn for their helpful comments and suggestions.

1. Many of the key informants reviewed the questionnaire to comment on the sensitivity and cultural appropriateness of the questions. Although we

received their support and encouragement, some of the key informants underestimated people's willingness to respond. The key informants were motivated to participate by what they considered to be the usefulness of the research in terms of formulating their outreach programs regarding issues that were most immediate to their community.

2. Because some of the key informants were very well known in their community, their ages were not given for the sake of anonymity.
3. This is not to imply that love marriages did not exist in Sri Lanka, but the majority of marriages are arranged with strong family involvement.
4. The conversations were short and concise and were not pursued further by the researchers out of respect for the respondents.
5. The level of violence against women that exists in Sri Lanka is unknown, but it does seem to be largely controlled by the family.

REFERENCES

Abeyesekera, Sunila. 'Abortion in Sri Lanka in the Context of Women's Human Rights'. *Reproductive Health Matters*, 8 (1997): 87–93.

Adrien, Alix, Gaston Godin, Paul Cappon, Sharon Manson Singer, Eleanor Maticka-Tindale, and Dennis Willms. 'Overview of the Canadian Study on the Determinants of Ethnoculturally Specific Behaviours Related to HIV/AIDS'. *Canadian Journal of Public Health*, 87, suppl. 1 (1996): S4–S10.

Beiser, M., P.J. Johnson, and R.J. Turner. 'Unemployment, Underemployment and Depressive Affect Among Southeast Asian Refugees'. *Psychological Medicine*, 23, no. 3 (1993): 731–43.

Berg, Bruce L. *Qualitative Research Methods for the Social Sciences*, 2nd ed. Boston, Mass.: Allyn and Bacon, 1995.

Bernard, H. Russell. *Research Methods in Cultural Anthropology*. Newbury Park, Ca.: Sage Publications, 1988.

Gill, Dhara S. and Bennett Matthews. 'Changes in the Breadwinner Role: Punjabi Families in Transition'. *Journal of Comparative Family Studies*, 26, no. 2 (summer 1995): 255–63.

Guruge, Sepali and Gail Donner. 'Transcultural Nursing in Canada'. *The Canadian Nurse*, 82, no. 8 (1996): 36–40.

Jegatheeswaran, Sivajini. Personal communication. Wellesley Hospital. March 1997.

Kenward, Wendy Lee. 'Justice for Tamil Women'. *Kinesis*, Feb. 1996, p. 6.

Kendall, P.R.W. *The Sri Lankan Tamil Community in Toronto*. City of Toronto Department of Public Health, Health Promotion and Advocacy Section. Series of Ethnocultural and *Health Profiles of Communities in Toronto* no. 6, 1989.

Lynam, Judith M. 'Support Networks Developed by Immigrant Women'. *Social Science and Medicine*, 21, no. 3 (1985): 327–33.

Meleis, Afaf I. 'Between Two Cultures: Identity, Roles and Health'. *Health Care for Women International*, 12 (1991): 365–78.

Meston, Cindy M., Paul D. Trapnell, and Boris B. Gorzalka. 'Ethnic and Gender Differences in Sexuality: Variations in Sexual Behavior Between Asian and Non-Asian University Students'. *Archives of Sexual Behavior*, 25 (1) (1996): 33–71.

Mueller, D. 'Social Networks: A Promising Direction for Research on the Relationship of the Social Environment to Psychiatric Disorder'. *Social Science and Medicine*, 14A (1980): 147–61.

SACEM. *Tamils: Ten Years that Made a Difference: 10th Anniversary Publication for the Aid of Ceylon (Sri Lankan) Minorities*. Toronto, 1994.

Singer, S.M. *et al.* 'Many Voices – Sociocultural Results of the Ethnocultural Communities Facing AIDS Study in Canada'. *Canadian Journal of Public Health*, 87, suppl. 1 (1996): S26–S32.

Stier, Haya. 'Immigrant Women Go to Work: Analysis of Immigrant Wives' Labor Supply for Six Asian Groups'. *Social Science Quarterly*, 72, no. 1 (1991): 67–82.

Wanasundera, N.P. *Cultures of the World: Sri Lanka*. New York: Marshall Cavendish Corporation, 1991.

9 Gender Implications of Immigration: the Case of Russian-Speaking Women in Israel

Larissa I. Remennick

INTRODUCTION

Gender and immigration have seldom been studied in tandem, although the experiences and challenges faced by male and female immigrants are as different as they are in other life contexts. The countries of origin and resettlement may significantly differ in the extent and forms of patriarchy and in gender roles, adding a unique facet to women's experiences of acculturation. Given that male dominance as a norm predominates throughout the world, immigrant women may face a double disadvantage as immigrants and as women on the job market and in all kinds of social and personal relations.

Some research has been done (usually as part of a broader research agenda) on male–female differences in the adaptation process, employment, mental health, social support and family patterns among Asian, African and Latin American immigrants in North America and Europe (Banchevska, 1981; Beiser and Wood, 1986; Buijs, 1993; Avison, 1995; Noh and Avison, 1996). Fewer studies have looked specifically into women's experiences of immigration and adjustment, particularly in the US and Canada (Arnopoulos, 1979; Lynam, 1985; Anderson, 1985, 1987; Schwartz Seller, 1994). Most of these studies addressed the problems faced by the women who entered host countries as 'family class' immigrants and were defined as 'dependants' of their husbands or other male relatives. Many of those women had little formal education and did not work outside of the home prior to coming to North America. Facing severe economic problems as new immigrants, many of these women had to join the labor market, typically in the lower levels of the occupational pyramid. The inferior status of those women in the labor force, where they do menial service jobs, is

163

aggravated by their subordinate status in the family. Coupled with deterioration of traditional support networks, this double disadvantage is often expressed in higher mental morbidity of female immigrants (Anderson, 1985; Beiser and Wood, 1986; Buijs, 1993).

Several qualitative studies have shown that immigrant women face more problems and barriers in their acculturation process than do their male partners. Joan M. Anderson has explored the experiences of female immigrants from Greece and India in the English-speaking region of Canada, particularly around the issues of their paid and unpaid work, perceptions of health and help seeking, and social support networks used by immigrant women. Having found the ubiquitous role of patriarchy in shaping women's lives (in its Eastern form inside the home, and Western-style male dominance in the public realm), Anderson argued that

> Women's everyday experiences … cannot be attributed solely to their 'cultural differences', but must also be understood within the context of the larger social organization and the ideological structures generated from outside of their experiences. (Anderson, 1987, p. 413)

During the late 1980s and 1990s, massive immigration from the former Eastern Bloc countries to North America, Israel and Western Europe became a prominent feature of the global political scene. So far, few studies have explored the problems of East European immigrant women in the course of their encounter with Western or westernized cultures. Their experiences are presumably quite distinct from those of third world women given their different background, particularly higher education and universal participation in the labor force in the former Soviet Union and other socialist countries. At the same time, immigrant women of any origin may experience a similar set of problems due to their downward social and occupational mobility (Segura, 1996). This chapter explores the intersection of immigration and gender as exemplified by the experiences of the former Soviet women who moved to Israel with the immigration wave of the early 1990s.

Among some 650,000 Soviet Jewish immigrants of the last wave, about 150,000 are women between the ages of 20 and 50 (*Immigrant Absorption*, 1996), that is, the period of life when economic and sexual-reproductive activities all peak and overlap. In addition to the problems of physical, psychological and social adjustment to the new environment – common for all immigrants – women face a new set of norms surrounding the issues of sexuality, child-bearing and family life (still viewed in both the former Soviet Union and Israel as primarily feminine domains). These less apparent aspects of migrant experiences are probably similar across western or westernized countries hosting Soviet and East European immigrants. This chapter aims at drawing a sketchy profile of gender-related problems experienced in public and private domains by recent female immigrants from the former Soviet Union in Israel; each of these definitely merits a separate study.

Migrant experiences in the country of resettlement are often defined in terms of continuity (or socio-cultural retention) versus change (integration or assimilation). Multinational studies in diverse immigrant communities, including those in Israel, indicate that the first generation of adult migrants largely preserve the features of culture and lifestyle of their country of origin, and real integration begins only with the second generation (Markowitz, 1992, 1993; Chiswick, 1993; Ro'i *et al.*, 1997). This observation is especially applicable to the marital, sexual and child-bearing behaviors, which may be more resistant to change than other aspects of social behavior (Peritz and Baras, 1992; Kahn, 1994; Sabatello, 1995; Remennick *et al.*, 1995; Sean-Shong Hwang and Saenz, 1997). Women from the former Soviet Union, who experienced a unique gender system of state socialism, are no exception to this rule. Before analyzing the specific problems faced in Israel by the Russian-speaking women,[1] it is necessary to provide a brief background on their life in the Soviet Union.

BACKGROUND

Until very recently, the notion of gender itself, let alone gender studies, was an alien term in the Soviet cultural thesaurus. Apart from official statistics on women's status, employment and maternity, hardly any in-depth anthropologic or psychosocial research has been done in this area by Soviet scholars. A 'woman's question' in the socialist societies was claimed to be settled once and for all, and powerholders turned a blind eye to many bitter problems experienced by women in both the domestic and public realms (Posadskaya, 1994; Buckley, 1997). In practice, Soviet-type 'emancipation and equality' meant that gender divisions ceased to exist and women were treated by the state as badly as men: doing the same hard work for equally low salaries, similarly abused by the state and party bureaucrats, getting equally miserable health care insensitive to their specific needs, and so on. Maternity-related policies, praised as an achievement of socialism (job-protected paid leave, day care facilities, etc.) reflected an economic need to keep women employed, combined with the state's interest in higher birth rates, rather than egalitarian or feminist considerations (Voronina, 1994). By way of backlash to this 'sexless equality' imposed from the state and resulting in severe exploitation of women, the advocacy of more traditional gender roles, the recognition of women's 'otherness' and specific needs gained much popularity in late Soviet years (Buckley, 1997). These moods may partly explain total unpopularity of Western-type feminism among East European women (Watson, 1997).

Despite universal access to higher education and employment, the partitions between male and female occupations in the white-collar domain were high enough (the images of female pilots, directors and diplomats promoted by the Soviet media were as fake as the rest of its imagery). As elsewhere, the feminization of certain occupational niches (such as health care and education) caused a gradual decrease in their status and prestige. Although the educational level of Soviet women was somewhat higher than that of men, their careers typically ended in the lower or middle tiers of the professional pyramid. Few political and nomenclature posts were occupied by women (usually by the virtue of token representation), but even when allowed to enter higher administrative ranks women took small part in decision-making, unless they were turned into 'men in skirts' (Voronina, 1994).

Although the notion of 'sexual harassment' was non-existent in the Soviet legal lexicon, women in lower service or clerical jobs were sometimes compelled to provide sexual services for their bosses, albeit the whole issue was carefully silenced. In the educated circles (schools, the academia, medical system, etc.), gender relations at work were usually more egalitarian and overt sexual pursuits were rather uncommon and unwelcome. This balance was abruptly changed by the advent of the private market forces during post-communist years (Khotkina, 1994).

All the above-said points to the very peculiar and controversial nature of the Soviet-type patriarchy. As was true of most other aspects of the Soviet system, a wide gap existed between the external manifestation, or the facade, of the various domains of social life and their deeper, core contents. Despite women's relative economic independence, the traditional Russian patriarchy continued to flourish under socialism, albeit in disguised and mutant forms. This was especially apparent in the realm of marriage and family life, which was far less affected by emancipatory ideas than the labor market. While being an equal breadwinner, an average Soviet woman also carried out most household and childcare chores. Yet, paradoxically enough, by virtue of this infamous double burden, Soviet women gained a lot of power in the private domain. Reflecting their continuous and harsh 'training', women generally managed better than men under tense and unstable conditions of the daily micro-economy (in 'hunting' for food and other supplies in constant shortage, for example). Additionally, women were often better oriented in the corridors of Soviet bureaucracy and took responsibility for most 'social functions' (contacts with welfare, educational, housing, medical and other authorities). Logically enough, their 'know-how' often put women in a position of an actual family head and a key decision-maker, while their male partners were rendered passive and dependent. For this reversal of gender roles in everyday life, a special Russian term has been coined – 'the infantilization of men' (Posadskaya, 1994; Kon, 1995).

Given a central role of the family as a 'shelter' from the omnipotent and intimidating system, relatively early and almost universal marriage was a typical feature of Soviet lifestyle. Many early marriages were induced by sexual urges seeking legitimation and/or by pregnancy (Maddock *et al.*, 1994; Kon, 1995). Premarital sex, always occurring but illicit and clandestine, lately became fairly common, especially in big cities. Apart from the normative constraints, an important obstacle to premarital sex was the scarcity of housing and lack of entry for unmarried couples to hotels and other facilities, seen by Soviet authorities as potentially catering to sexual needs. Unable to resist multiple internal and external pressures (low income, lack of housing, male violence and alcoholism), Soviet families were increasingly unstable, one-third typically ending in divorce. Reflecting the high divorce rate, about 18 percent of women and ten percent of men were divorced by age 40–9, excluding those remarried. Most divorces were initiated by women, whose universal employment and relative economic independence enabled them to abandon relationships they considered unsatisfactory (Kon, 1995; Borisov and Sinelnikov, 1995).

Despite their socio-economic and cultural diversity, most former Soviet people share conservative views and emotional discomfort about sexuality. For years, sex has been a taboo subject in Soviet culture, science and education; the only acceptable context for raising sex-related issues (again, with many constraints) was the medical one. As a result, most Soviets grew up ignorant of sexual matters, believing that sexuality was spontaneous and required no special knowledge or skills (Kon, 1995). An extension of these views was the lack of consistent contraceptive practice, which, juxtaposed with low fertility, resulted in the dominance of abortion as a birth control instrument. The lack of alternatives reflected the virtual absence of social policy in the area of women's health, coupled with the firm prejudice towards modern contraceptive methods shared by both doctors and women. Hence, throughout the Soviet period, women were compelled to perform repeated abortions, with severe implications for their health and well-being (Remennick, 1993).

Fertility among the urban population of the former Soviet Union was below the level needed for demographic replacement from the 1970s onwards. By the early 1990s it had dropped dramatically (in Russia to 1.3 children per woman), which is partly explained by the overall socio-economic crisis and the growing instability of marriage (Borisov and Sinelnikov, 1995). Some 15–17 percent of annual births are to unmarried mothers, which adds to the pool of one-parent families. Since single motherhood has always been common in the former Soviet Union (historically, due to wars and political purges targeted mostly at men; lately, because of frequent divorces), it has generally existed in a tolerant social climate (Borisov and Sinelnikov, 1995). Among Jewish women, the proportion of never-married was higher than in the general population (Toltz, 1995), probably reflecting higher marital assertiveness related to the above-average education of Jewish women. The number of children in Jewish families was as low as in the rest of the urban residents, or even lower (Toltz, 1995).

Due to the almost complete assimilation of the Soviet Jews (Toltz, 1995), their mentality and behavioral patterns are similar to these of general urban population (Jews were in fact the single most urbanized ethnic group in the former Soviet Union). No tangible differences exist between Jews from different parts of the country – the uniformity of Soviet socialization has been more powerful than local variations. The only distinct groups are, in fact, the Jews of European descent and those originating in the Caucasus or Central Asia. The latter group, comprising some ten percent of the Soviet Jews and about 25 percent in the last immigration wave (Immigrant Absorption, 1996), is much less educated, more patriarchal and observant of the Jewish tradition.

Gender roles and family life in the Israeli-Jewish society are markedly different. Only two-thirds of the women are employed outside the home (often part-time), and they are usually considered secondary breadwinners. Both education and income are typically higher in men, although in younger generations these gaps tend to narrow (Azmon and Israeli, 1993). Reflecting the influence of the Jewish tradition, Israeli nationalism, and demographic pressures in the Middle East region, Israeli society is family-centered and strongly encourages higher fertility, at both institutional (state agencies, social services, health care sector) and individual/normative levels. Marriage is universal and divorce rates, albeit growing, are still relatively low. The total fertility rate is among the highest in the developed world: around three children per woman, that is, more than double that in the Soviet immigrants. Out-of-wedlock births comprise less than one percent of the total (Peritz and Baras, 1992). At the same time, the secular majority of Israelis are fairly tolerant towards premarital sex and the cohabitation of young adults. Information on sex is widely available to youngsters, and the overall climate surrounding sexuality is one of acceptance.

As is often the case with new immigrants, or any newcomers in general, the sexual and reproductive conduct of former Soviet Jews, which apparently differed from the mainstream Israeli norms, became the focus of public attention. The image of a 'Russian' woman as an alien 'other', stressing her sex appeal as a threat to local male mores, and her non-familial orientations, became one of the key elements in the popular discourse on the last immigration wave. The institutional response to this challenge emerged in the form of frantic efforts to 'educate and acculturate' by means of the 'melting pot' policies applied to the earlier immigration waves. Little attempt was made to understand the culture and values of immigrants, let alone accept some of them as a potential enrichment of the local scene, that is, to 'bridge the gap from both sides' (Amir *et al.*, 1997). These feelings of the hosts are heightened by immigrants' apparent unwillingness to alter their life-style in the desired direction, seeking shelter in the strong, multifaceted Russian subculture (Zilber, 1997).

In the context of this dramatic cross-cultural encounter, the present article examines the experiences and attitudes of recent female immigrants, illustrating them with examples from our two recent studies. The first study, conducted in the Greater Tel Aviv area in 1993,[2] examined experiences and attitudes of young ex-Soviet women in the matters of marriage, fertility and birth control. Briefly, the mean age of respondents was 29, they were recruited to the study by means of 'snowballing' (that is, relying on informal social networks), and their socio-demographic background was similar to that of the new immigrant women of this age interval in general. Over one-quarter were university students. Most other women before emigration were professionals or white-collar workers. Although over 80 percent of the non-students were employed at the time of the study, only about one-quarter had a skilled job, while others held various menial jobs, often part-time. This was in line with the general employment situation among Russian immigrants in the early 1990s, whereby unemployment rates were two to three times higher among women compared with men, and only about 30 percent of those holding academic degrees worked in their field (Naveh *et al.*, 1995; *Immigrant Absorption*, 1996).

The second study (Remennick, 1997) explored health-related attitudes and behaviors relevant for the early detection of female cancers among Russian immigrants over age 35. This study included a survey in the representative national sample of 'Russian' immigrant women and in-depth interviews with women and their health care providers. The socio-economic profile of the second sample was roughly similar to the above-described, that is, most women before emigration were educated urban professionals or public servants. The employment situation and self-rated wealth in these women were even worse than in the first sample due to their older age (on the average, 49 years). Below I discuss some of the integrated findings of the two studies.

'RUSSIAN' WOMEN IN ISRAEL: FACETS OF THE PROBLEM

All immigrants of the last wave faced problems of physical, socio-cultural and occupational adjustment in the new country, where limited economic resources were strained by the mass influx of newcomers. A dramatic fall in professional, and hence socio-economic status, as compared with the country of origin, is another common immigrant problem. For women, this inevitable process has an additional gender-related aspect.

Downward Occupational Mobility

The change in social and/or occupational status, as measured by occupational retention, job quality and income, is the most common ramification of resettlement, especially under conditions of mass immigration (Flug *et al.*, 1997). Most independent immigrants, let alone refugees, undergo temporary process of marginalization in the host society, while many have slim chances to regain their former occupational status in their lifetime.[3] The extent of downward mobility is determined by demographic characteristics of immigrants (age, gender, ethnicity), their economic and personal resources at the baseline (financial capital, education, professional experience, language command) and the absorbing capacity of the host country's economy.

Social and occupational mobility have objective and subjective dimensions. Objective measures of downward mobility among immigrants include the rates of general unemployment and structural unemployment (that is, having a job unrelated to one's training and qualification), their position on the national income ladder, and various indices of affluence (house and car ownership, for example). Immigrants' subjective experiences of downward mobility are shaped by their pre-emigration occupational status and affluence, and the expectations they have developed regarding their work and income in the host country. At the same time, the perceived change in social status is influenced by comparison with members of one's reference group, that is, other immigrants in comparable circumstances. Finally, from the individual point of view, some facets of the status may be more important than others: for example, occupational retention, even in a junior position, for some people mean more than income or promotion prospects (Naveh *et al.*, 1995; Segura, 1996; Flug *et al.*, 1997).

Several studies that looked into the issues of occupational mobility among immigrant women described the experiences of the women with little formal education and low occupational aspirations (Chicana and Mexican women in California, for example – Segura, 1996). Many of these women considered themselves successful and upwardly mobile due to their modest expectations (for example, they were happy if their per hour pay was slightly above the minimum required by law), especially when they saw that other women they knew were doing worse. Little is known about the experiences of social mobility among East European immigrant women, whose prior occupational history may have created a higher level of ambitions.

Reflecting high educational level of Soviet Jewry, about 6 out of 10 recent immigrants (men and women alike) hold academic degrees, and all but few had non-manual occupations before emigration (*Immigrant Absorption*, 1996). Hence, a general problem of this immigration wave is a disparity between its educational and occupational profile and structural opportunities of the Israeli economy. The local labor market in the areas of science, technology, education, medicine, media and culture is highly saturated, and new jobs are opening very slowly. Coupled with a traditional male worker preference on the part of Israeli employers, this means that immigrant women suffer more dramatic downward occupational mobility than men. Many 'Russian' women have engineering, construction and other Soviet-type heavy industry specialities, many of which are considered non-feminine in Israel, while others are not in demand. A further common barrier is the Hebrew language, especially its professional applications, which many adult immigrants have little hope of mastering in their lifetime. Therefore, thousands of younger women engineers had to seek requalification, while older ones had to live on unemployment benefits often supplemented by part-time manual or caring work (baby-sitting or care for the elderly, for example). The latter occupation has become a 'Russian' specialty in Israel, since demand is vast and qualification and language requirements are minimal.

Another numerous and problematic group are women with language- and culture-dependent professions such as teachers, physicians, lawyers, journalists and specialists in humanities and arts. The Israeli academic and cultural market, which is very limited and based on a Hebrew-English language mix, is unable to absorb most of these women, many of whom used to be established professionals in their field. Thus, an entire layer of intellectuals have lost their professional identity (and hence much of the personal one), and have been marginalized and forced into the bottom niche of the social structure. Having to work in menial service jobs, these women face a completely different social environment from the one before emigration.

Our interviews took place within two to three years of respondents' arrival in Israel. All but few women spoke of the drop in their socio-economic condition, as measured by relative income, housing quality, type of employment, and perceived social status before and after immigration. This may partly reflect the higher-than-average socio-economic status of Jews in Soviet society, making the perceived change more dramatic. Almost one-half of respondents at the time of the interview were either unemployed or had an unskilled job. Younger women (mainly college students) told similar stories about their mothers or elder sisters.

Less than one-quarter of the women had permanent professional jobs. Salaries were universally low, around the minimum required by Israeli law. There was a clear age gradient in the way women discussed their adjust-ment in Israel and perceived prospects: younger interviewees expressed more satisfaction and optimism than older ones. Women in their forties did not expect any major improvement in their professional and social status, and many considered it hopeless even trying to regain it (especially representatives of competitive occupations or those culturally-linked – for example, physicians, economists, musicians, teachers of humanities). Respondents ascribed similar problems and moods to their male partners.

Many married women said that they received less support in their profession-oriented efforts which required a temporary loss of income (taking a refresher course or starting a job as a volunteer, for example) than they gave their husbands in similar circumstances. With younger couples, a male partner would more often encourage a woman to study, to start a new job, or to take any other step towards positive professional mobility.

Gender-related Problems

Sexual Harassment
It is difficult to provide a clear-cut description of the pre-emigration expe-rience of Russian immigrants with sexual harassment. Since Soviet society declared itself to be asexual, or sex-blind, all kinds of sexual misconduct and deviance took a clandestine form and were never brought into the open (Kon, 1995). Yet, this morbid trend was counterbalanced by the economic reality, rendering women equal, if not principal, breadwinners.

This put women in a position of power, allowing them to negotiate sexual relations and to stop unwanted sexual advances. At the same time, social stratification of the Russian-Soviet society always implied a wide cultural gap (including different norms of sexual conduct) between the educated 'intelligentsia' and the 'masses' (Shalin, 1996). In the educated circles, to which most Soviet Jews belonged, blatant expression of sexual interest in a public setting (workplace, transport, etc.) was perceived as offensive and indecent. This does not mean, of course, that dating never occurred between co-workers, or that some women did not build their careers on providing sexual favors to their bosses. Yet, overt sexual harassment in the workplace was uncommon in this social layer, at least before the advent of the free market, with its built-in disadvantage for women (Khotkina, 1994; Watson, 1997; Buckley, 1997).

Thus, it can be safely argued that most Russian Jewish immigrants were socialized in a relatively egalitarian gender culture of the Soviet intelligentsia. In Israel, all these female engineers, museum workers and musicians have suddenly found themselves in the midst of a Levantine male culture – which sees little point in restraining or disguising sexual interests, especially toward dependent and apparently helpless 'Russian' newcomers. Women with a Russian accent are often approached with sheer sexual offers – called 'sweeties' and invited for 'a cup of coffee' (a local euphemism for sex) in the street markets, public gardens or buses, in apartments they rent (by the owners), and, of course, in their new places of work. This is not to say that local women are never treated similarly, but many of them had been socialized to perceive it as a natural part of gender conduct. The term 'sexual harassment' appeared in the Israeli media and legal discourse only recently and mainly as a result of American influence. This problem has suddenly been 'discovered' by Israeli society and, as soon as it has been named, sexual harassment turned out to be very common (Hirschberg, 1995; Sawicki, 1995).

Making things worse for the ex-Soviet female immigrants, the latest Jewish emigration has coincided with an influx of illegal sex workers from Russia via international organized crime channels. The deteriorating Soviet empire has become one of the major world exporters of sex workers, and Israel is an easy target country due to its unselective immigration policy towards any holder of Jewish documents. Russian-speaking 'girls' with false Jewish papers or outdated tourist visas fill the massage parlors and nightclubs of Tel-Aviv, reinforcing prevalent stereotypes of Russian women as a whole.

On the other hand, the process of marginalization and the confusion over old versus new sexual norms, may actually lure some younger immigrants into dress code and behavior that may be interpreted by local observers as 'loose' and provocative.[4] The Israeli media has also contributed greatly to this image, publishing courtroom stories about sex trade and sex crime with many Russian names mentioned. Finally, the alleged connection with the omnipotent 'Russian mafia' completed the demonization of the newcomers. Such publicity has done a severe disservice to the vast majority of true immigrant women – Israelis with the Russian accent (Sawicki, 1995).

What aggravates this problem for 'Russians' (beside their double dependence as women and as immigrants) is their unpreparedness to face harassment and their lack of verbal and other cultural tools to resist it. They are often shocked by such attacks and lose whatever Hebrew words they might know, their silence being perceived by offenders as a sign of consent. In general, paternalistic and 'joshing' behavior towards women is common among Israeli men (or, rather, their less sophisticated majority), and in most cases it goes unopposed (Hirschberg, 1995).

Almost every other woman in our study complained of sexual harassment on the part of Israeli men on whom they were dependent via work relations or otherwise. In most cases, it was a 'mild' harassment, which, on meeting resistance, gradually ceased. But in several cases the 'obstinate' women lost their jobs, or were otherwise punished (for example, forfeit of a promised promotion or salary increase).

Street harassment has also been a permanent reality for many young women; most of our respondents had developed tools of their own to cope with it – some preferred to ignore it; others had learned from local women all kinds of repartee answers. One woman recalled how on one occasion, responding to a 'cup-of-coffee' proposal by a realty agent, she asked what made him think she was easily available. 'An experience with other "Russians"', he answered, 'that's the way you are'. The woman noted how degraded she felt, having nothing to argue in return.

In this manner, the occupational and status-related problems faced by Russian women in Israel attain clear gender aspects. Male immigrants, experiencing similar downward social mobility, are spared at least these problems. As studies in other countries suggest, job loss, lack of promotion and low job satisfaction are not the only costs of sexual harassment in the workplace. Women living under the shade of constant unwanted sexual advances may experience substantial damage to their psychological health and well-being, including such outcomes as depression, anxiety, sleep disturbance, sexual dysfunction, and other problems (Fitzgerald, 1993). The same is probably true of any victims of sexual harassment, regardless of the context in which it occurs.

Changes in Sexual Conduct

Our interviews strongly indicate an on-going change in sexual norms and behavior among younger immigrant women, especially students. Although clandestine sexual activity among Soviet adolescents and young unmarried adults always occurred, it was never regarded as legitimate by their parents and other adults, and was scarcely discussed between generations. The only accepted framework for sexuality was early marriage. Most young singles arrived with this attitude in Israel, where they became exposed to far more liberal ideas about premarital sex.

As elsewhere in the developed world, the secular majority of Israelis now marry later in life, after having completed their education and obtained stable jobs. Premarital relationships, often beginning in the final grades of high school (age 17–18), continuing through the years of mandatory army service and well into the mid- or late-20s, have become a normal feature of sexual behavior of Israeli youth. Parents of Israeli teenagers are increasingly tolerant of overnight stays in their homes by their children's boyfriends or girlfriends. After army service, many young men and women (most of whom become students) rent apartments together. Usually, cohabitating couples stay together for at least several years, if they do not eventually marry. Contraceptive means in these unions are readily available and widely used.

Soviet immigrant parents find this openness shocking, while youngsters adopt the behavioral pattern rapidly. Most younger women in our group felt very positive about this new legitimation of premarital sexuality, although some worried that it might discourage young men from marriage for a long time. 'Women still want a more stable and mutually obliging union' – commented one of the young women who had been cohabitating with her Israeli-born partner for over two years, adding that:

> Cohabitation is very comfortable for men since they get all they want from a woman – sex and services – while keeping their freedom and avoiding childcare and domestic chores for years. And a girl meanwhile is getting older, her chances of marrying diminishing. ... These 'free' relationships are also ... asymmetric, as ever for men and women.

Women in their late teens and early twenties usually did not express such concerns. Their problem was getting along with their parents, who often objected to overt cohabitation with no clear intention to marry (typically, toward boys such feelings were much weaker). Nevertheless, most women students in our group said they had a full sexual relationship with their boyfriend, and in many cases shared living quarters with him.

Most boyfriends were ex-compatriots, with whom they 'shared a common language and interests, as well as our past, whether it was good or bad', as one woman put it. A few women whose partners were Israeli-born, said that 'it was challenging, but exciting, to overcome all the differences between us'.

Most women noted that they started using contraception early in a relationship, switching over time from ad hoc methods (condoms, withdrawal) to permanent and more effective ones. Many young women in this group were taking contraceptive pills, despite lingering health fears inherited from their mothers (let me remind that, for decades, contraceptive pills were not accepted by Soviet medicine). They said that the example of their Israeli friends, and some 'Russians', had been more persuasive than parental concerns or fears in causing them to break with the age-old sexual norms. 'We have to become like our Israeli mates if we do not want to stay "backward Russians" forever. Our parents cannot understand it', – was the universal feeling, as expressed by one of the women. Few respondents below the age of 25 intended to marry soon, saying that they would like 'to live for themselves before taking over the whole set of marital and parental obligations'. This also reflects an attitudinal shift, given universal acceptance of early marriage in Soviet culture.

When married women were asked about changes in their sexual life upon migration, a recurrent theme in many cases was the growing tension between the spouses as a result of general adjustment stress and poor living conditions. In part, this reflects the fact that, due to high housing costs, many families have to share small apartments with parents or other relatives. Lack of intimacy, strained nerves and fatigue are obstacles to a fulfilling sexual life, the lack of which is, in turn, an additional source of stress.

Child-bearing Plans
As indicated above, fertility among 'Russian' immigrants is about half that of native Israeli couples. Among our respondents who had children, their average number was 1.56. A clear disparity in child-bearing plans was seen between older women (30 +), who did not intend to increase their families, and younger unweds or newly-married women who were oriented more toward the Israeli norms (2 to 3 children desired versus 1 to 2 among older women). Older women said that they could not jeopardize the quality of parental care and the educational prospects of the existing children by having another child. Many felt that three or four children (an Israeli norm) was too much for a working mother; it was a strain on the personal and material resources of the parents, often resulting in neglect of the child. Among women with one child, another common reason for not

having a second child was lack of a male partner or problems with a current relationship.

The reluctance of the 'Russians' to bear more than one or two children and their strong emphasis on the quality of their upbringing are seen by native Israelis as a reflection of parental (especially woman's) egoism in pursuit of non-familial life goals. Many Israelis fail to appreciate that a small family size is the norm in most industrial countries, and ex-Soviets belong in this sense to the rule rather than the exception. There are many jokes about 'single and priceless' 'Russian' children, surrounded by the tireless care of their mothers and grandmothers and growing up lonely individualists. Several mothers of single children in this group said that this attitude, expressed or implied by their Israeli acquaintances, provoked feelings of guilt and inferiority.

Younger women did not think about child-bearing in concrete terms: they felt that 'several kids around is great', as was 'having more brothers and sisters than we used to have as kids'. The next decade will show whether these plans will be implemented. The experience of the Soviet immigrants of the 1970s wave shows that their fertility has achieved an intermediate level between the Soviet and Israeli standards (Sabatello, 1995).

Another hot issue adding to the stigmatization of 'Russian' women is their repeated use of abortion as a birth control method.[5] Socialized in the country with easy access to abortion, viewed largely as a medical issue with few moral overtones, Russian immigrants face new legal and financial barriers to pregnancy termination. Since birth control practice has deep cultural roots and cannot change overnight, many women experience great distress having to deal with unplanned pregnancies. Overestimating the severity of the Israeli law,[6] some prefer not even to apply for an official approval of pregnancy termination and seek 'grey market' services, provided by private gynecologists (including unemployed 'Russian' doctors). In some cases, this may cause unnecessary suffering and health risks, which could be avoided by providing immigrant women with more information and family planning services. On the other hand, due to the basic discomfort about sexual issues, Russian immigrants underutilize the available counseling and aid in family planning issues. Only 20 percent of the women in our younger sample said they used Israeli family planning services at least once, while the actual need in these services is of course much higher. About 10 percent of the respondents said they knew other women who had had an illegal abortion in Israel, and about 20 percent (mostly older ones) said they would consider using such services themselves if needed. The latter finding causes particular concern, since illicit abortion services may put immigrant women at the risk of serious health complications and even death.

Single-Parent Families
Another recurrent theme in our interviews with divorced women having children (13 percent in the first study sample) was tacit disapproval of divorcees and an explicit definition of single mothers as 'social cases', in the institutional context and everyday communications alike. Divorce rates in Israel, albeit growing, still are among the lowest in the developed world. This reflects, along with legal constraints and economic dependence of women, a strong cultural norm to preserve marital ties at whatever personal cost. Frequent divorces and the high prevalence of single motherhood among the new immigrants (certainly exacerbated by emigration) are frowned upon by most Israelis, which further impedes these women in their pursuit of social integration. More than once divorced mothers in our sample encountered tacit disapproval on the part of immigration officials, social and welfare workers, school teachers of their children, and other representatives of the establishment, including hints that they were a burden on Israeli society. 'They see divorce as a woman's caprice, or her inability to adjust to men, to sacrifice her own wishes and ambitions for the sake of the family and children', commented one woman. 'They think we are all welfare cases, living on account of "good taxpayers," while this is not true for me and many others. We make our living ourselves like anyone else, and provide for all the needs of our children', said another single mother.

Altogether, the apparent differences between immigrant and host cultures in marital and child-bearing conduct create a serious locus of tension in immigrant women's lives. This is especially true when immigrants are aware of being permanently observed and judged by the veteran majority and representatives of the state bodies.

Health Problems
Downward socio-economic mobility and marginalization of the immigrant women cause changes in their health-related behavior. Our recently completed study in the national sample of 'Russian' women over age 35 (Remennick, 1997) has strongly indicated that health issues occupy a low place in women's personal agenda loaded with more immediate 'survival' problems – employment, financial insecurity, housing, family relations, children's adjustment, etc. As was the case in their pre-emigration lives, all working age women in our study carried the double burden of income-raising and home-making. On top of it, women tended to most of the resettlement-related chores (bureaucratic and monetary arrangements, housing search, etc.) in their families. Many women said this was a necessity because they had better social skills, somewhat better Hebrew command

and were generally more successful in 'public relations' than their male partners, if any. Physical and mental exhaustion were often a result of these hectic activities, leaving little room for preventive health motivation and self-care. In many women, the chronic stress found its expression in various psychosomatic complaints – fatigue, headaches, sleep and mood disturbances, lower back and bone pains, and other typical symptoms for which conventional biomedicine has no answer.

Middle-aged and especially retired immigrant women tend to under-utilize available health care resources,[7] especially in preventive matters, and postpone medical consultations until disease has advanced too far. They receive little preventive gynecological care, precisely in the age of the growing risks of female cancers, which partly reflects their reluctance to visit male gynecologists.[8] Other cultural barriers to health care use include poor Hebrew command, bureaucratic red tape in the health sector, lack of information about their rights as clients and perceived unfriendliness of the Israeli medical providers towards 'Russian' immigrants. Low level of social integration coupled with the above-described immigrant 'syndrome' of time pressures, limited personal resources and the lack of self-care motivation also result in retention of the pre-emigration life habits (high-fat diet, lack of exercise, smoking), which further augment health risks in the 'Russian' community.

Thus, the general marginality of immigrant women and their inability to navigate the male-dominated Israeli medical system may result in higher health risks and unrelieved suffering experienced by recent female immigrants. Indeed, the available survey data suggest that the morbidity levels among Soviet immigrants, including heart disease, hypertension, diabetes and some other common chronic conditions is higher than in indigenous Israelis while the utilization of the related health services is lower (Rennert, 1994; Nirel *et al.*, 1996).

CONCLUSION

The scope of this chapter permits only a brief and simplistic description of the principal gender-related problems experienced by ex-Soviet immigrant women in their encounter with Israeli society. The 'snapshot' format did not permit me to include more extensive interview quotes, depriving this human discourse of its flavor and individuality. The study could be further enriched by discussing gender-related experiences of other East European female immigrants. However, they are a small and widely dispersed minority in the recent immigration wave, and hence not readily accessible. Quite possibly, no major difference in feminine experiences between the two groups would have emerged, given similar socio-economic and cultural definitions of gender roles in the Eastern Bloc as a whole, and common acculturation problems in Israel.

The cultural conflict between the immigrants and the host society has many facets, and its gender aspect permeates them all. The marginalization of thousands of professionals compelled to make a living by unskilled labor has especially dramatic implications for women, since their downward mobility means not only low wages and poor working conditions, but also sexual harassment by male employers and co-workers. As was shown above, deterioration of health status and diminishing motivation for self-care comprise yet another, less apparent, aspect of women's immigration experience. The discomfort and tension experienced by immigrant women in the male-dominated Western medical systems is one of the universal findings in the studies among immigrant women, regardless of their ethnic origin (Anderson, 1985, 1987).

Since gender roles and sexual conduct exhibit remarkable cultural stability, immigrants' age is a key determinant of conversion to new norms. Younger women (usually those between the ages of 20 and 35) find it easier to accept the ways of the host society and to adopt them over time. In Israel, they master Hebrew faster, have wider contacts with local women via studies and work, and switch to new life habits during their first years in the country. This is especially apparent in the adoption of overt premarital sexual relations and cohabitation, protected by efficient contraceptive use. Conversely, older women are often isolated within the immigrant community, which precludes them from social learning and 'diversification' of their identity and life habits.

The countries which host large groups of immigrants tend to focus much attention on the sexual and reproductive conduct of the newcomers, often perceived as a threat to the mainstream norms and causing 'moral panic'. In Israel, these issues gain a special public emphasis because of the core existential values (demographic, ethnic, geopolitical) associated with them (Amir *et al.*, 1997). The last wave of Soviet immigrants, seen as a 'critical mass' because of its size and cultural impact on the Israeli society, poses a special challenge in that respect. The stereotyping of the 'loose sexual mores' of Russian-speaking women by the Israeli 'street' was caused both by actual marginalization of the young immigrants and by confusing them with Russian-speaking sex workers. Constant presence in the Hebrew-language media of the topics like 'Russian' prostitution, abortion, divorce and single motherhood made severe disservice to the majority of immigrant women. The apparent disparity between family and child-bearing patterns in immigrants and the Israeli majority caused ex-Soviet women to be labeled selfish and individualistic. The mainstream society has shown little tolerance towards such differences, let alone readiness to accept them.[9]

Instead, the emphasis is made on 'absorption', 'education', turning 'them' into 'us'. Israeli proselytism, both institutional and popular, leads many immigrants, who cherish their individuality, 'to close the door' to any local influence. This adds to the isolation of the 'Russian' community, perpetuating the vicious circle of 'cultural disengagement'.

Regretfully, recent attempt of political organization in the Israeli Russian community included too few women to make their voice heard. Both Russian/Soviet and Israeli political cultures are based on male dominance, and these two forces combined to keep women from the positions of power in the recently formed Israeli 'Russian party' ('Israel be-Aliyah'). For several reasons related to their past, former Soviet women, on their part, have retained a strong prejudice against political activism (Posadskaya, 1994; Watson, 1997). Men and women who lived under socialism, with its virtual absence of civil society, also lack the experience of creating voluntary associations on the basis of common interests and problems. Russian immigrants in the post-Soviet diaspora are as atomized and disorganized in Israel and in America as they were in Moscow, Leningrad or Kiev (Markowitz, 1993a, 1993b; Gold, 1997). Hence, it is sad but not surprising that, so far, 'women with the Russian accent' have made little collective effort to resist the negative stereotyping they are subjected to by the Israeli institutions and the media.[10]

In sum, the picture I tried to draw in this chapter points to the need to pay more attention, both in research and in various institutional contexts, to specific feminine aspects of immigrants' social integration. The question remains how unique are the described problems faced by Russian immigrant women in Israel, compared to America, Germany, and other host countries. My guess is that the problems are similar, but in Israel they are magnified and heightened by the scope of the last immigration wave and its potential impact on the Israeli society. Yet, different national contexts may shape different expressions of this cultural conflict around the issues of gender, sexuality and womanhood. The available studies on Soviet and post-Soviet immigrants in North America provide us with few clues because none of them, in my knowledge, looked specifically into women's issues (Markowitz, 1993a; Gold, 1997).

In any case, greater tolerance to cross-cultural differences in gender roles on the part of the mainstream society could strongly mitigate the problems experienced by women in the new country. Many pitfalls in communications between the newcomers and the hosts could be ameliorated by just know-ing more about one another. Being a dependent minority, immigrants are compelled to learn much and fast about the ways of the new country in order to survive, while the hosts are not similarly motivated to understand the immigrants. Creating more opportunities for personal acquaintance between immigrants and indigenous Israelis could substantially facilitate this process.

NOTES

1. 'Russian-speaking' is used throughout this article as a synonym of 'former Soviet' since language rather than ethnicity is the main unifying ground of the immigrants from the former Soviet Union.

2. For the detailed methodology and results of this study see L. Remennick *et al.*, 1995. 'Family Planning Practices and Attitudes Among Former Soviet New Immigrant Women in Israel'. *Social Science and Medicine* 41 (4): 569–77.

3. Of course, some immigrants experience upward social and occupational mobility in the new country, especially when they left their motherland young, before having achieved high socio-professional status.

4. For years deprived of fashionable clothes and cosmetics in their pre-emigration lives, some immigrant women tend to fall for a cheap glitter (the only one they can afford) in their clothes and overuse make-up, thus rein-forcing the image of 'looseness'.

5. It is estimated that Jewish Soviet women had much lower abortion rates than the rest of the female population in the former Soviet Union, presumably due to their higher educational level and better access to quality health services. Yet the estimated rate of about 2.2 abortions per lifetime among Soviet Jewish women is more than three times that of Israeli-born women (Sabatello, 1995).

6. The Israeli abortion law, which emerged in the late 1970s as a political compromise between the religious and the secular forces, postulates four grounds for pregnancy termination. They include the woman's age (below 17 or above 40), illegal nature of the pregnancy (incest, rape, pre- or extra-marital), threat to a woman's somatic or mental health, and suspected deformity of the fetus. In practice, though, many hospital-based abortion committees treat these regulations quite liberally, and approval is granted to over 90 percent of applicants.

7. All Israeli citizens, including new immigrants, have access to health care, including the main preventive procedures (Pap tests for early detection of cervical cancer, mammography), although a co-payment is required in some cases.

8. In the former Soviet Union, most gynecologists were women. Preventive gynecological care (annual breast examinations and Pap-tests) was an

integral part of Soviet medicine, and most women were subject to mandatory health screening via their workplace or local clinics.

9. Interestingly, while disapproving of small number of children and single mothers among the 'Russians', most Israelis are unaware of the fact that these demographic characteristics are typical rather than deviant in the post-industrial world. High fertility and strong family orientations are unique features of the Israeli culture.

10. Few initial steps in this direction have recently been taken by the Zionist forum of the ex-Soviet Jewry, which publicized its campaign for the 'improvement of the public image of Russian immigrant women', along with the training courses in 'social leadership' for these women. Many Russian women, though, scorned this campaign, arguing that the stance of self-defense ('we are not prostitutes and welfare cases!') is even more humiliating.

REFERENCES

Amir, D., Y. Elimelech and L. Remennick. 1997. The Israeli 'Melting Pot' and the Politics of Sexuality: The Case of Russian Immigrant Women. In Y. Ro'i *et al.* (eds), *Russian Jews on Three Continents*. London: Frank Cass.

Anderson, J.M. 1985. Perspectives on the health of immigrant women: A feminist analysis. *Advances in Nursing Science*, 8 (1): 61–76.

——. 1987. Migration and Health: Perspectives on Immigrant Women. *Sociology of Health and Illness*, 9 (4): 410–38.

Arnopoulos, S. 1979. *Problems of Immigrant Women in the Canadian Labour Force*. Ottawa: Canadian Advisory Council on the Status of Women.

Avison, W.R. 1995. Roles and Resources: The Effects of Work and Family Context on Women's Psychosocial Resources and Psychological Distress. In J.R. Greenley (ed.), *Research in Community and Mental Health*. Greenwich, CT: JAI Press.

Azmon, Y. and D.N. Izraeli (eds). 1993. *Women in Israel. Studies of Israeli Society, Volume VI*. (Series published by the Israel Sociological Society.) New Brunswick, NJ and London: Transaction Publishers.

Banchevska, R. 1981. Uprooting and Settling: The Transplanted Family. In D. Schwartz (ed.), *Strangers in the World*. Bern, Switzerland: Hans Huber.

Beiser, M. and M. Wood. 1986. *Canadian Task Force on Mental Health Issues Affecting Immigrants and Refugees: Review of the Literature on Migrant Mental Health*. Ottawa: Health & Welfare Canada.

Borisov, V.A. and A.B. Sinelnikov. 1995. *Marriage and Fertility in Russia: The Demographic Analysis*. Moscow: Institute of Family Studies. (Russian).

Buijs, G. 1993. *Migrant Women: Crossing Boundaries and Changing Identities*. Oxford, Providence: Berg.

Chiswick, B.R. 1993. Soviet Jews in the United States: An Analysis of Their Linguistic and Economic Adjustment. *International Migration Review*, 27 (102): 260–87.

Fitzgerald, L.F. 1993. Sexual Harassment: Violence against Women in the Workplace. *American Psychologist*, 48 (10): 1070–6.

Flug, K., N. Kaliner-Kasir, and O. Gur. 1997. The Absorption of Soviet Immigrants into the Labour Market: Aspects of Occupational Substitution and Retention. In *Russian Jews on Three Continents*. London: Frank Cass.

Gold, S.J. 1997. Community Formation among Jews from the former Soviet Union in the US. In *Russian Jews on Three Continents*. London: Frank Cass.

Hirschberg, P. 1995. A Blind Eye to Sexual Harassment. *The Jerusalem Report*, Jan. 26.

Immigrant Absorption: Situation, Challenges and Goals. 1996. Jerusalem: Government of Israel, Ministry of Immigrant Absorption.

Kahn, J.R. 1994. Immigrant and Native Fertility During the 1980s: Adaptation and Expectations for the Future. *International Migration Review*, 28 (3): 501–19.

Khotkina, Z. 1994. Women in the Labor Market: Yesterday, Today and Tomorrow. In A. Posadskaya (ed.), *Women in Russia: A New Era in Russian Feminism*, New York, London: Verso.

Kon, I.S. 1995. *The Sexual Revolution in Russia. From the Age of the Czars to Today*, New York: Free Press.

Lynam, M.J. 1985. Social Support Networks Developed by Immigrant Women. *Social Science and Medicine*, 21 (3): 327–33.

Maddock, J.W., M.J. Hogan, *et al.* (eds). 1994. *Families Before and After Perestroika*, New York: Guildford Press.

Markowitz, F. 1992. *A Community in Spite of Itself. Soviet Emigres in New York. Washington*, DC: The Smithsonian Institute Press.

——. 1993a. *A Community in Spite of Itself. Soviet Emigrés in New York. Washington*, DC: The Smithsonian Institute Press.

——. 1993b. Israelis with a Russian Accent. *Jewish Journal of Sociology*, 35: 97–114.

Naveh, G., G. Noam, and E. Benita. 1995. *The Employment and Economic Situation of Immigrants from the Former Soviet Union: Selected Findings from a National Employment Survey*. Jerusalem: JDC-Brookdale Institute of Gerontology and Human Development.

Nirel, N., B. Rosen, R. Gross, *et al.* 1996. *Immigrants from the Former Soviet Union in the Health System: Selected findings from National Surveys*. Jerusalem: JDC-Brookdale Institute of gerontology and Human Development (Hebrew).

Noh, S. and W.R. Avison. 1996. Asian Immigrants and the Stress Process: A Study of Koreans in Canada. *Journal of Health and Social Behavior*, 37 (2): 192–206.

Peritz, E. and M. Baras (eds). 1992. *Studies of Fertility in Israel*. Jerusalem: The Hebrew University (Institute of Contemporary Jewry).

Posadskaya A. (ed.). 1994. *Women in Russia: A New Era in Russian Feminism*. New York, London: Verso.

Remennick, L.I. 1993. Patterns of Birth Control. In I. Kon and J. Riordan (eds), *Sex and Russian Society*. London: Pluto.

Remennick, L., D. Amir, *et al.* 1995. Family Planning Practices and Attitudes among Former Soviet New Immigrant Women in Israel. *Social Science and Medicine*, 41 (4): 569–77.

Remennick, L.I. 1997. *Patterns of Risk and Preventive Behaviors Associated with Female Reproductive Cancers Among Recent Immigrants from the Former Soviet Union in Israel*. Scientific Report to Israeli Cancer Association.

Rennert, Gad. 1994. Implications of Russian Immigration on Mortality Patterns in Israel. *International Journal of Epidemiology*, 23 (4): 751–6.

Ro'i, Y., N. Levin-Epstein, *et al.* (eds). 1997. *Russian Jews on Three Continents*. London: Frank Cass.

Sabatello, E. F. 1995. Continuity and Change in Reproductive and Abortion Patterns of Soviet Immigrants in Israel. *Social Science and Medicine,* 40 (1): 117–24.

Sawicki, T. 1995. The Russian Nightmare. *The Jerusalem Report,* Jan. 26.

Schwartz Seller, M. 1994. *Immigrant Women,* 2nd ed. Albany: State University of New York Press.

Sean-Shong Hwang and R. Saenz. 1997. Fertility of Chinese Immigrants in the US: Testing a Fertility Emancipation Hypothesis. *Journal of Marriage and the Family,* 59 (February): 50–61.

Segura, D.A. 1996. Chicana and Mexican Immigrant Women at Work: the Impact of Class, Race, and Gender on Occupational Mobility. In E. Ngan-Ling Chow, D. Wilkinson, and M. Baca Zinn, (eds), *Race, Class, and Gender: Common Bonds, Different Voices.* London: Sage.

Shalin, D.N. 1996. Intellectual Culture. In D. Shalin (ed.), *Russian Culture at the Crossroads. Paradoxes of Postcommunist Consciousness.* Boulder, CO: Westview Press.

Toltz, M. 1995. Trends in Soviet Jewish Demography Since the Second World War. In Y. Ro'i (ed.), *Jews and Jewish Life in Russia and the Soviet Union.* London: Frank Cass.

Voronina, O. 1994. The Mythology of Women's Emancipation in the USSR as the Foundation for a Policy of Discrimination. In A. Posadskaya (ed.), *Women in Russia: A New Era in Russian Feminism.* London: Verso.

Watson, P. 1997. (Anti)feminism After Communism. In A. Oakley and J. Mitchell (eds.), *Who's Afraid of Feminism?* London: Penguin.

Zilber, C. 1997. Little Russia in Israel. *Yediot Aharonot,* June 1 (Hebrew).

10 Social Services for Immigrant Women in European Nations; Including Lessons from the Council of Europe's Project on Human Dignity and Social Exclusion

Brigitte H. Bechtold and
Ludmila Dziewięcka-Bokun

INTRODUCTION

In Europe, immigrant women and their children face varying legal situations and economic experiences by nation and region of settlement. Their economic well-being depends on a multitude of overlapping influences, including the length of time that immigrants and their descendants have spent in the host nation, the legal system and how it applies to women in general, the availability of social services, the host nation's economic situation, as well as differences in treatment under existing legislation both in the country itself and in supra-national organizations. As far as the last influence is concerned, special attention must be given to the European Union's efforts to create the required environment for the creation of the European Monetary Union, as regulated by the Treaties of Maastricht (1991) and Dublin (1996), which on the one hand leads to reinforcement of 'Fortress Europe' with respect to immigrants and asylum seekers, and on the other imposes requirements of austerity in public finance and, hence, a cutback in social services and access to these services by immigrants and their families.

We will begin our analysis with an overview of European immigration patterns and compare the demographic profile of immigrant women with those of the receiver nations. We then turn our attention to general factors affecting the economic status of female immigrants in the traditional and the new receiving countries of Europe, including the approaches taken to women's rights and relevant regulations imposed by the European Community that affect women migrants. The factors studied include different patterns in nations' approach to assimilation of immigrants, the degree to which countries and regions have been committed to the formation of welfare states, the letter and the spirit of women's equality under the law, and the influence of supra-national organizations.

In the next part of the paper, we describe the influence of European integration and the move to the common currency, which is rather directly reducing the generosity of social protection programs. We also address the potential importance of the Council of Europe's Project on Human Dignity and Social Exclusion to gather data on social well-being of Europeans in terms of access to health, education and pensions. The main lesson of this data gathering effort is that immigrant women are to a large extent still invisible in official statistics, and the importance of targeted surveys of immigrants' experience and access to social life is becoming more and more apparent. Our conclusions are summarized in the final section and deal primarily with the need to maintain social services for immigrant women in the face of demands for austerity in the provision of social services imposed by the European Union's efforts to establish the EMU.

POSTWAR IMMIGRATION PATTERNS

European migration is not a new phenomenon. It has been an established part of the social history of Europe, practiced by members of all social groups, by women and men (Jackson and Moch, 1996, p. 55). In the current century, migration patterns must be viewed in light of a dramatic decline in the natural growth rates of Europe's population, especially in the post-World War II period. Table 10.1 presents the current rate of natural population increase and the net migration rate of selected countries.[1] The sum of the two last columns, when positive, indicates a rising population. Several nations have negative natural population growth. Overall population growth is negative in 12 nations, of which 11 are in Eastern Europe (p. 9). For the majority of European nations, overall population growth rates are low, between zero and 10 percent. Natural rates of increase are generally either decelerating or even negative, with the latter heavily concentrated in the former socialist countries of Eastern Europe (p. 11). Even in Turkey, whose population exhibits the largest natural

Table 10.1   Changes in Europe's population[1] (selected countries, 1995)

Country or region	Population (thousands) (*Jan. 1996*)	Natural increase (%)	Migration rate (%)
Belgium	10,143 (+)	0.01	0.21
France	58,265 (+)	0.34	0.08
Germany	81,539[4] (+)	−0.14	0.39[5]
FRG[2]	66,007[4] (+)	−0.04	0.43[5]
GDR[3]	15,531[4] (−)	−0.66[5]	0.23[5]
Italy	57,333 (+)	−0.05	0.16
Luxembourg	413 (+)	0.04	1.12
Netherlands	15,494 (+)	0.35	0.01
Sweden	8,838 (+)	0.11	0.14
United Kingdom	58,334 (+)	0.21[5]	0.14
Bulgaria	8,385 (−)	na	−0.51
Czech Republic	10,321 (−)	−0.21	0.10
Poland	38,609 (+)	0.12	−0.05
Romania	22,656 (−)	−0.16	−0.09
Russian Federation	147,976 (−)	−0.57	0.34
Turkey	62,171 (+)	1.58	0.14

Notes and Sources:
[1]Data are summarized from the Council of Europe (1996). Rates of change are for 1995. The level of the population is for January, 1996. In parentheses, we indicate whether the population as a whole is rising (+) or declining (−).
[2]FRG denotes the Federal Republic of Germany, before reunification.
[3]GDR denotes the German Democratic Republic, before reunification.
[4]Data are for 1995.
[5]Data are for 1994.

population growth rate, a marked deceleration is taking place. Indeed, the rate decreased from 1.62 percent to 1.58 percent in just the last year. Even migration has slowed in 1995, and migration to the popular receiving nations in northern and western Europe is in decline. The feared large waves of immigrants from Eastern Europe have not materialized, notwithstanding refugees from the war zones of Bosnia and Chechnya. Nevertheless, western Europe's immigrant population can only be considered as large. Indeed, Schnapper (1994, p. 127) reports that, in the 30 years following 1945, as many as 30 million persons, corresponding to eight percent of the population, became permanent residents of western Europe. To this must be added the large number of persons who, though born elsewhere, are automatic recipients of rights to nationality in some nations. More than three fourths of the 14.8 million non-national residents in the

EU's member states (up from 12.8 in 1987) resided in three receiving countries, notably 5.9 million in Germany, 3.6 million in France and two million in the United Kingdom.[2] However, these three countries have very different public policy approaches to the immigrant population.[3]

Some detail of women's migration patterns compared with those of men within the European Union (EU) is displayed in Table 10.2.[4] With few exceptions, women comprise less than half of the non-national populations, and the male/female gap is generally larger for immigrants originating in non-EU countries (Eurostat, 1995, p. 31) and it is the greatest in France (Delacourt and Zighera, 1992, p. 134). A large concentration of Asian and African immigrant women, respectively, in the United Kingdom and in France largely results from these countries' colonial histories (Eurostat, 1995, p. 32). Overall, women still immigrate most often because of reunification of families, rather than on their own accord. With the exception of Luxembourg, where they comprise more than a third of the active female labor force, foreign women's labor averages only seven percent of female labor market participation, with much stronger than average participation in Denmark, Germany, Spain, Ireland and Greece (Delacourt and Zighera, 1992, pp. 138–9). Generally, foreign men also hold the relatively better jobs in industry and the distributive trades,[5] with women heavily represented in domestic services. This all demonstrates the slow rate at which women are achieving equality in European labor markets and society, where traditionally males have encountered relative ease of access to labor markets in receiving countries, whereas these labor markets were

Table 10.2   Female and male non-nationals in the European Union[1]
(percent of the country's total population, 1992)

Country	From other EU		From outside EU	
	Men	*Women*	*Men*	*Women*
EU	1.7	1.4	3.4	2.8
Belgium	6.1	5.0	4.0	3.3
Germany	2.2	1.6	6.4	4.6
France	2.5	2.1	4.7	3.4
Italy	0.2	0.2	0.9	0.6
Luxembourg	29.5	27.7	3.5	3.4
Netherlands	1.1	1.0	4.3	3.3
United Kingdom	1.4	1.4	2.0	2.2

[1]Compiled from Eurostat, 1995, p. 30. Data are for 1992, or latest available.

closed to immigrant women, and sometimes even to women nationals. Of course, an equally enormous obstacle may have be the traditional society of the country of origin. Either way, they are vulnerable as a social group and are largely dependent on their male relatives for access to support, including social services. Even where social benefits are granted on the basis of entitlements other than the person's employment, entitlement may be linked to a person's legal right to be in a country, a right that may disappear when an employed spouse leaves.

EUROPEAN-WIDE AND NATIONAL RIGHTS OF IMMIGRANT WOMEN

Supra-national legislation concerning basic human rights and social entitlements, to the extent that it exists, provides some protection for immigrant women. More extensive protection is provided by national legislation specifically geared to women's rights. We will look at each of these in turn.

In western Europe, a supra-national system of human rights was forged in the years following the end of World War II. It began with the European Convention of Human Rights and Fundamental Freedoms, passed by the Council of Europe in 1950 but ratified as late as 1974 by France (Therborn, 1995, p. 100). Contrary to the UN Declaration of Human Rights of 1948, the Convention had judicial power, in the form of the European Court of Human Rights (1959). Furthermore, the seventh section of the so-called Helsinki Declaration of 1975 outlined fundamental human freedoms to be respected in east-European nations within the borders set up at Yalta. Thus, freedom of belief/religion, thought and conscience was provided, albeit in a declaration that was not enforceable (p. 101).

Immigration patterns described above show that the postwar immigration waves took place in a social environment that was still characterized by patriarchy in family life and in labor markets. For example, on the eve of World War II, it was legal in almost every European country to fire a woman upon marriage. Therborn (p. 105) describes several types of patriarchy that were legally practiced in European nations in the early decades of the twentieth century. Among these, traditional church law was especially dominant in Albania, Bulgaria, Greece and Russia, although patriarchal views also dominated in the Protestant nations of the Netherlands, Switzerland and Germany. Secular law in France, Belgium, Italy, Luxembourg, Romania and Spain was dominated by the Napoleonic Code of 1804, under which the husband had the power to govern the family (p. 106). Therborn reports (p. 109) that, '[t]he French High Court of

Appeal (Cour de Cassation) upheld in 1962 the right of a husband to prohibit his wife to practise a profession, and denied in 1969 the right of the wife of an adulterous husband, a wife who had been denied a divorce, to set up a separate domicile'. Similarly, in Belgium during the 1960s, it was possible for a husband to divorce an adulterous wife, while a wife could only sue for divorce on grounds of adultery, if she could prove that her husband had committed adultery in the conjugal bed! Legal rights of wives were achieved in three 'waves' according to Therborn (p. 108). A first group of countries, including Scandinavia and the USSR, granted legal equality of husband and wife by 1929. This group also included the United Kingdom, one of the major immigrant recipient countries. By 1950, the remaining central and east European countries granted legal equality, followed in 1959 by the Federal Republic of Germany, whose new constitution included an equal rights clause and a Constitutional Court (p. 108). In 1959, this Court struck down the *Stichentscheid principle* of family law (which granted the decisive vote in family matters to the husband) as unconstitutional. Other important immigrant receiving countries (Belgium, France, the Netherlands) granted legal equality relatively late, by 1975 and 1985 (p. 108). For immigrant women, protection under legal equality legislation thus generally came late in the major countries of immigration.

Eastern Europe Before the Fall of Communism

The orthodox Marxist feminist view has consistently been that oppression of women is a byproduct of the patriarchal capitalist system, so that its replacement by socialism or ultimately communism, will automatically liberate women together with male workers.[6] However, radical and socialist feminism has argued convincingly, and the experiences of women in socialist nations have shown abundantly, that patriarchy flourishes in many alternative economic environments. Thus, socialism imposed on the women the familiar multiple burdens also found in the United States and other capitalist nations.

Until 1990, and varying from country to country, some 60 to 90 percent of women were employed and their share of the total labor force ranged from a low of 36 percent in Romania to a high of 48 percent in Czechoslovakia. Across the board, women were better educated than men, and female college enrollment ranged from 40 percent in Czechoslovakia to 58 percent in Bulgaria (Dornberg, 1995, p. 76).

Women did not merely yield to economic pressure to help cover basic living costs. They enjoyed being in the public sphere, and 40 percent of women stated they would not quit their jobs even if their families could get by with one paycheck (Dziewięcka-Bokun, 1996, p. 51). Men and women did not seem bothered by the fact that women were not receiving equal pay and were rarely in positions of administration or managerial status, even in female dominated professions like education and health care where women constituted 96 percent of the entry level college students (From Plan to Market, p. 72); moreover, women still were paid less than men, and jobs were still gender-defined. In Czechoslovakia, for example, one man in four with a university degree but only one woman in 30 with a degree was an executive or in a managerial job (Dornberg, 1995, p. 76). Although the laws of all the countries prescribed equal pay and equal opportunity of job placement, they were not complied with. In Czechoslovakia in 1990, women's average pay was 29 percent lower than that of men (p. 76). In Hungary, although women accounted for 42 percent of the total labor force, men outnumbered women in the better paying skilled jobs nearly four to one (p. 76).

Discrimination against women was also typical in social life, as demonstrated by the automatic arrest of any single women found in the company of a man in Romanian hotel rooms, by the lack of availability of birth control and sex education, and the resultant use of abortion as a method of birth control in those countries where it was legal.

After the Fall of Communism

Women's emancipation was not a priority compared to democratization, although economic transition affects women differently than men. Under the socialist regime, women were expected to work full time, but the state provided day care and health care. Now, women are no longer seen as having social duty to work, but reform has also brought a dramatic decline in affordable child care facilities and deterioration in health care systems, and even maternity leave is threatened. Working mothers cannot keep their jobs without such facilities, but the government budget is too strapped to take over providing these services.

Women are the biggest losers in other ways as well. There was practically unanimity on this assessment among twelve central and eastern European research correspondents of the Council of Europe during the October 1996 workshop held in Wrocław (Poland). Women's pensions are practically fixed incomes that have not kept pace with rising prices. The Czech Republic has a divorce rate of around 30 percent (Dornberg, 1995, p. 77). In state-owned companies, it was practice to garner a husband's wages if he failed to pay alimony or child support, but this is no longer being done. And there is as yet no welfare system to help divorced mothers if ex-husbands and fathers do not pay. According to Navarová (1990), women under communism gained and under capitalism retained the 'privilege' of two full-time jobs: one in the company, the other at home. Discrimination in employment and pay has continued following the collapse of communism. An alarming trend is that women constitute almost half of the employed (49.6 percent), but only four percent of new job entrants are women (Sztanderska, 1994, p. 5). Women's political representation in central and eastern Europe has not improved either following 1990; if anything, it has been reduced. After the fall of the socialist regime, women's participation in politics and their participation in parliament decreased by 25 to 30 percent (Funk and Mueller, 1993, p. 12). Women occupied 24 percent of the Czech parliament before the 'velvet revolution' but today account for only seven percent of the representatives in the Czech National Council (Dornberg, 1995, p. 77). Poland had a woman prime minister, Hanna Suchocka, for about one year, and another woman, Hanna Gronkiewicz-Waltz, is president of the National Bank of Poland, a position that makes her one of the country's most powerful and influential figures. But every other Central and East European cabinet in the mid-1990s had at most one woman-tokenism as bad as or worse than under communism.

Since indigenous women in the economies of central and eastern Europe are not seeing an improvement in their legal and social status after the fall of communism, immigrant women can hardly be expected to fare better. They too are caught in the spiral of an ideology that favors their domesticity, discrimination in labor markets, and reduction in state-provided social services.

Eastern Europe: Social Services for Women

Political and economic rebuilding in central and eastern Europe since 1989 has not yet been accompanied by any coherent vision of social services development. Citizens' needs and expectations concerning social services stand in sharp contrast to the increasing financial constraints and fiscal crises, as well as prohibitive costs for ordinary citizens if social services were to be financed through the private sector (Pestoff, 1994). The new political environments combine strong confidence in market forces, shown by post-communist neo-liberals with a lasting societal belief that the state should secure and take care of the social security and standard of living of the individual, including adequate housing, day-care for children, medical care and access to vacation sites. Under the 'old' regimes, full employment guaranteed that such services were available to everyone, although at various levels and of different quality. The 1990s have thus far witnessed a significant deterioration of already inadequate social services, and subsidies for purchases of basic goods and services or certain social insurance benefits are gradually replaced by very targeted social welfare schemes.

The present political climate discourages display of interest in social policy, since it is associated with the policies of the former regime. 'Stressing social policy topics means risking being labeled as "leftist" or "old timer", thus threatening any prospect for a political career' (Laczko, 1993, p. 100). It means that the poor or vulnerable, the non-unionized unemployed and immigrants increasingly find themselves without political champions.

The problems are exacerbated by the absence of a tradition of self-help organisations and independent voluntary non-profit sector, as well as the absence of a 'donation culture'. In some countries, the church plays a significant role in the provision of social welfare services. Since Catholicism is associated with reactionary social policies, this trend too is likely to create serious social problems for a government to resolve. The Roman Catholic church in Poland seeks to reclaim property and ideological authority with the goal of regaining its prominent position in society, rather than to ease the path of post-socialist evolution. An additional influence of the Church comes from conservative arguments that communism destroyed the traditional family by allowing women to enter the labor force at the same rates as men. A just society, it is argued, requires that women stay at home with family and men go out to earn money. Nowhere in eastern Europe has such a position been translated to state policy; their economies still need female labor power, and there is no tendency by employers to pay higher 'family wages' to male workers.

It is obvious that social services systems in post-socialist Europe are subject to changes in access patterns, and there a need the development of an information infrastructure of the state, scope and quality of social services provided. Such information would include legal frameworks and institutional networks for immigrants. Knowing what is possible to get and what is impossible would help regulate the immigrant situation in each individual country. When there is little political interest in solving social problems of the country citizens, however, there is even less interest in looking for solutions to problems faced by the immigrant population.

POSITIVE AND NEGATIVE IMPACT OF THE COUNCIL OF EUROPE

The Council's Resolutions Favoring Immigrants

Since the 1960s, the Council of Europe's Committee of Ministers[7] has passed a number of resolutions and recommendations that extend social services to immigrant workers and their families, regardless of nationality status. The progression in these resolutions reflects actual migration patterns, with the earlier ones focusing on the male immigrant as the employed worker, while wives and children are considered as dependents, and the more recent resolutions in which women immigrants are focused on as workers as well. While the resolutions do not carry the weight of binding legislation, they bring to bear pressure on national governments to abide by them.

Extensive social services for migrant workers and their families were advocated in recommendation R(68)2, with a general guideline that social services available to nationals should be extended to migrants, language instruction should be provided, and the reunification of immigrant families in the receiving state should be encouraged. A specific recommendation to improve the population's attitudes towards immigrants in receiving countries was also included (Council of Europe, 1994, pp. 22–3). Thus, the focus was on integration. In a later resolution, the Council urged measures to enhance assimilation of immigrants in the firms where they work R(69)9, including union membership and benefits such as access to low-cost housing, crèches[8] and community centers (pp. 41–2). In 1970, the Council urged that social services for migrants must include extensive access to education for their children, including special courses to hasten integration, language classes, and even the opportunity of completing a portion of this education in the country of origin free of cost (p. 70). Social integration was again the focal point of recommendation R(88)6, when juvenile delinquency among migrant families, and among second-generation migrants was addressed with a recommendation that states act in a manner to foster the social integration of these juveniles (p. 243). Non-discriminatory treatment in housing and equal access to rental dwellings and home ownership was the focus of R(88)14, and R(90)14 recommended the preparation of information brochures on social rights and obligations of migrant workers and their families, extending the group of potential recipients of this information to include 'refugees and stateless persons' (pp. 250, 264).

Three general observations can be made regarding the work of the Council of Europe. First, the recommendations may foster strong social services for migrants and their families, often with special additional services to promote integration into the home country and to counteract discrimination. Second, special attention is given to increasing tolerance thresholds of the indigenous populations. As a result of these two aspects, it is now possible in Belgium, for example, to have one's vacant real estate in a non-urban area confiscated (for compensation) to provide housing to immigrants.

Unfortunately, the reality of immigrant life in most receiving nations is still characterized by discrimination and less than equal access to social services. Even where national law reflects the Council of Europe's recommendations, immigrants have access only to inferior housing.[9] Promises of access to language instruction and crèches often turn out to be just that, with immigrant women and children appearing on long waiting lists of social services that are available in name only.

Third, while the Council of Europe's recommendations do not single out women, or specifically state that women immigrants are never themselves workers, they assume that females among the immigrant population are the dependents of male migrant workers and that adult females and children usually follow these males to the receiving country after some period of time has elapsed.

There are two main counterpoints to the Council of Europe's beneficial impact on immigrants' access to social services. The Schengen agreements of 1985 and 1990 have effectively battened down the hatches of the European fortress, while the efforts to establish the requirements to a common currency in the European Union are giving rise to increasing austerity measures, most of which come at the expense of reduction in social services, including those provided to immigrants. We will briefly consider the implications of each of these policies.

The Schengen Agreements: A Closer Watch on Immigrants

In post-war Europe, inter-country agreements to allow free movement of persons go back to a Benelux agreement of 1960 that eliminated internal passport controls for these three nations,[10] as well as the Nordic Passport Control Agreement forged in 1957 between four Scandinavian countries (Hoogenboom, 1992). Free movement of persons was also part of the European Economic Area Agreement (EEA), signed by 19 countries in 1992 in Oporto Portugal (Blanchet, 1994), and it was central in the EC Treaty, article 3(c) of which articulates the community goal of free movement of persons (de Zwaan, 1993, p. 335), and of the Maastricht Treaty of 1993, although it is yet to materialize as a reality in the xenophobic human environment of the 1990s. Prior to the Treaty, the Schengen Agreement[11] was signed in 1985, and was operationalized in the Schengen Convention of 1990.

Basically, the agreement allows free movement of persons *within* the area, while simultaneously strengthening border controls at the *external* borders, a policy consistent with the fear of new waves of immigrants from central and eastern Europe, as well as from war-stricken zones.[12] Free movement implies the right to reside or to work in the area. Right to residence is not equivalent to rights of free movement. It applies to students and persons who are no longer employed. Although the agreement specifies that the right to free movement extends to spouses and children, women immigrants tend to be disadvantaged, because their free movement is often dependent on that of their employed spouse (Hoogenboom, 1992). Four main policies make up the detail of the agreement, namely (a) abolition of checks at internal borders, (b) policing and security measures, (c) the Schengen information gathering network and (d) protection of personal data (Boeles, 1993 and de Zwaan, 1993). For the time being, however, there are still border checks, and they tend to be tougher for immigrants than in earlier years. At the external borders, an additional restriction appears in the form of fixed opening hours. Aliens must not only possess a valid visa or residence permit but must be able to prove adequacy of financial resources to support the stay. Aliens who are not welcome in one country are automatically refused entry to all other countries in the agreement. Moreover, carriers (for example, airlines) can be held financially responsible for transporting illegal aliens, and the first Schengen institution to become operative was *Europol*, the common police force. Progress to free movement of persons is thus still a utopia.

Moving to the Euro: At the Expense of Immigrants?

In their open letter of 12 June 1997, addressed to the leaders of the member states of the European Union, a group of European economists described the economies of the 15 member states as characterized by poverty, unemployment, social exclusion and environmental crisis. The European Monetary Union, to go into effect at the end of the century, requires adherence to several convergence criteria. They are by now familiar criteria in economic circles and include caps on government budget deficits, inflation and interest rates. Even taken by themselves, these criteria have been criticized by many economists as not having the requisite effect on growth, employment and price stability. However, viewed in the social sphere, they are disastrous given the economic situation in the member countries. Austerity in government spending automatically translates in a reduction in social programs. In Germany, the austerity measures were the reason for the general demonstrations by workers in Bonn during June 1996. As the letter's authors state, the Euro is equated with 'austerity policies and social suffering. It is high time that politicians realise: the peoples of Europe have the right to an economy that serves the interest of human beings' (Reuten *et al.*, 1997). Similar concerns were raised by the social scientists who were the signatories of the European Statement on Poverty, published in March 1997.

The message of these concerns is simple. Instead of focusing on integration based on emphasis on traditional macroeconomic variables such as exchange rates, government deficits, inflation rates and so on, government policymakers must begin to shift their focus to variables that express the state of human beings living in their societies. Macroeconomic variables, by their very design, measure only the economic activity of those parts of the economy that reflect the dominant groups. Accordingly, poverty, lack of access to social services, and the increasing marginalization of groups such as immigrants and asylum seekers, is often not at the forefront of policymakers' concerns.

THE NEED FOR TARGETED SURVEYS ON IMMIGRANTS' ACCESS TO SOCIAL LIFE

The Human Dignity and Social Exclusion Project

The Human Dignity and Social Exclusion (HDSE) project was initiated in 1994 by the Council of Europe as a two-year survey research effort (1995–7) to discover levels and trends in poverty and social exclusion, the connections between exclusion and human and social rights, and concrete principles and standards for action in the 36-plus countries of the Council of Europe. As director of research Katherine Duffy (1996, p. 3) pointed out, 'the HDSE project can be a central part of a process of providing a coherent European perspective on poverty and social exclusion and the consequences for policy and action'.

The HDSE project reveals immigrants as one of the most socially ignored groups, mainly because it provides very limited information on immigrants' living and working conditions and does not specify any women and/or children related issues. One reason for it is the absence of immigrants from official statistics, population censuses, household surveys, etc. which mostly use the sampling method based on a selection of respondents from a pool of people who have an official address, a dwelling, which very often is not the case with immigrants. Until recently, immigration has been almost unknown as a social problem in Central and Eastern Europe, and no specific effort has been made thus far to collect comprehensive data for this population sub-group. The concomitant lack of data on women immigrants and social services provided to meet their basic needs is indicative of the intention of authorities to measure social progress only in terms of the improvement of their countries' citizens. What's more, absence of specific questions and related answers in the HDSE concerning women immigrants' situation combined with more detailed information on women as a group more affected by the transition processes allow us to assume that immigrant women are being marginalized more frequently than others. The social and economic position of a significant part of immigrant women tends to make them almost entirely dependent on their husbands, fathers or men, unless they try to cope on their own as singles or single mothers. The paradox consists of the very fact, discussed by the HDSE project research correspondents, that immigrant women are the major supplier of household services. This would mean that they are forced to take a bigger burden than men.

The HDSE project does give some limited information on immigrants in Central and Eastern Europe. Notably, in Romania, data was unavailable for 90 percent of the survey questions. The most striking feature of this project is that it used citizenship as the criterion for coverage and that, consequently, only a few of the multitude of questions appeared concerning the situation of immigrants, and none specifically concerned women immigrants. Questions focused on the following areas: education, employment (including employment of foreigners and child labor), social protection, health care, and homelessness.

According to the HDSE survey, immigrants' health status is not worse than that of the indigenous population. Only in Hungary is their health perceived as significantly worse than that of Hungarians. However, in Estonia, Hungary, Latvia, and Poland, access to and utilization of health care services by immigrants is described as much inferior to the rest of society. In the long run, therefore, the Hungarian immigrants case may become the norm for all of Central and Eastern Europe.

Non-nationals are entitled to minimum incomes granted by the state only in the Czech Republic, Estonia, Latvia, Lithuania, and Romania. In the field of education, the HDSE survey questionnaire contained one question, 'What is the law concerning compulsory school attendance in cases where the parents are illegally resident in the country?' Children and adolescents are prohibited from attending school in Hungary, Slovak Republic, and Poland. In Albania and Estonia, there is compulsory attendance for those children and adolescents. They are allowed to attend school in Czech Republic, Latvia, Lithuania, and Slovenia.

Case Studies on Immigrant Women in Individual Receiving Nations

Migrant women are generally in a more vulnerable position than men because the legality of their stay in the receiving country is more often than not linked to that of their spouses.[13] For those migrant women who are independent, income, employment and housing requirements that need to be met for residence requirements are typically generated from male wage earners' experiences, making it very difficult for these women to meet them (Boyd, 1995, p. 93). Access to social programs, where available, is not without penalty. Migrants can benefit from social programs without jeopardising their residence rights in some countries (for example, Sweden), but not in others (United Kingdom and Germany).[14] Problems of 'measurability' abound when trying to assess the ways in which existing laws and practices discriminate against women immigrants (Tapinos, 1995, p. 101). In France, for example, priority cards for immigration were refused to foreign women who were either pregnant or were mothers of young children (p. 101). Even when one studies the exact letter of such applicable regulations, the exact same rule may have different meaning in different countries (p. 102).

In France, the integration of female Algerian immigrants into French society is characterized by a combination of traditional integration in the domestic sphere, combined with employment in the public sphere (Boulahbel-Vollac, 1995). Algerian women combine traditional sex roles in their marriage with informal economic activities and utilization of available social services in such a way that their knowledge of the receiving country's institutions is fostered and integration into the receiving country's society is accelerated (p. 116). Integration of immigrant women from north Africa (Morocco) and Turkey into social life in the Netherlands was addressed by Schoorl (1995). Most of these women have experienced an apparent improvement in economic position relative to their country of origin. Those who are employed are so mostly in full-time jobs. Although immigrant women are still subject to traditions in the domestic sphere, they have lowered fertility rates compared to their home countries. This changeover to smaller family size and increased female independence is slow, however, as many women enter the country only after they already have born several children (Schoorl, 1995, p. 150).

Germany presents a unique case. The Federal Republic of Germany has traditionally viewed its immigrants as guestworkers who would eventually leave the country. Of course, this policy wish has not quite materialized, although it has added to tensions relative to the rather large contingent of immigrants from Turkey and other areas. Now, East Germans must be integrated into the new Germany. This integration is not automatic, and there is still a discriminatory *Wessie* and *Ossie* distinction, with the latter category denoting the less sophisticated, less industrialized, more primitive citizen. Of all eastern bloc countries, the GDR was by far the nation that provided the most extensive social protection to women, including single women. For example, a single mother could receive up to three years of paid maternity leave under socialism. Furthermore, from their fifth month of pregnancy, prospective single mothers were able to enter public housing in which services were provided to them at no charge. In addition to having lost access to these privileges, women from the former GDR now face the added problem of almost being outsiders in the German system of social protection. There are, of course, showcases of women starting businesses in the western part of Germany, and even women who have become ministers in parliament, for example, the minister of social affairs in the State of Brandenburg. These triumphs come at a cost, however. Whenever a woman enters the cabinet, she may not be free to act out policies if she also sees a need to keep an official party policy. Regardless of the single cases of immigrant women involved, overall the 'immigrants' from east to west Germany will live in an unequal position for some years to come.

CONCLUSION

Free movement of persons and equal access to social services in the European community has been a consistent part of the rhetoric of social and economic integration. Through the talks, agreements and recommendations, the recognition surfaced that a democratic society cannot stop immigration and that coordination of immigration policies is needed. Unfortunately, the combination of feared waves of immigrants accompanying the move to free markets without a state network of social protection in the post-socialist nations, government austerity plans fostered by the drive to the *Euro*, the increased flow of refugees and asylum seekers resulting from armed conflicts, and, finally, the lack of adequate data on the needs of immigrants, especially women, have served to push attention to social services of immigrant families to the fringes of consciousness.

These problems are more critical in the post-socialist nations than in western Europe. So far, Ringen (1993, p. 10) writes, 'there has been much destruction but less creation'. Post-socialist governments and societies must look towards a new, more active role for social services, contributing more not only in supporting economic development and restructuring but also in ensuring that sustainable social progress is also made.

Immigrants in all post-socialist countries do not know where, when, and in which form to obtain assistance. Offices that could supply information to potentially needy persons proved to be completely incapable of managing this task. The HDSE revealed a serious information gap in the areas of labor markets, housing, education, health, and social security for both the indigenous and the immigrant population. Undeveloped information infrastructure can be seen as another cause making migrants more and more marginal in the labour market and in society. 'Social centers', possibly staffed in part by volunteer workers, are sorely needed to handle the increasing number of immigrants in difficult circumstances who require urgent help.

The information gap obvious in the HDSE and in official statistics of the European area in general is partly filled by surveys targeting specific immigrant populations. However, these are not sufficiently comprehensive, and a Europe-wide survey of marginalized groups such as immigrant women is sorely needed. Fortunately, this need is beginning to surface, since '[a]s the migration process unfolds, female migration sheds its induced or subordinate nature to become a critical element in the dynamics of [European] integration' (Tapinos, p. 115).

NOTES

1.   The data in Tables 10.1 and 10.2 are derived from the Council of Europe's *Recent Demographic Developments in Europe* (1996). As of June, 1996, the Council's member countries numbered 39, including the fifteen members of the European Union, and the nations of central and eastern Europe, including Bulgaria, Hungary, Poland, Romania, and the Russian Federation, as well as several other nations.
2.   See Eurostat, 1995, p. 30.
3.   The high percentage of foreign nationals in Luxembourg, and to a lesser extent in Belgium, is due to the status of these countries in EU governance, and requires no special attention in this chapter.

4. The European Community comprised 12 nations in 1992 and 15 nations in 1997.
5. Delacourt and Zigheri report (p. 140) that the United Kingdom employs nearly 25 percent of foreign female workers in the industrial sector. Elsewhere, the percentage averages ten percent. In another exception, Greece has more foreign females than males employed as non-manual workers in the distributive trades (p. 140).
6. This view is summarized in Yedlin (p. 10).
7. The Council of Europe includes ministers from more nations than the exact number comprised in the European Union. In fact, at present, representative ministers from the Russian Federation have a seat on the Council.
8. Crèches are daycare facilities, often provided with government funding, for infants and small children who have not yet reached kindergarten age.
9. This is the case, for example, in several of Brussels' neighborhoods, where cramped substandard housing is 'designated' for immigrants (Kesteloot, 1995) and in large towns in Germany (Van Weesep, 1995).
10. The Benelux consists of the nations Belgium, Netherlands and Luxembourg.
11. So named after the town of Schengen in Luxembourg, where the agreement was signed. As of today, ten member countries of the European Union have signed the agreement. They are the five original members (Benelux, France and Germany), augmented by Austria, Greece, Italy, Portugal, and Spain.
12. In fact, the agreement could rightly be called a *Schanken* agreement, the German word for gates at railroad crossings.
13. This pattern is changing more and more. In Italy, a country that has changed its status from a sending country to a receiving country, Filipino immigrant women are generally employed as domestic servants (Barsotti and Lecchini, 1995).
14. Boyd (1995, p. 93) reports that, in the United Kingdom, the Secretary of State's decision to allow a wife and her children to accompany her spouse includes her 'ability … to maintain herself and children or to be maintained by relatives or friends without charge to public funds, not merely for a short period but for the foreseeable future'. In Germany, an alien can be expelled if he/she requires social assistance for longer than a transitory period (p. 93).

REFERENCES

Barsotti, Odo and Laura Lecchini. 1995. The experience of Filipino female migrants in Italy, in *International Migration Policies and the Status of Female Migrants* (Proceedings of the United Nations Expert Group Meeting on International Migration Policies and the Status of Female Migrants, San Miniato, Italy, 28–31 March 1990). New York: United Nations (ST/ESA/SER R/126).

Bergmann, A., ed. 1926. *Internationales Ehe- und Kindschaftsrecht*. 2 volumes. Berlin: Verlag des Reichsbundes der Standesambten Deutschlands.

Blanchet, T., *et al.* 1994. *The Agreement on the European Economic Area: A Guide to the Free Movement of Goods and Competition Rules*. Oxford: Clarendon Press.

Boeles, P. 1993. Data Exchange, Privacy and Legal Protection, Especially Regarding Aliens, in *Free Movement of Persons in Europe*: *Legal Problems and Experiences*, H.G. Schermers *et al.*, eds. Dordrecht, Netherlands: Martinus Nijhoff.

Boulahbel-Villac, Yeza. 1995. The Integration of Algerian Women in France: A Compromise Between Tradition and Modernity, in *International Migration Policies and the Status of Female Migrants* (Proceedings of the United Nations Expert Group Meeting on International Migration Policies and the Status of Female Migrants, San Miniato, Italy, 28–31 March 1990). New York: United Nations (ST/ESA/SER R/126).

Boyd, Monica. 1995. Migration Regulations and Sex Selective Outcomes in Developed Countries, in *International Migration Policies and the Status of Female Migrants* (Proceedings of the United Nations Expert Group Meeting on International Migration Policies and the Status of Female Migrants, San Miniato, Italy, 28–31 March 1990). New York: United Nations (ST/ESA/SER R/126).

Brinton, W. 1990. The Helsinki Final Act and Other International Convenants Supporting Freedom and Human Rights, in W. Brinton and A. Rinzler, eds., *Without Force or Lies*. San Francisco, CA: Mercury House.

Commission of the European Communities, Directorate General V: Employment, Social Affairs and Industrial Relations. 1993. *Social Services and Social Exclusion*: *Report of the European Community Observations on National Policies to Combat Social Exclusion*, G. Room *et al.*, eds. Lille, France: European Economic Interest Group.

Council of Europe. 1994. *Texts Drawn up by the Council of Europe in the Field of Poverty and Social Exclusion*: *Resolutions and Recommendations of the Committee of Ministers*. Publication CDOS III.5 (94) 4. Strasbourg: Council of Europe Publishing Office.

———.1996. *Recent Demographic Developments in Europe*. Strasbourg: Council of Europe Publishing Office.

Delacourt, M.-L. and J.A. Zighera. 1992. *Women in the European Community*. Luxembourg: Office for Official Publications of the European Communities (Eurostat).

Dornberg, John. 1995. *Central and Eastern Europe*. Phoenix, AZ: Oryx Press.

Duffy, Katherine. 1996. *Human Dignity and Social Exclusion*: *Report to the Council of Europe*. Strasbourg: Council of Europe Publishing Office.

Dziewięcka-Bokun, Ludmila. 1996. *Human Dignity and Social Exclusion – Poland. Report to the Council of Europe*. Wrocław, Poland. Mimeograph.

Einhorn, Barbara. 1993. *Cinderella Goes to the Market*. London: Verso.

Esping-Andersen, Gøsta. 1990. *The Three Worlds of Welfare Capitalism* Cambridge: Polity Press.

European Statement on Poverty. 1997. Bristol, UK: University of Bristol, School for Policy Studies.

Eurostat. 1995. *Women and Men in the European Union*: *A Statistical Portrait*. Luxembourg: Office for Official Publications of the European Communities.

Flora, P., ed. 1983. *State, Economy, and Society in Western Europe, 1815–1975*. Frankfurt: Campus. (Has data on higher education comparisons in Western Europe.)

Funk, Nanette, and M. Mueller. 1993. *Gender Politics and Post-Communism*. New York: Routledge.

Ganghofer, R., ed. 1992. *Le droit de famille en Europe*. Strasburg: Presses Universitaires de Strasburg.

Helsinki Declaration. 1992. Chapter 4 in *Human Rights and International Law*. Strasbourg.

Hoogenboom, T. 1992. Free Movement of non-EC Nationals: Schengen and Beyond, in H. Meijers *et al.*, eds., *Schengen: Internationalization of central chapters of the law on aliens, refugees, privacy, security and the police*. Leiden, Netherlands: Stichting NJCM-Boekerij.

Human Development Report – Poland '95. 1996. Warsaw: UNDP.

Husbands, R. 1992. Sexual Harassment Law in Employment: An International Perspective. *International Labour Review*, 131 (6): 540–9.

International Labour Office. 1993. *International Survey of Social Services*. Geneva: ILO.

Jackson, James, Jr. and Leslie Page Moch. 1996. Migration and the Social History of Modern Europe, in *European Migrants: Global and Local Perspectives*, Dirk Hoerder and Leslie Page Moch, eds. Boston: Northeastern University Press, pp. 52–69.

Kesteloot, C. 1995. The Creation of Socio-spatial Marginalisation in Brussels: A Tale of Flexibility, Geographic Competition and Guestworker Neighbourhoods, in *Europe at the Margins: New Mosaics of Inequality*, C. Hadjimichalis and D. Sadler, eds. New York: Wiley.

Kirk, M. *et al.*, eds. 1975. *Law and Fertility in Europe*. 2 vols. Dolhain: Ordina.

Laczko, F. 1993. Social Policy and the Third Sector in East-Central Europe, in *Societies in Transition: East-Central Europe Today*, vol. 1., S. Ringen and C. Wallace, eds. Prague: CEU.

Mazey, S. 1988. European Community Action on Behalf of Women: The Limits of Legislation, *Journal of Common Market studies*, 27 (1).

Navarová, Hana. 1990. *What did Socialism Give to Women?* Mimeograph.

Nee, V. and D. Stark, eds. 1990. *Remaking the Economic Institutions of Socialism: China and Eastern Europe*. Stanford: Stanford University Press.

Peschar, J., ed. 1990. *Social Reproduction in Eastern and Western Europe*. Nijmegen: Institute for Applied Social Sciences.

Pestoff, V.A. 1994. Institutional Changes in Basic Social Welfare Services in Central and East Europe – an overview. Krakow, Poland: unpublished conference paper.

Pugliese, Enrico. 1995. New Integrational Migrations in the 'European Fortress', in *Europe at the Margins: New Mosaics of Inequality*, Costis Hadjimichalis and D. Sadler, eds. New York: Wiley.

Reuten, Geert, *et al.* 1997. *Open Letter to the Heads of Government of the 15 Member States of the European Union*. Amsterdam, Netherlands: University of Amsterdam.

Ringen, Stein. 1993. *Democracy, Science, and the Civic Spirit: An Inaugural Lecture*. Oxford: Clarendon Press; New York: Oxford University Press.

Schmidt, F. 1978. Discrimination Because of Sex, in Schmidt, F., ed., *Discrimination and Employment: A Study of Six Countries by the Comparative Labour Law Group*. Stockholm: Almqvist & Wicksell.

Schnapper, Dominique. 1994. The Debate on Immigration and the Crisis of National Identity. *West European politics*, 17 (2): 127–39.

Schoorl, Jeannette J. 1995. Comparing the Position of Moroccan and Turkish Women in the Netherlands and in the Countries of Origin, in *International Migration Policies and the Status of Female Migrants* (Proceedings of the United Nations Expert Group Meeting on International Migration Policies and the Status of Female Migrants, San Miniato, Italy, 28–31 March 1990). New York: United Nations (ST/ESA/SER R/126).

Sztanderska, Urszula. 1994. *Determinanty sytuacji kobiet na rynku pracy. Referat na konferencje* (Determinants of Women's Status in the Labor Market). Warsaw, Poland: unpublished conference paper.

Tapinos, Georges Photios. 1995. Female Migration and the Status of Foreign Women in France, in *International Migration Policies and the Status of Female Migrants* (Proceedings of the United Nations Expert Group Meeting on International Migration Policies and the Status of Female Migrants, San Miniato, Italy, 28–31 March 1990). New York: United Nations (ST/ESA/SER R/126).

Therborn, Göran. 1995. *European Modernity and Beyond: The Trajectory of European Societies, 1945–2000*. London: Sage.

United Nations. 1996. *From Plan to Market*. World Development Report. New York: Oxford University Press.

Van Weesep, Jan. 1995. Housing the Guestworkers, in *Europe at the Margins: New Mosaics of Inequality*, Costis Hadjimichalis and D. Sadler, eds. New York: Wiley.

Yedlin, Tova. 1980. *Women in Eastern Europe and the Soviet Union*. New York: Praeger.

Zwaan, J.W. de. 1993. Institutional Problems and Free Movement of Persons: The Legal and Political Framework for Cooperation, in *Free Movement of Persons in Europe: Legal Problems and Experiences*, H.G. Schermers, *et al.*, eds. Dordrecht, Netherlands: Martinus Nijhoff.

11 Conclusion: Policy Considerations for the Twenty-First Century
Gregory A. Kelson

INTRODUCTION

When I first developed the idea for this book in 1996, I envisioned a tool that could be used not only by scholars of international migration, but also by those who were responsible for formulating and implementing policy that would affect women who migrate. It has been noted that most of the world's refugees are female (DeLaet, this volume; Kelly 1993). In the United States, for example, 'about one half of the immigrants admitted ... for permanent residence were women' between fiscal years 1983 and 1993 (Johnson, 1995). Because of this factor, we can no longer ignore how women are affected by international migration. The authors who have contributed to this volume have attempted to show many of the aspects of how international migration affect the lives of women.

In Part I of this volume, we looked at the economic aspects of international female migration. The contributors to this section gave us a varied view of the role that women play upon moving to their host countries. Nandini Assar, for example, tells us how women perform most of the labor in motels owned by Indian-Americans. In contrast, Kathleen Staudt notes that women at the Juárez–El Paso border are more enterprising and have the full support of their husbands.

In Part II, we looked at the social aspects of international female migration. In the four chapters that make up this section, the authors give us first-hand knowledge of how moving to a new country affects their customs and their way of thinking. The chapter by Morrison, Guruge and Snarr, for example, tells us how the Tamil community quickly adopted Western thinking in terms of dating, marriage and sexual choice soon after moving from Sri Lanka to Canada.

In the pages that follow, I will revisit each of these chapters looking closely at the economic and social aspects of international female migration.

I will then offer recommendations for policy that should be developed worldwide based on the contributor's writings.

I. ECONOMIC IMPLICATIONS

How immigrant women have contributed to the economy of their host societies has been the major theme of the five chapters that examine the economic status of immigrant women. In many cases, women are the major breadwinners – assuring that the economic success of their families are stable. Women have assisted in family businesses headed by their husbands, or have set up their own businesses with the assistance of a male relative.

Establishing credit for women to go into business has always been a problem in most Western countries. The problem gained so much notice that several paragraphs in the 1995 Beijing Platform for Action specifically recommend making credit more accessible for women. In the Juárez–El Paso area, however, the Mexican Federation of Private Associations (FEMAP) developed a community bank model to assure financing for women who started their own businesses. FEMAP's community bank model works – Kathleen Staudt tells us that by using peer pressure as loan guarantees (similar to the Asian Grameen Bank model), 'repayment rates always exceed ninety percent' (Staudt, this volume). Several countries could learn from FEMAP's success.

Another aspect is how immigrant women contribute to the family business and thus the economy of the host country. In the United States, it has been noted that Indian-Americans have become very successful in the motel business (Assar, this volume). However, women are still expected to perform their traditional roles in addition to assisting their spouses in the motel industry. The major work in the hotel/motel industry, according to Assar, consists of cleaning and laundry, 'skills in which women are already trained and socialized, and which are easily incorporated as an *extension of the domestic domain*' (Assar, this volume) (emphasis mine).

Contrasting this is when women work in the family business and want to go out on their own to go into business. In most cases, this cannot be done without support (financial or otherwise) from a male relative (usually the woman's spouse). Ip and Lever-Tracy found interesting data to support this. They note that even when a woman had her own business, the male relative had a major voice in the running of the business. Take note of one study that they conducted and the conclusion that they found:

> [Two women in the study] said that they generally chose to follow their husband's advice because they found it good and in a third case, where

a previously full-time husband had largely retired, he said that 'she more or less runs [the business], but I decide'. (Ip and Lever-Tracy, this volume)

However, this was not always the case. Ip and Lever-Tracy, in the same study, also found nine cases where women did have a greater say in the business, regardless of her husband's input, 'the majority view was that although she might seek advice or engage in discussions, in the end, "it's really her business", "I discuss problems with my husband, use him as a sounding board, but I decide"'.

Finally, in formulating an economic policy for women migrants, looking at the traditional roles that women play must also be considered. We must look at the traditional gender roles of women and if they can leave those roles behind for new roles in their new society. The chapters by Shu-Ju Ada Cheng and Cecilia and Gabriel Manrique highlight this important aspect.

In looking at how the international sexual division of labor affects gender roles, Shu-Ju Ada Cheng points out two major characteristics that can affect migration flows. First, she notes, the percentage of women in migration flows are increasing. Secondly, 'migrant women are mainly concentrated in certain occupations, such as the service industry, manufacturing industry, sex industry and domestic service' (Cheng, this volume). Because of this, she concludes that:

the concentration of women in certain female-dominated occupations in the migration process is an extension of the sexual division of labor that has already existed at the national level of both labor sending and receiving countries. The sexual segregation in the global labor market among the migrant population has served to reinforce the division of labor by gender at the international level through the migration process. (Cheng, this volume)

But it has always been my assertion in international migration that women do not have to accept these traditional roles. Many women leave their homelands with advanced degrees and could very easily practice in their chosen professions in their new host society. But what of those who simply want a better life for themselves and their family? Many turn to Western-style education to get ahead.

The chapter by Cecilia Manrique and Gabriel Manrique takes a critical look at women from the third world in American tertiary education. In looking closely at this chapter, we can see how immigrant faculty from non-European countries suffer from recent anti-immigration bias. With the difficulty in hiring qualified American citizens for tenure-track faculty positions, many colleges are now considering qualified candidates from other countries, especially third world countries. This can have many advantages, especially to foreign students, who can find a faculty member that they can identify with culturally. However, Manrique and Manrique point out:

> [Many American] students have questioned [the foreign faculty member's] credentials for teaching 'American' subjects (e.g., American history, American government, English composition), and how students have openly questioned their policies and the qualifications. Being visibly different from the majority can also lead to their exclusion from the greater campus and community thereby negating or retarding their potential benefits that can be derived from their presence. Immigrant faculty refer to the 'chilly campus climate' where enclaves form that tend to exclude the immigrant. (Manrique and Manrique, this volume)

For a female immigrant faculty member, this can be very distressing. This wave of anti-immigrant sentiment can impede not only the faculty member's teaching but also her research. And, in the patriarchal system of tertiary education in the United States, tenure decisions can also be affected.

The common theme of the chapters in this section have dealt with keeping women in their traditional roles and not offering opportunities for advancement. Limited opportunities for business establishment, business financing, access to credit, denial of education, and traditional gender roles for women can have a negative affect on women who migrate on their own and not as a family where a man heads the household. Policies in this area must address this facet of international female migration, assuring more equality to women.

II. SOCIAL IMPLICATIONS

Coming into a new host society can be very troubling for a new immigrant. How she assimilates into the host culture, what values of her culture will she keep or leave behind, and how quickly she adopts new cultures will depend on several factors. The four chapters that make up this section took a critical look at these factors, many known for years, others more recently recognized.

In the chapters by Lynn Morrison, Sepali Guruge, Kymberly Snarr and Lisa Simons, we look at two of these factors, namely adopting or leaving behind cultural values and assimilation into the host society.

The case of the Tamil population in Toronto, as highlighted by Morrison, Guruge and Snarr, is an excellent case study. One of the questions that this chapter sought to answer, which I will focus on here, was '[a]re Tamils in the midst of a cultural transition and becoming more "Canadianized" and how does that impact on their marriage patterns and sexual behaviors' (Morrison, Guruge and Snarr, this volume)? The question would not be so much becoming more 'Canadianized' as it would be becoming more 'Westernized'.[1] This becomes true in two areas: marriage and sexual decision-making. The authors point out that most Tamil men will not marry Tamil women who have been in Canada for four or five years because of the Western values that they have adopted. One of the women in their study words this best:

> The men feel that when the women come here and they lived here long in Canada they are beginning to get the western influence and the marriages may not last long. Or they might think that they have gone with boyfriends and girlfriends and they might have more freedom. So they like to have the girls from back home [in Sri Lanka] who have been brought up the traditional way, traditional outlook so they might stay home to look after the children, not go to work. (Morrison, Guruge and Snarr, this volume)

In terms of sexual decision-making, the authors found that both genders accepted Western ideals of respect for the right to refuse to have sex, although that was not the case for everyone in their study. The authors point to a 30-year-old female who told them '[m]any times [in discussing sex with her husband] I just try to say no, I just don't want to have it. I try to sleep with the child, just tired' (Morrison, Guruge and Snarr, this volume).

Lisa Simons, however, brings a new perspective into this discussion in her chapter on the mail order bride industry. Citing the fact that 'more [American] men want mail order brides today because of men's unhappiness with American women' (Simons, this volume), the mail order bride industry have become one of the fastest ways for women from the Philippines to migrate to the United States. Simons does warn, however, that many of the firms that advertise mail order brides, especially those found on the Internet, where she did most of her research, can be fronts for women who want to find a way to leave their homeland for a new life in the West. However, another avenue is opened when the men, who are enthused with the idea of having a non-feminist wife who is 'joyful and fun, mellow, soft, sincere, vulnerable, zestful, compassionate, loyal. ...' (Simons, this volume), physically and mentally abuse the women, knowing that their options are limited for assistance. This was also a factor brought out by Morrison, Guruge, and Snarr. There is also the prospect that once these 'mail order brides' are in the United States and become permanent citizens, they will use that status to bring family members to the US under family reunification policies (Simons, this volume).

The last two chapters in this section, Larissa Remennick's chapter on Russian women in Israel and Brigitte Bechtold and Ludmila Dziewięcka-Bokun's chapter on the Council of Europe's Project on Human Dignity and Social Exclusion, requires more extensive discussion.

Larissa Remennick, herself a Russian immigrant now living in Israel, gives us an excellent account of assimilating into a new host society. She prefaces this by noting that for the 150,000 Russian women who migrated to Israel in the 1990 who face 'problems of physical, psychological and social adjustment to the new environment... women face a new set of norms surrounding the issues of sexuality, childbearing and family life (still viewed in both the former Soviet Union and Israel as primarily feminine domains)' (Remennick, this volume).

Remennick notes how many female Russian immigrants who hold college degrees have difficulty obtaining jobs in Israeli society because of patriarchal customs. She notes that women must often take 'part-time manual or caring work (e.g., baby-sitting or caring for the elderly)' because of limited job opportunities and 'traditional male worker preference on the part of Israeli employers' (Remennick, this volume). There is also the problem of going into 'non-feminine' occupations in Israel (engineering, construction, etc.) which reinforces gender roles in Israel.

Another aspect of life that Remennick notes that was also brought out slightly in the other chapters in this section is the problem of sexual harassment. With international trafficking of women for prostitution at an all-time high, many men will get the impression that immigrant women are eager and willing to perform sexual acts. For many immigrant women who have no desire for this, it becomes troubling because they must continue to live under this type of harassment.

In describing the Council of Europe's Project on Human Dignity and Social Exclusion (HDSE), Brigitte Bechtold and Ludmila Dziewięcka-Bokun noted that it 'provide[d] very limited information on immigrants' living and working conditions and does not specify any women and/or children related issues' (Bechtold and Dziewięcka-Bokun, this volume). In noting the limited amount of social services for migrant women and children in the European Union, this project was very important as it reinforces the invisibility of women who migrate on their own accord.

III. RECOMMENDATIONS AND CONCLUSION

With the wealth of information provided to us by the authors in this volume, the questions we ask now are: how do we pull all of this together? What are the direct policy implications? What should policymakers focus on as we approach the twenty-first century? This section will attempt to answer these questions.

A. Recommendations

In putting this volume together, the editors agreed to categorize each of the two chapters into one of two sections: economic and social implications. As such, in offering my policy recommendations, I will also keep these sections separate. What I hope to do here is not attempt to give final policy recommendations, but to give policymakers topics for further discussion and implementation of policy concerning international female migration.

1. *Economic Policies*

Perhaps the most important aspect under this heading would be the availability of credit to women. The Beijing Platform for Action, approved at the Fourth World Conference on Women in 1995, in stating that governments should '[S]trengthen women's economic capacity and commercial networks', recommended

> adopt[ing] policies that support business organizations, non-governmental organizations, cooperatives, revolving loan funds, credit unions, grassroots organizations, women's self-help groups and other groups in order to provide services to women entrepreneurs in rural and urban areas.

Many women who migrate with their families do so under family unification policies. We have seen, within the pages of this volume, that women contribute tremendously to the success of the family business, especially the hotel/motel industry. But there is still a bias to give more opportunities to start new businesses to men than to women. But, if we look at the success of FEMAP in helping women start new businesses, it is definitely the model that countries could follow. Albeit, with the anti-immigrant sentiment in most Western countries, especially in the United States, most countries are trying to avoid it because it is considered political suicide.

Another issue is women who come into a host society with advanced degrees. In other words, women who are trained in medicine, engineering, and the social sciences are not allowed to practice their chosen professions once they come into their new countries. Licensing provisions aside, law should be enacted that provide for women in certain professions to be able to practice. There should be reciprocity agreements between countries that allow a woman with an advanced degree to be able to practice her trade in her new country.

2. *Social Policies*

Another aspect of international female migration that must be examined is how women adapt to their host society. Building on that is how male spouses accept the fact that their wives and daughters are becoming more 'Westernized'.

Many women migrate into a new country with the same custom and traditions from their former country. They may not be used to the fact that a woman can own a business, is free to pursue an education, can say no to sexual advances, and so forth. Morrison, Guruge and Sepali noted in one of their case studies that most men would rather marry a woman from Sri Lanka rather than marry a woman who has lived in Toronto for a few years and picked up the ideals of that country.

This can many times lead to domestic violence between couples. The man will want to continue being the breadwinner for the family and want his wife to stay home and take care of the home and the kids. The wife, on the other hand, embracing Western and feminist ideals, will want more independence and the ability to make her own decisions. The male spouse will usually lose control and resort to domestic violence to keep everything under the status quo in his opinion. In 1994, the United States Federal Bureau of Investigation estimated that a woman is beaten in the United States every 18 seconds (Mertus 1995). Indeed, '[in] many states in the United States, husbands are free to rape their wives without fear of legal reprisal' (Mertus 1995).

There is also the problem of women who do not come into a new host society under their own right. That is, they come into a new host society under family reunification laws. The women are dependent on their husband for their permanent residency status. Because of this, women are forced to remain in abusive relationships in order to maintain their immigrant status. If they do find enough strength to leave the relationship, they can be subject to deportation.

What I recommend here is a system that would support a woman's right to leave these abusive relationships. Mechanisms must also be found to enable the abusive spouse to be prosecuted under the laws of the host society, with no retribution to the woman. And finally, laws should be enacted that would allow a woman to apply to permanent residency status on her own behalf, regardless of her marital status.

B. Conclusion

The main purpose of this volume was to bring out of 'invisibility' the status of women in the study of international migration. It is our hope that this will be an area where more study can be done. It is also my personal hope that policymakers will no longer ignore this aspect of immigration and will look very seriously at implementing policies as we approach the twenty-first century. As long as women want more opportunities for education, employment, and child care opportunities, migration will increase. We need to make sure that we, as a society, will be ready to accept them as productive members of our society.

NOTES

1. In my own work dealing with gender-based persecution and political asylum, I have found that many women try to escape certain persecutions such as female circumcision or the social mores of their homeland once they have had a 'taste' of Western culture (Kelson, 1995). See also *Fatin v. INS*, 12 F.3d 1233 (3d Cir. 1995) (case of Iranian woman seeking asylum in the US after admitting that she was a feminist and had adopted Western values).

REFERENCES

Johnson, Kevin R. 1995. Public Benefits and Immigration: The Intersection of Immigration Status, Ethnicity, Gender, and Class. *UCLA Law Review*, 42: 1509–75.

Kelly, N. 1993. Gender-Related Persecution: Assessing the Asylum Claims of Women. *Cornell International Law Journal*, 26: 625–74.

Kelson, G.A. 1995. Granting Political Asylum to Potential Victims of Female Circumcision. *Michigan Journal of Gender and Law*, 3: 257–98.

Mertus, J. 1995. State Discriminatory Family Law and Customary Abuses. In Julie Peters and Andrea Wolper, eds., *Women's Rights, Human Rights: International Feminist Perspectives*. New York and London: Routledge.

Index